Conversation and T

Conversation and Technology

From the Telephone to
the Internet

Ian Hutchby

Polity

First published in 2001 by Polity Press in association with Blackwell Publishers Ltd.

Editorial office:
Polity Press
65 Bridge Street
Cambridge CB2 1UR, UK

Marketing and production:
Blackwell Publishers Ltd
108 Cowley Road
Oxford OX4 1JF, UK

Published in the USA by
Blackwell Publishers Inc.
Commerce Place
350 Main Street
Malden, MA 02148, USA

ISBN 0-7456-2110-4
ISBN 0-7456-2111-2 (pbk)

A catalogue record for this book is available from the British Library.

Library of Congress Cataloging-in-Publication Data

Hutchby, Ian.
　　Conversation and technology : from the telephone to the internet / by Ian Hutchby.
　　　p. cm.
　　Includes bibliographical references and index.
　　ISBN 0-7456-2110-4—ISBN 0-7456-2111-2 (pbk.)
　　1. Communication and technology.　2. Conversation analysis.　I. Title.
　　P96.T42 H88 2000
　　302.3′46—dc21　　　　　　　　　　　　　　　　　　　　　　　00-040087

Typeset in 10¹/₂ on 12 pt Times New Roman
by Best-set Typesetter Ltd., Hong Kong
Printed in Great Britain by MPG Books, Bodmin, Cornwall

This book is printed on acid-free paper.

Contents

1

Introduction: Technologies for Communication

For some, the title of this book may pose a question: what does conversation have to do with technology? It is easy to think of technology in relation to the mechanical, the automatic, the inanimate, the electronic, the inorganic, the constructed, the non-thinking, the impersonal, the asocial. This seems quite different from conversation, one of our most common forms of social interaction, which seems by contrast spontaneous, involved, active, lived, mindful, sociable and deeply interpersonal. Indeed, it might be proposed that the very thing which distinguishes humankind from other species is our capacity not just to use language (after all, many other species are now known to use relatively complex forms of symbolic communication) but to use language in the form of ordinary conversation; to talk about ourselves and our interests, activities, desires and so on purely for the sake of talking to each other. Chat, in other words, may well be one of the most significant defining characteristics of the category 'human'. In what sense, then, can technology and conversation be brought together?

It does not take a great deal of reflection to see that there is, in today's world, a multiplicity of ways in which conversational practices interface with technological devices. For instance, artefacts such as the telephone and the internet – one so established as to be all but invisible to sociologists, the other so novel as to all but fill the cultural horizon for many – function primarily as technologies through which communication of certain sorts is enabled. In different ways, both of them function as channels by means of which individuals or groups can be situated in co-presence, yet an abstract form of co-presence, in which space and often also time separate the participants.

Computer technologies such as expert systems and those for supporting cooperative work-based tasks also operate as media for communication of a certain sort. Such systems, typically deployed in workplace environments, are designed ostensibly to assist or complement human workers in carrying out specific tasks. But they do not operate independently of human work and communication, and the humans who work with them need to find ways of incorporating into their interactions with each other the demands and constraints that emerge from the design of the system. At the same time, there are ways in which the technological artefacts themselves can be seen as 'participants' in the interaction, at least in the sense that their outputs (such as words or pictures on a screen) can become oriented to as 'contributions' which are the subject of mutual, active and collaborative sense-making on the part of humans.

We also increasingly communicate *with* certain forms of technology. Although they have not yet reached particularly high levels of conversational sophistication, speech-generating computers and artificial intelligence systems are increasingly encountered in information-seeking and other basic service encounters. Designers of more advanced systems are attempting to build computers which could hold 'conversations' with humans, and this prompts the question of what those conversations will look like, whether they will manifest any significant differences with human–human conversation; and also, significantly, what are the implicit assumptions about the nature of human interaction which underlie the design of such systems?

Together, I will label these forms of technology 'technologies for communication'. The telephone, the videophone, internet conferencing, computerized expert systems, artificial intelligence systems based on natural language, are all technologies through which, around which and with which humans attempt to communicate. Such communication incorporates an enormous range of activities, from holding a conversation with a friend to trying to extract information from a database by 'conversing' with a computer. But because, in each case, the interaction involved is interpersonal or (very broadly) conversational, these are not simply communications technologies but, in an important sense, technologies *for* communication.

The existence of technologies for communication poses a question: what is the nature of the communication that takes places when humans interact through, around, or with them? Put more broadly, what is the relationship between forms of technology and structures of social interaction? In this book, my aim is to explore what this particular category of technologies can tell us about that relationship. In the following chapters I explore the multiplicity of ways that technologies for communication can become implicated in our ordinary conversational practices while, at the same time, those very practices may not only adapt to but also shape the cultural meanings and communicative purposes that such artefacts have. My central argument is that we can learn more about the nature of human communication by observing how it is affected by technology, and, correspondingly, we can learn more about the social nature of communications technologies by thinking about how they both rely upon and transform basic human communicative patterns.

There are a number of prongs to this argument. Two significant questions that are raised immediately concern the nature of technology and the nature of human communication. It is not my aim to answer these questions by means of definitive, metaphysical statements on what I take to be the 'essential' nature of these things. Rather, I will take an analytical stance on technologies and their relationship with human communication. In other words, I want to argue for a particular way of conceptualizing technology, and a particular method of studying communication, which together help us to understand the ways that technologies can impact on the interactive social world of humans, and how humans can find ways of managing those impacts.

As I outline in detail in the first few chapters of the book, this involves taking issue with certain aspects of the recent radical sociology of technology, centred as it is around an uneasy social constructivist consensus. The main thrust of this consensus has cast into doubt the very validity of asking questions about the nature of technologies and communication, and the impacts of technologies on social life. Technologies, in the constructivist way of thinking, can only amount to what humans make of them in and through their uses of them; or at least, that is deemed to be the most appropriate way for sociologists to approach them. As I will argue in chapter 2, this is to overlook the very materiality of technological artefacts and to downplay the extent to which humans' uses of artefacts are not just shaped but constrained by aspects of that materiality. Materiality here need not be thought of only in physical terms. We may, for instance, be able to conceive of the telephone as having a materiality affecting the distribution of interactional space through the promotion of what I will call conversational 'intimacy at a distance' (see chapter 5). Likewise, we can conceive of the interfaces of expert systems or internet conferencing software as having a materiality affecting navigation through a technically bounded interactional space as people attempt to orient themselves in the sequential order of a particular interaction.

This inevitably implies a conception of what communication is, how it is produced and how best to analyse it. As I outline further in chapters 3 and 4, my perspective derives from conversation analysis (Sacks 1992; Psathas 1979; see also Atkinson and Heritage 1984; Hutchby and Wooffitt 1998), an approach which is distinctive on both conceptual and methodological grounds. Conversation analysis (CA) is characterized by the view that there are discoverable rules, procedures and conventions which underlie the orderly production of talk in interactional circumstances. These conventions comprise a form of social organization which makes for the very possibility of mutually intelligible communication. Methodologically, CA takes the view that this underlying social organization cannot be discovered using conventional sociological research techniques such as interviews, surveys, or even participant observation and the conscientious taking of field notes. Rather, it is viewed as available to observation in the details of naturally occurring interactions, which are recorded using audio and video equipment and then carefully transcribed.

Taken together, these angles on the relationship between technological artefacts and the social organization of communication enable us to think anew about fundamental questions such as the nature of human sociality and the phenomenon of intersubjectivity. The question of how humans manage to act in concert, how we are able to understand one another, and the extent to which it is possible for us to 'know' the intentions, mental states or consciousness of another person is one that has concerned philosophers since the beginnings of systematic human inquiry and, latterly, social theorists as well. One effect of the advent of 'conversational' machines – machines that exhibit features of humanness – is to raise again, from a different angle, the issue of whether there are any specific characteristics of being human (Woolgar 1985). Along with that, the spectacle of a human being engaging in conversation with a computer may prompt us to think differently about the nature of human intersubjectivity, understanding and co-communication.

Clearly, an issue that has been around as long as the problem of intersubjectivity does not lend itself to easy or straightforward solution. In fact, it might be more accurate to say that the very longevity of the problem reflects the fact that, as it is conventionally stated ('How is it possible for me to know whether you are really the same as me, as opposed to being, for example, a machine, a robot, an automaton or an alien?'), it has no answer. It is certainly not my aim in this book to suggest any definitive answer. Instead, drawing on a range of writing on the topic, I will outline what seem to be the two principal alternative models or frameworks through which human intersubjectivity and social interaction have been accounted for.

I call these the 'computational' and the 'interactional' models. The former focuses mainly on internal processes, centred in the brain, as the explanatory basis for human action; while the latter, of which CA is a constituent, rejects this view and focuses instead on how intersubjectivity is ongoingly constructed and negotiated in the public space between interactants. Thus, while the computational model addresses itself to furnishing ostensibly causal explanations for human interactive behaviour, the interactional model aims rather to provide a robust framework for analysing intersubjectivity as an interpersonal accomplishment. The writings of Wittgenstein (1958), Schutz (1962) and, more recently, Garfinkel (1967) and Sacks (1992) all suggest that this model provides the most appropriate framework for thinking about human intersubjectivity and interaction. I will propose that the interactional model also provides the best basis for analysing the ways in which non-human technological artefacts can become important elements in the patterns of ordinary human conduct.

As these brief preliminary remarks suggest, I range across a wide terrain of theoretical thought and empirical research in the following chapters. It is worth considering at this point why such a large body of work looms in front of us once we start to think about conversation and technology. One way of accounting for it is to suggest that the era we live in is seeing great, and rapid, changes in the very nature of social interaction.

Technologized interaction?

I began with a question: why might there be a link between technology and social activities such as conversation? In fact, sociologists have always argued against the notion that the 'technological' equates with the 'asocial' (see chapter 2). But, more recently, the idea has grown up that the properties of new technologies themselves – particularly information and communications technologies – mean that we in the developed capitalist world are currently entering a phase of what might be called 'technologized interaction'.

For instance, the advent and rapid expansion of the internet, on which people can engage in computer-mediated 'chat' from their bedrooms, studies or offices with any number of anonymous logged-on others, has led some to suggest that the nature of human subjectivity is undergoing a process of fundamental change. Poster (1995), one of the leading proponents of this view, argues that electronic communications technologies allow the physical body to be separated from 'presence' to such an extent that our common-sense notion of the self is being fragmented, since identities can no longer meaningfully be pinned to their concrete individual 'owners'. Turkle (1995) in some respects goes further. She has always been fascinated with the way in which some computer programmers search for an almost symbiotic relationship with their machines (see Turkle (1986)). In a similar vein, her more recent ethnography of regular participants in real-time internet games such as MUDs (multi-user domains) prompts her to claim that 'as human beings become increasingly intertwined with the technology and with each other via the technology, old distinctions between what is specifically human and specifically technological become more complex. Are we living life *on* the screen or life *in* the screen?' (Turkle 1995: 21, emphasis in original).

But the internet is only the most high-profile phenomenon involved in the idea that we are at a moment of technologized inter-action. The telephone is a much more well-established technology for enabling spatially – indeed globally – distributed conversation. Since its development, and its rapid and widespread uptake in the early years of the twentieth century, the telephone has become a technol-ogy for communication that is so familiar as to be all but invisible as an object for sociological attention (a notable exception is the work of Hopper (1992) which I discuss further in chapters 5 and 6). Yet one thing we might be encouraged to ask is: what does the existence of the telephone mean for the nature of interpersonal interaction? Some time ago, Pool (1981) edited a collection of studies which traced some of the ways in which the adoption of the telephone could lead to shifts in cultural patterns of living and socializing. But, for the most part, these studies paid little attention to the details of what people could be seen (or rather heard) to *do* on the telephone. By far the most radical aspect of the telephone as a technology for communi-cation is that its invention enabled people, for the first time ever, to talk to each other as if they were co-present when in fact they were not. While most of us now take this experience in our stride, traces of its strangeness still show in the unease or confusion that very young children sometimes manifest when they first begin to encoun-ter telephone conversation.

So what of the details? What are the structures of telephone interaction like and how, if at all, do they differ from the more primary patterns of co-present interaction? (I call these patterns 'primary' because they obviously precede in temporal terms, and out-weigh in terms of global distribution, the phenomenon of telephone conversation.) Patterns of talk-in-interaction change as people adapt to developments in the circumstances and the possibilities for talk. What kinds of adaptations can people be said to have made – and still be making – to the contingencies of talking on the telephone?

The idea of technologized interaction gains further impetus from the way in which technologies, both large and small, with which we are required to interact in various ways are now pervasive in almost all aspects of our daily lives. Consider, for example, the automated telling machines which most people in developed capitalist societies now use as their principal mode for gaining access to cash. Or the increasing prevalence of automated answering systems which are encountered whenever we make a telephone enquiry to a bank or airport. Indeed, emerging cultural practices such as home banking or teleshopping rely in large part on computer systems that are able to recognize basic elements of ordinary speech and generate appropriate (if pre-programmed) responses. Of interest not merely in technical or engineering terms, these 'interactive' technologies are worthy of investigation because they invite us to ask some fundamental questions about human sociality in a society where much of our interaction is mediated by technological forms.

To what extent, then, are we 'technologized' conversationalists? How far are our conversational practices configured by technologies for communication and interaction; or from the opposite angle, how far may we as competent conversationalists be configurers of the communicative properties of these technologies? In an era which has seen more than a century of extraordinarily rapid technological innovation and development, a commonplace assumption, particularly in populist treatments of the question, is that information and communications technologies are so deeply embedded in cultural existence that the shape of our lives is determined by them (Toffler 1981). This is also reflected, albeit in a less explicitly deterministic fashion, in contemporary theories of the 'information society' (Webster 1995). Critics of the various forms of technological determinism have asserted, by contrast, that information and communications technologies have no effects outside the interpretive constructions made of them by humans (Grint and Woolgar 1997).

In my view, neither of these extremes is solely adequate for thinking about the relationships between forms of communications technology and human interaction. Instead we need to develop a framework that argues both that technologies for communication do indeed bring into existence – in the sense of enable and promote – new forms of participatory possibilities in human interaction, new categories of what might be called 'localized social identities', and that these new forms of interaction are at the same time the product of humans' active appropriation and configuration of the technology in pursuit of their own purposes. How we might develop such a model is explored in chapter 2.

In the process, as already mentioned, we must address other questions. For example, what are the assumptions about the nature of human communication that are embedded in the design of technologies for communication? What are the effects that these assumptions have on the situated, practical actions through which communication is accomplished? How do the configuring properties of technologies such as telephones, expert systems and speech-based computers interrelate with the normative structures of social interaction? It is only through a consideration of these questions that we can come to an understanding of the relationship between conversation and technology and its contemporary sociological significance.

The relevance of conversation

As these remarks suggest, there is a particular relevance in thinking about the nature of ordinary conversation for our understanding of how technologies for communication function in everyday life. This connection is not entirely novel. Some years ago, it was observed that 'new technology has brought with it the idea that we no longer simply use machines, we interact with them' (Suchman 1987: 1). Focusing on computerized 'help' systems, Suchman argued that the operation of such machines is an activity less akin to a mechanical process and more like a linguistic or discursive one. That is, in using a modern computer, the actions we engage in involve not so much the operation of switches or levers with some determinate physical outcome as engagement in a form of dialogue with the machine. Most people who use a computer nowadays will be familiar with graphical user interfaces (GUIs) such as those used in Macintosh or Windows operating systems. These make extensive use of what are called 'dialogue boxes'. At certain points, such as when we create or save a file, when we move a file from one location to another, or when we ask the computer to do something that it cannot do or does not understand, the system presents us with a set of choices and asks us which we would prefer.

Note that I have started to talk here of a human 'asking' the machine to 'do something' which the machine may 'not understand', and of the machine 'presenting' the human with choices about actions and 'asking' for a preferred option. Part of Suchman's point was that the very design features of information technology artefacts make it extraordinarily easy to slip into this type of anthropomorphic language. GUIs are of course designed with precisely this kind of conversational metaphor in mind. Related to the metaphor of conversational turn-taking (asking and answering; offering options and choosing preferences – see chapter 4), GUIs also frequently aim to simulate on the screen features of the non-computer world outside the screen. Users of modern personal computers take it for granted that their computer screen is a 'desktop' on which there reside 'folders' which in turn contain 'documents'. The folders themselves are represented by little pictures (known as icons) that look like the cardboard folders the user may have in the metal filing cabinet across the office. In order to 'throw away' a document (that is, erase a file from the computer's disk) we can use a pointer to 'pick it up' and 'drop it' into a little icon of a wastebasket. When the wastebasket has things in it, its lid may be lifted off and scrunched up papers can be seen inside. When 'emptied', the lid is replaced.

To most people reading this book, no doubt all this will seem quite commonplace. Yet the idea that we interact with machines rather than just using them brings with it a question: precisely *how* do humans interact with such devices? What is the nature of human–machine interaction? And what are the most appropriate methods for engaging in the analysis of that interaction?

As Suchman herself saw, the fact that technological devices may be designed with an interactional metaphor in mind means that techniques for analysing human–human interaction may fruitfully be applied to human–machine interaction. Extending this slightly, I suggest that the same techniques may be used to analyse human–machine–human interaction: that is, interaction that is somehow mediated by technologies for communication.

Suchman (1987) used aspects of CA to analyse interaction with one form of technology, a supposedly 'user-friendly' xeroxing machine. But I will range much further and wider in the domain of technologies for communication, using the techniques of CA to develop what is hopefully a general account of the ways in which such artefacts may become involved in everyday interpersonal interaction. In this account, conversation becomes not simply a metaphor but an analytical baseline from which I will gauge the nature of the relationship between forms of technology and structures of interaction.

Outline of the book

I begin in chapters 2 and 3 by exploring the two poles around which the book's arguments are set out: the social study of technology as a specific phenomenon, and the sociology of interpersonal communication and social interaction. These chapters are designed to take issue both with prevailing dichotomies in the social study of technology and with notions in communication studies deriving from cognitive science and information theory. In chapter 2 I discuss the main theories put forward in the recent sociology of technology. Most of these embrace one form or another of social constructivism. However it should be noted that Grint and Woolgar (1997) have recently taken issue with what they see as an underlying essentialism in even the most constructivist accounts, which suggests that technological artefacts possess properties which are beyond the reach of sociological analysis. I argue that while Grint and Woolgar's relativist standpoint is a powerful one, it actually deflects attention away from some of the most sociologically important features of technologies for communication.

Chapter 3 proceeds to consider how social interaction, and especially conversation, is best conceptualized. Noting the extent to which technological metaphors have informed models of human communication, I outline in more detail the basic distinction between computational and interactional models of communication. I discuss how these models have informed research in various traditions over the past few decades: principally, parts of linguistics, cognitive science and communication studies. I argue that the most radically interactional model of communication is to be found in the field of CA (Hutchby and Wooffitt 1998). This is then introduced in detail in chapter 4.

The remaining chapters present empirical accounts of various technologies for communication and their relationship with the structures of interaction. Chapters 5 and 6 focus on the telephone as a 'technology of sociability'. I discuss the extent to which the invention and widespread adoption of the telephone in modern culture has transformed the nature of social interaction. Drawing on literature which addresses both the social impacts of the telephone, and the nature of telephone conversation as social interaction, I develop two arguments. First, that the telephone has brought into existence not only new forms of interaction but also new forms of identity which participants need to negotiate competently. Second, that arguments which stress either telephone technology's configuration of its users, or users' configuration of telephone technology, are equally limited. We are both configured by, and configurers of, the telephone as a communication technology. This is a position that informs my discussions of other technologies in subsequent chapters.

In chapter 7 I turn to look at computer technologies and how people interact around them in various workplace settings. I look at how novel forms of workplace technology such as collaborative video links can be seen to encourage the development of apparently new forms of interpersonal interaction. However, as in the following two chapters, my overall argument is that humans who attempt to communicate via these technologies are still reliant upon everyday interactional competencies, which in turn leads to many of the problems that are experienced in computer-supported collaborative working. In the second part of the chapter I look at the contributions made by ethnomethodological and conversation-analytic perspectives on human interaction around 'intelligent' machines. Here Suchman's (1987) work receives a more extended treatment. I also examine recent studies of service encounters which illustrate both positive and negative impacts of so-called 'expert' systems on the delivery of public services.

Chapter 8 address a range of issues around the question of artificial intelligence (AI) and human–computer interaction (HCI). An initial concern here is with the various designs and design strategies which underlie attempts to construct computers that can engage in 'conversations' with humans. These are now moving out of the purely experimental domain and into the arena of public services such as banking or airport enquiries services. As well as providing some empirical analyses of issues raised when humans attempt to engage in interaction with computers that give the appearance of conversational competence, I discuss some of the conceptual and philosophical issues around the very possibility of human–computer conversation. I consider the arguments within ethnomethodology and CA which oppose those in the AI and HCI community who believe that social studies of interaction can represent the basis for truly conversational computers, and discuss how this debate itself raises issues about the nature of social interaction and communication.

Chapter 9 focuses on new forms of interaction currently being brought into existence via the internet. Mirroring the argument of chapter 5, in which we saw how the telephone enables and promotes new forms of identity and of participation in social interaction, I suggest that computer-mediated communication (CMC) is effecting similar transformations. In the first part I discuss CMC in relation to questions of identity, social interaction and the formation of social relationships; then, in the second half, I look at multi-user 'conversations' in real-time Internet Relay Chat (IRC), and adapt the basic perspective of conversation analysis to investigate the nature of participation in this novel arena for social interaction.

2

The Communicative
Affordances of
Technological Artefacts

My aim in this book is to investigate whether there may be specific forms of social interaction that have grown up around what I am calling technologies for communication. The argument centres upon a complex interplay between the *normative structures* of conversational interaction and the *communicative affordances* offered by different forms of technology. In chapters 3 and 4 I say more about the idea of normative structures of conversation. In this chapter, the focus will be on how the notion of communicative affordances relates to other perspectives in the sociology of technology.

Analysing the ways in which technologies for communication can become involved in ordinary interactional processes entails developing a specific view of the relationship between technology and social processes. The issue for this chapter therefore is to disentangle my position from other theories in the recent sociology of technology. I start by outlining some of the key social constructivist responses which have been made to what is seen as the technological determinist consensus in earlier sociology of technology. Then, in order to situate my own argument in relation to these perspectives, I turn to some major critiques which claim to be presenting a more rigorous social constructivism. One approach focuses on the idea that technologies should be seen as 'texts' which have no necessary characteristics at all but are meaningful only in and through the 'readings' that social actors give them (Grint and Woolgar 1997). From a slightly different angle, others have suggested that the focus of attention should be shifted away from the question of what is social about technologies towards that of how technologies are situated within concrete social contexts of action, and how social actors knowingly constitute those artefacts, and their actions in relation to them, as 'technological' (Button 1993). My own approach draws on the concept of 'affordances' (Gibson 1979) in order to propose an alternative which takes account of the constraining, as well as enabling, materiality of artefacts.

The social dynamics of technology

Recent years have seen a resurgence of interest in technology as an object of sociological investigation. Technology has always figured in the list of sociology's key topics, along with themes such as power, bureaucracy, work, class, and more recently, deviance, gender and ethnicity. But technology has now taken on a new lease of sociological life in the form of 'social studies of science and technology'. This is an offshoot of the more well-established sociology of scientific knowledge (Woolgar 1991). The main aim of social studies of science and technology is to argue that technological artefacts, in both their form and their meaning, are socially shaped, as opposed to being the clearly defined products of particular inventors or innovators. As two of the key figures in the development of the field have put it:

> Technologies do not have a momentum of their own at the outset that allows them . . . to pass through a neutral social medium. Rather, they are subject to contingency as they pass from figurative hand to hand, and so are shaped and reshaped. Sometimes they disappear altogether: no-one felt moved, or was obliged, to pass them on. At other times they take novel forms, or are subverted by users to be employed in ways quite different from those for which they were originally intended. (Bijker and Law 1992: 8)

As this quote suggests, most of the work in this field is not about technology in the abstract, but about the complex relationships between technologies and the social and interactional circumstances in which they exist and through which they attain their meaning. This is in stark contrast to earlier sociological concerns with technology which focused on the development of factories, the introduction of machines and the increasing automation of work. The explicit aim was to develop a critical, and political, account of the effects of these processes in terms of class division and the nature of the labour process (for example, Braverman 1974). Underpinning much of the theory was a particular conception of the social impacts of new technologies, often described as 'technological determinism': the view that forms of technology actively cause new forms of social relations to come about.

Whether in a strong or a diluted form, this view courses through much of the populist discourse about the social 'impacts' of new information and communication technologies. Toffler (1981), one of the most well-known 'sociologists of the future', has argued that the invention of computers heralded a 'Third Wave' in Western culture, following the First Wave of agriculturalism and the Second Wave of industrialism, in which just as profound a set of social and cultural changes will be caused as came in the wake of the preceding Waves. This view also influences many of the more serious sociological accounts that have been produced in recent years. Poster (1995), for instance, takes a similar, if theoretically more sophisticated, line to Toffler when he argues that the current 'era of electronic exchange' is the third in a series of communication eras that have characterized human societies (the others are the era of 'oralism', prior to the development of writing systems, and the era of 'written exchange' which allowed rationalism and science, with their objective representations of the world, to flourish). What is being brought about by the era of electronic mediation, for Poster, is a fragmentation of the self and a resulting crisis of identity in which there is an increasing separation between the things that we can be or have done to us in the world, and our physical presence in any given social space.

It is, of course, very easy to think in these terms. Indeed, in the previous chapter I talked of an era of 'technologized interaction' which is possibly being brought about by the advent of technologies for communication. I tried not to assume that such an era was actually upon us; in fact one of the aims of this book is to question whether or not that might be the case, and if so, what are the different roles played by technology and conversation in the process. Yet technological determinism is easily identifiable as the *bête noire* of recent developments in science and technology studies. This is a field which is riven by often fierce theoretical and epistemological debates; however, if the different schools are united by one thing it is their opposition to the view that technologies have determinate, causal effects on social change.

Responses to technological determinism have taken a number of forms. One of the key ideas is that common-sense dichotomies between the 'technical' and the 'social' need to be challenged. Sociologists need to recognize and to analyse the ways in which social processes and technological artefacts are interrelated and intertwined. Thus, contrary to technological determinism, in which the inherent characteristics of a technology are thought to have determinate causal effects on social structures, precisely what the characteristics of the technology are, as well as their relationship with social structures, are both seen to be negotiated outcomes of a whole range of social factors and processes.

There are two main tendencies in research into the social shaping of technology. On the one hand, there are those who argue for a focus on *interaction* between social and technical elements; and on the other, those who propose a conception of socio-technical *networks*. The second approach ultimately denies that there is a meaningful distinction between the social and the technical, while the first embraces this distinction, arguing, in contrast to technological determinism, that it is the social which affects the technological. I will look briefly at each in turn before coming to some critical assessments which argue that neither approach is as radically anti-determinist as it appears.

The socio-technical dimension: from interaction to networks

As an example of the interactionist approach I will focus on Winner's ([1977] 1984) early and very influential article in which he proposes that technological artefacts are social in the sense that they can embody forms of order, or structures of social relations. Artefacts, in other words, 'have politics'. Winner is concerned to take issue with the view that technologies, if they do not determine social change, must therefore be neutral conduits which could be open to any interpretation, any use, which humans chose to lend them. For Winner, technological artefacts can never have such social neutrality: any artefact is always and inevitably 'entrammelled in the political ribbons of its designers and users' as Grint and Woolgar (1997: 21) neatly put it.

Winner proposes that technical arrangements can be seen as forms of social order, as 'embody[ing] a systematic social inequality, a way of engineering relationships among people that, after a time, becomes just another part of the landscape' (1984: 29). This can be so 'intentionally' or 'unintentionally'. For instance, by designing the entrance to a building in a particular way, an architect may unintentionally restrict the access of wheelchair-bound people. Going further still, Winner suggests that technologies can be intrinsically linked to definite patterns of social relations. The example he uses is the atom bomb, which he argues 'needs' to be embedded in a rigidly hierarchical system of command (such as the military), since without a clear line of authority there would be too much uncertainty surrounding the use of such a highly lethal technological artefact. A more everyday example (though not one discussed by Winner) might be the automobile. In order for the number of motorists that exist in advanced industrialized societies to continue successfully to use their cars, there needs to be a highly structured set of social relations (often partially formalized in the shape of written highway codes) governing the organization and behaviour of cars on the roads.

Winner's article was influential because it suggested that there are manifold ways in which the order of physical components, in the shape of technological artefacts, and the order of social and political relations can be deeply intertwined, often in the most taken-for-granted ways. For Winner, artefacts do not determine the form of social relations, but they cannot avoid embodying certain ideologies (principally, those of their creators) and hence encouraging, and even 'preferring', certain kinds of social outcomes.

An alternative perspective argues that the two categories at work in the interactionist approach, the 'technological' and the 'social', along with the traditional distinctions between them, need to be dissolved. In this view, rather than thinking in terms of socio-technical interaction, the relevant way of thinking is in terms of socio-technical networks; or as Hughes (1988) describes it, a 'seamless web' of society and technology. The argument in fact originates from Hughes's work detailing the complex processes by which technologies whose form and function we take for granted, such as the electric light, came to be accorded the forms which nowadays appear to be their 'natural' attributes.

One of Hughes's most important ideas was that the most successful developers of large-scale technologies were those who did not merely design devices, but also designed societies into which their devices would fit (Hughes 1983). Certain key inventors of the early industrial era became successful entrepreneurs because they were not just concerned with the technical characteristics of their inventions but with the social, economic and political contexts in which they could be deployed. More than that, as technologies such as urban lighting systems grow into, and in the process alter, these contexts, the technologies themselves become social forces in the sense that they need to be organized and managed. As Hughes writes:

> As the power systems grew even larger, managers . . . rationally organ-
> ised large numbers of engineers, electricians, administrative personnel

and others. . . . . They analysed the social and industrial structure of the market to define markets and determine differential pricing. They regularly recorded consumption patterns of consumers in order to predict and respond to loads. [They were] applying social science in their response to the social factor. (Hughes 1988: 11)

In short, the technologies are seen as heterogeneous collections of technical, social, human, and conceptual phenomena in which the specifically 'technological' characteristics of the web are increasingly difficult to pin down. Latour (1998) later argued that large-scale urban technologies in fact spawn second-order, scaled down models of society in which the continuously monitored behaviour of those using the technologies feeds back in a never-ending loop into the managers' conceptions of how the technology, and its users, should be functioning. That monitoring itself rapidly becomes technologized, especially with the development of computers and video surveillance cameras. Nowadays, in order to organize a major urban utility successfully, those who manage it come to develop what Latour describes as small 'virtual societies' in which the day-to-day activities of a city's inhabitants are technologically transformed into predictable flows of demand on the system's capacities.

Thus, in order to understand the social dynamics of technologies, we have to dissolve the very categories of 'technology' and 'society'. For Latour, both of these are *'artefacts* created simultaneously and symmetrically by analysts' for the purpose of explaining the 'effects' of technology on society. 'The first thing that should be done in order to . . . render history less opaque is to get rid of these twin artefacts, technology and society' (1988: 22, emphasis in original). He suggests that case studies such as Hughes's, among others, 'shift the attention away from the two artefacts of society and technology . . . and lead us to a socio-technical position in which we see the innovators, or entrepreneurs, appealing from one set of alliances with human actors to another set of alliances with non-human actors, thus increasing the heterogeneity of the mixture at each turn of the negotiation' (ibid.).

The terminology here – particularly the references to 'human actors' and 'non-human actors' – is typical of the approach known as 'actor-network theory'. Actor-network theory represents a small but important wing within the contemporary sociology of technology. Its aim is to try and find a way of describing the constitution of heterogeneous networks which avoids making a priori assumptions about the 'natural' properties of *any* of the elements. That is, not only does it refuse to assume that there are any natural or inherent properties of technologies, it takes exactly the same stance with regard to the social aspects of networks, including humans. Actor-network theorists 'avoid making the commonsense assumption that people, entrepreneurs or machines are naturally-occurring categories' (Bijker and Law 1992: 13). The focus of study becomes the processes by which the boundaries around these categories are drawn in the course of technological innovation and dissemination. The procedure is to highlight connections between human and non-human elements, none of which have any necessary priority.

This approach originated in the work of Callon (1980, 1986a, 1986b). Subsequent important contributors include Latour (1987) and Law (1987). A small but elegant example is Latour's (1992) account of the actor network that is involved in hotel managers' attempts to get guests to return their room keys to the desk before leaving the hotel. Here a number of actors (or more strictly, 'actants', since the latter term carries fewer associations with human-centred common-sense assumptions) are recruited in a network which effects a 'program' – making sure keys do not leave the hotel – to combat what Latour describes as hotel guests' 'anti-program' – keep your key with you to ensure easy access to your room. These elements include verbal instructions, signs on the wall, and ultimately, the attachment of a large weight to the key to make it uncomfortable to carry around. For Latour, the key, the signs, the instructions, and the weight are all equally active members of this network along with the humans; but at the same time, their identities as participants in the network are constituted precisely by the network itself. The weight's role in the construction of the 'program' is not simply a function of its being a 'weight', but is given by its relationship to all the other actants within the network.

The main difference between actor-network theory and the earlier systems approach developed by Hughes is that while Hughes tended to assume that there is a distinction between human elements and non-human elements, such as steel, copper, machinery, cables, gases, fuel and the rest, and that the humans are the only active parties in the building of systems, actor-network theory rejects both these assumptions. It begins from the stance that 'actors may be human or non-human . . . they are infinitely pliable, heterogeneous . . . they are free associates, know no differences of scale . . . there is no inertia, no order . . . they build their own temporality' (Latour 1997: 6). In short, it discards all the conventional sociological categories and distinctions – human/non-human, large-scale/small-scale, order/disorder, temporal development/stasis – which underpin most other accounts of the social dynamics of technology.

Technologies as texts

While there are many ways in which these perspectives differ from each other, the key similarity between them is that they are all variants of social constructivism. That is, whether the account is posed in terms of socio-technical interaction or socio-technical networks, the basic idea is that there are no inherent or necessary features of technological artefacts which lead to determinate social consequences. Rather, the precise nature of the social dynamics of technologies is treated as an issue that is open for empirical sociological investigation.

In a radical intervention in the social constructivist perspective, however, Grint and Woolgar claim that all of the approaches outlined above, including actor-network theory, are flawed by what they describe as 'a residual technicism' (1997: 37). This means that they are not as constructivist, nor as distinct from the varieties of technological determinism, as they believe. This residual technicism is found in the continued adherence to the view that, at some level, technological artefacts have capacities which cannot be affected by human interpretive actions, and hence are beyond the purview of sociological investigation. For instance, while socio-technical interactionists want to say that the specific functions, and hence the social 'effects', of a given technology are bound to social factors such as the ideologies informing its design or the division of labour within which it is deployed, they still maintain that there are particular features of technologies which do have some kind of social effect. For Grint and Woolgar, this means that these writers end up 'struggling with a dualism between "technology" and "the social". Does technology . . . determine, or is it determined by, the social?' (1997: 21).

This is so even when there is an explicit denial of, or attempt to transcend, this dualism. Grint and Woolgar discuss an article by Orlikowski (1992) in which she draws on Giddens' structuration theory to argue that technological artefacts simultaneously have an objective reality and are socially constructed in human interpretive actions. Giddens (1984) developed the notion that social structures – the institutional arrangements that both precede individuals in time and spread beyond them in space – represent the conditions within which we can meaningfully engage in social action. Yet, crucially, our social actions are not just framed by but simultaneously reproduce (and possibly modify and develop) those very structures. In other words, social institutions may seem as if they are 'always there', but they would simply cease to be if our actions ceased to orient to them and reproduce them (Giddens 1981).

Orlikowski (1992) draws on this theory in order to construct an account of the social dynamics of technology which argues that the meanings and 'effects' of artefacts are constituted in humans' interpretive accounts of them, yet these accounts are framed, or constrained, by the structural characteristics – the 'objective reality' – of the technology itself. However, for Grint and Woolgar,

> it could still be said that what counts as objective reality is also a social construction. In other words . . . 'objective reality' and 'social construction' are not two aspects of the same artefact – if they were it would imply that we could separate out the two – *they are different ways of saying the same thing.* (1997: 23, emphasis added)

What they are arguing is that what counts as 'the technology' is just as much the outcome of interpretive accounts – some more persuasive than others – as is what counts as the technology's 'uses' or 'effects'. They note that,

> For example, telephone technology was used originally to broadcast concert music. It was not axiomatic to its design that the telephone system would ultimately be restricted primarily to two-way personal communication, nor serve as a communication channel for students undertaking distance education, nor carry faxes, nor act as an electronic surfboard for the internet. The original use of telephone technology, and indeed its use now, was and is the result of interpretations and negotiations, not determinations. (1997: 21)

On the face of it, it might be thought that this approach has much in common with actor-network theory. There also, we found a scepticism about the characteristics of technologies and an unwillingness to accord any necessary, objective characteristics to technical artefacts. Yet Grint and Woolgar are equally critical of actor-network theory, asserting that it too is susceptible to 'technicism', or the idea that technologies ultimately have features specific to themselves. They discuss one of the foundational studies in the actor-network approach, Callon's (1986b) analysis of the attempts by a French company (EDF) to develop an electric car (the VEL) in competition with another company (Renault).

According to Callon, the actor network within which the VEL was developed, promoted and ultimately withdrawn from production involved a range of actants including batteries, zinc, potential users, city streets, the Renault motor company, engineers, catalysts, platinum and so forth. The two companies, EDF and Renault, sought to build different actor networks out of these consituents in order for their own technology to become the accepted one. The key point which Grint and Woolgar pick up on is the moment at which, in Callon's account, one element 'deserted' the network prepared by EDF, thereby playing into the hands of Renault. This element was the motor parts called catalysts: 'the catalysts refused to play their part in the scenario prepared by EDF: although cheap (unlike platinum), the catalysts had the unfortunate tendency of quickly becoming contaminated, rendering the fuel cell unusable' (Callon 1986b: 90, cited in Grint and Woolgar 1997: 31).

As Grint and Woolgar point out, this description implies that the catalysts had specific 'actual properties' – the tendency to become contaminated – which were not affected by their socially constructed role within the network. In other words, we once again find a retreat to technicism. Grint and Woolgar's proposal is that 'the "actual property" of catalysts [should] be treated as a construction (or accomplishment) and hence as part of the situation to be explained' (1997: 31).

> Who says catalysts had this unfortunate tendency, how and why did they say so, and why does this particular version prevail? A ... rendering ... in line with the initial scepticism about essential capacities of technical entities, might proceed by suggesting that what was initially construed (by EDF) as the attractive property of a solid ally, later became recast (by Renault) as the deficient weakness of a deserter. (ibid.)

Their alternative is to suggest that technologies should be treated as 'texts' which are 'written' (i.e. configured) in certain ways by their developers, producers and marketers, and have to be 'read' (i.e. interpreted) by their users or consumers. The writers of these technology-texts seek to impose particular meanings on the artefact, and to constrain the range of possible interpretations open to users. On the other hand, users seek to produce readings of the technology-text which best suit the purposes they may have in mind for the artefact.

Neither the writing nor the reading of technology-texts is determinate: both are open, negotiated processes. Although there may be ways that technology-texts have 'preferred' readings built into them, it is always open to the user to find a way round this attempt at interpretive closure. A good example, discussed further in chapter 5, is, once again, the telephone. As Frissen (1995) points out, one of the early ways that the telephone was marketed to a mass audience was as an instrumental tool useful for business negotiations (for men) and the management of household services (for women). However, women in particular began to 'read' this technology in quite a different way – as a tool for sociability, for chatting – and after a while the manufacturers, forced to accept this new reading, began to market what was essentially a 'different' technology to the one they had begun with.

The affordances of technological artefacts

The strength of Grint and Woolgar's approach over those introduced earlier is that they focus attention on the discourses through which technologies are made to 'become' what they are. In their case study of the design and production of a new personal computer system (1997, chapter 3), the procedure is to look at how not only the technology, but also its users, are configured or even invented in the daily course of meetings involving the different departments within the company. The analytic policy is to consider how the various discourses surrounding the project, from verbal contributions in meetings to the instruction manuals prepared for the system's eventual users, involve a battle of persuasive rhetoric in which one account is seen to win out over others.

However, some significant problems arise when we consider this idea a little more closely. The text metaphor appears to assume that technologies are 'open' forms. Although Grint and Woolgar are critical of actor-network theorists, they share with them a commitment to the idea that technological artefacts have no intrinsic properties, and that what they are is a matter for negotiation and persuasive rhetoric. But the unavoidable upshot of this commitment is that the artefact can be made to be anything in the world as long as the account is persuasive enough (or the network sound enough). Of course, this is not their explicit claim. Yet it can be found even in passages where they disclaim any commitment to absolute relativism. For example: 'In disassociating the upshot of reading and interpretation from any notion of the inherent quality of the text (what it actually says, what it actually means), we do not mean to suggest that any reading is possible (let alone that all readings are equally possible), *although in principle this is the case*' (Grint and Woolgar 1997: 72–3, emphasis added). But how far *is* that the case? How far, for example, are a fruit machine and a telephone open to the same set of possible readings? While both have many common aspects (for instance, both may routinely be found in pubs, both might need money putting into them to get them going, both may make bleeping noises), it seems clear that there are things which one can do that the other cannot. A telephone allows vocal signals to be transmitted along wires; a fruit machine does not. A fruit machine allows money to be won at specific moments of alignment of three barrels with pictures painted on them; a telephone does not.

Grint and Woolgar would doubtless argue that these descriptions themselves rely on a whole array of other constructions, both technological and cultural (for instance, 'transmission', 'winning' and so on), which are in turn the prior outcomes of persuasive negotiations. Indeed, they spend an entire chapter arguing against an objection by Kling (1992) that their position fails to acknowledge the fact that a bullet fired from a gun has effects on flesh and bone that are intrinsic to the gun and bullet, and cannot be altered by social constructions. Yet while they demonstrate again and again that there are manifold social factors involved in producing the outcome of whether someone gets shot dead or not (or even what it means to be 'dead'), they ultimately fail to dismiss the simple point that 'physical objects like guns and roses have some capabilities which are not only arbitrarily derived from the talk about them. It is much harder to kill a platoon of soldiers with a dozen roses than with well placed high speed bullets' (Kling 1992: 362, cited in Grint and Woolgar 1997: 154).

The issue is more complicated still. At various points Grint and Woolgar claim that 'the social constructivist argument does not deny that material artefacts have constraining influences upon actors' (p. 23), that their point is 'not to suggest that machines do not have effects' (p. 33) and that the technology-as-text metaphor 'does not mean that any interpretation is as good as any other' (p. 32). Yet because of their preferred focus, it is not clear what the status of such 'materiality' might be nor where such 'effects' might derive from. The problem is that the textual metaphor leads them to focus almost entirely on the question of *representations* of technologies. A general strategy is to observe that a given technological form (for instance, a bridge) can be represented in at least two competing ways and then show that both these representations are based on some conception of 'inherent' characteristics, whereas the more appropriate procedure is to analyse the discursive practices through which one interpretation wins out over another.

For example, in his influential paper cited earlier, Winner (1984) discusses the case of a series of bridges on Long Island, New York, which were designed by the civic architect Robert Moses to take traffic over the parkways linked to Jones Beach, a public park also designed by Moses. Apparently, however, these overpasses were designed to be very low-hanging, offering only nine or ten feet of clearance from the parkway. The consequence of this, according to Winner, was that buses, at some twelve feet tall, could not pass along the parkways; neither, therefore, could they get to Jones Beach. Winner argues that this was not simply a technical design feature of the overpasses – it was a political design feature, since at that time the main users of public transport were black and working-class people. Hence the effect of the overpasses was to exclude all but the car-owning middle and upper classes from using the parkways and associated recreational areas.

Woolgar and Cooper (1999) present a critique of this argument that, from a certain perspective, could be seen as a decisive refutation. That is, they reproduce as part of their article bus timetables which demonstrate that buses do indeed run along the parkway to Jones Beach and therefore that Winner could not have been correct. Characteristically, however, they seek to distance their argument from any claims about the 'real facts of the matter' and maintain that, of course, their own account is just as much of a persuasive construction as was Winner's original claim about the bridges. The timetables themselves become a playful element in this: they are not reproduced at the point where they are mentioned in the main body of the article, being supposedly 'lost' at the time of writing. Instead they make a 'surprise' appearance, quite separately, at the very end, under the heading 'Stop Press'. The 'material proof' offered by the timetables is thus distanced from the rhetorical construction of the authors' case.

There are a number of problems with maintaining an emphasis on representations. For one thing, as Button (1993) has pointed out, the focus on interpretive representations of technologies both inevitably relies on, and systematically leaves out of account, our common-sense recognition of the artefact as a particular type of artefact in the first place. For Button, the technology-as-text argument is flawed principally because it fails to acknowledge that *any* account of, say, a bridge is 'irremediably tied to the ordinarily constrained description of the technology "as a bridge". . . . To pursue the persuasiveness of one account over the other is then to direct our attention away from the ordinary constraints involved in describing some technology "as a bridge"' (Button 1993: 21). Button is not proposing that there are indeed inherent or objective characteristics of technologies. Rather he is saying that the range of descriptions that can sensibly be made of an artefact, the range of interpretations that can be made and still be recognized as rational, as opposed to being contrary or downright wacky, is constrained by the common-sense understandings of ordinary actors in everyday life.

I want to raise a different objection to the technology-as-text metaphor. Juxtaposing different 'readings' of a bridge, or of a computer, or of an aeroplane, certainly shows that humans are capable of interpreting the capacities of technologies in varying ways. It also appears to undermine the idea that the 'effects' of technologies derive from their inherent characteristics. But the inevitable question that then arises is: does the aeroplane lend itself to the same set of possible interpretations as the bridge, and if not, why not?

It seems clear that the answer to this question is no. The reason is that different technologies possess different *affordances*, and these affordances constrain the ways that they can be read. The physical capabilities of aeroplane and bridge are different, and because of this, they afford different (though overlapping) ranges of meanings. By ignoring the different affordances which constrain both the possible meanings and the possible uses of technologies, Grint and Woolgar deny themselves the opportunity of empirically analysing precisely what the 'effects' and 'constraints' associated with technological forms are. While they admit to the possibility of such effects and constraints, ultimately it is not clear where, in their view, these phenomena emerge from. Interpretations and representations are by definition defeasible, open to contestation. To what degree could these lead to 'constraining influences' and 'effects', terms which seem to imply the existence of precisely those objective features of technologies which Grint and Woolgar are so concerned to question?

The concept of affordances is associated with the work of Gibson (1979) in the psychology of perception. For Gibson, humans, along with animals, insects, birds and fishes, orient to objects in their world (rocks, trees, rivers, etc.) in terms of what he called their affordances: the possibilities that they offer for action. For example, a rock may have the affordance, for a reptile, of being a shelter from the heat of the sun; or, for an insect, of concealment from a hunter. A river may have the affordance, for a buffalo, of providing a place to drink; or, for a hippopotamus, of being a place to wallow. Affordances may thus differ from species to species and from context to context. However, they cannot be seen as freely variable. While a tree offers an enormous range of affordances for a vast variety of species, there are things a river can afford which the tree cannot, and vice versa.

Gibson argued that there are many types of affordances: affordances of the natural environment; affordances of artefacts; affordances of other species within the environment; affordances of other members of our own species; and so on. He used the concept to argue against the view, associated principally with Koffka's (1935) school of gestalt psychology, that the perception of an object in the world is based on the needs or desires of the observer, not on the object 'itself'. Koffka believed that we encounter things in the world in terms of their 'demand-character':

> The postbox 'invites' the mailing of a letter; the handle 'wants to be grasped'; the chocolate 'wants to be eaten'; things in experience 'tell us what to do with them'. In short, the value of something [does] not have any 'physical' reality. The valence of an object [is] bestowed upon it by a need of the observer [or user – IH]. . . . Koffka [argued] that the postbox has a demand-character only when the observer needs to mail a letter, for only then is he *attracted* to it. Thus the value of something is assumed to change as the need of the observer changes. (Gibson 1982: 409, emphasis in original)

By contrast, in Gibson's theory,

> the *affordance* of something is assumed *not* to change as the need of the observer changes. The edibility of a substance for an animal does not depend on the hunger of the animal. The walk-on-ability of a surface exists whether or not the animal walks on it. (ibid., emphasis in original)

In this sense, the uses and the 'values' of things are not attached to them by interpretive procedures or internal representations, but are a material aspect of the thing as it is encountered in the course of action. We are able to perceive things in terms of their affordances, which in turn are properties of things; yet those properties are not determinate or even finite, since they only emerge in the context of material encounters between actors and objects. Thus, for Gibson:

> An important fact about the affordances of the environment is that they are in a sense objective, real and physical, unlike values and meanings, which are often supposed to be subjective, phenomenal, and mental. But actually, an affordance is neither an objective property nor a subjective property; or it is both if you like. . . . An affordance points both ways, to the environment and to the observer. (Gibson 1979: 129)

The full range of affordances of any object cannot be available to immediate perception; although Gibson argued that some affordances, especially of objects in the natural environment, can be immediately perceived. But particularly when it comes to humans, for whom objects can be tied in with complex sets of concepts and the rules and conventions of their use, there is an important sense in which we must learn about the affordances a thing offers (Gibson 1979: 141). Similarly, affordances can be laminated or compounded. For example, a young child may become interested in a camera found around the house. The camera may be found to have a catch, which affords undoing, and a hinged door, which affords opening. Yet carrying out these actions will lead to problems if the camera contains a roll of film, which is a material affording the development of still photographic images but only if exposed to light under highly restricted conditions. The child may thus learn that there are both social and technological rules delimiting the affordances of the camera's door: namely that you do not open it while a film is inside unless you want to destroy the film.

The notion of affordances can enable us to transcend some of the unresolved difficulties in the constructivist technology-as-text metaphor. Let us return briefly to the earlier quote about the telephone from Grint and Woolgar: '. . . telephone technology was used originally to broadcast concert music. It was not axiomatic to its design that the telephone system would ultimately be restricted primarily to two-way personal communication . . . The original use of telephone technology, and indeed its use now, was and is the result of interpretations and negotiations, not determinations (1997: 21)'. Focusing for the moment on the last sentence, the question that arises here is: what is it that these interpretations are interpretations *of*? While it may be the case that the telephone was not originally marketed as a means of two-party interpersonal communication, the point is that it *affords* that form of interaction. The interpretations and negotiations that are referred to here are precisely interpretations of the affordances of the artefact: the possibilities for action that it offers.

Another way of seeing the problem is to think in terms of the relevant 'slots' which delimit the possibilities for actions in a particular sequence. In ordinary conversation, a question is a type of action that delimits the range of possible rational actions to be produced 'next' by a co-participant in the sequence of talk. A question, in other words, affords the production of something that is recognizable as, or can legitimately be interpreted as, an 'answer', or as something which attempts to evade giving an answer. Thus, the question already provides the structural possibilities for the next move in a conversation: you may choose to answer or not, but whatever you do can be heard as an action in response to the affordances offered by the question (I say more about this in chapter 4).

In Grint and Woolgar's approach, this relationship is inverted. That is, they seek to view technologies in terms of the interpretations that are made of them by social actors of various sorts, but the technologies themselves are seen as essentially formless 'first moves' in the sequence. It is the interpretation which makes of the technology what it is, rather than there being elements of the technology which constrain the possible range of interpretive moves that can be made in 'second' position. It is this idea of technology as a *tabula rasa* which is only given meaning and structure through actors' interpretations and negotiations that the concept of affordances allows us to challenge.

It might be objected that my suggestion that we focus on the affordances of technological artefacts is simply to fall back into a form of technological determinism. Note that earlier I suggested that the 'physical capabilities' of different artefacts may be different, and that therefore different ranges of affordances are associated with each. Does this reference to capabilities not mean that there are, after all, the kinds of determinate properties to technologies which social constructivists argue against? In a way it does. To focus on affordances in the way I suggest *is* to accept that there are features of artefacts that are not constructed through accounts. In my view, it is these features that provide the very conditions of possibility for competing accounts to be sensibly made. However, this is not to fall back into a form of technological determinism, because it is not to claim that human actors are necessarily caused to react in given ways to technological forms. Rather, it is to stress that the range of possibilities for interpretation and action is nowhere near as open for either 'writers' or 'readers' as the technology-as-text metaphor implies.

Grint and Woolgar, along with actor-network theorists, might go on to object that the very features that supposedly distinguish the aeroplane irremediably from the bridge are merely outcomes of the socially situated process of design and the negotiated interpretive stabilization through which the technology has become 'what it is'. My proposal that the bridge affords a range of possibilities for action that are different from the aeroplane is merely to state the obvious: for that is precisely the way that both bridge and aeroplane have been designed to have practical and social meaning, or use value. This is a more serious objection. But in responding to it, we will see in clear terms the difference between my position and those outlined above. It is not that I am suggesting a focus on affordances negates work on the socially constructed nature of artefacts; nor am I proposing to reinstate some notion of the 'natural' properties of what are, after all, man-made objects. Rather, the difference lies in the fact that I am proposing a shift in analytic focus for the sociology of technology: a change in empirical footing.

Affordances and the 'impact' of technologies on social interaction

Recall Grint and Woolgar's argument against Orlikowski (1992), outlined above. Their position relies on the rhetorical stance that 'objective realities' and 'social constructions' are the same thing: that is, what counts as objective reality is also a social construction. If this were not the case, 'it would imply that we could separate out the two' (Grint and Woolgar 1997: 23).

However, this is only an issue if we continue to rely on accounts and representations of technology. If, on the other hand, we turn the analytic focus towards what people do with technologies in ordinary everyday life, towards the precise details of how technological artefacts become involved in everyday conduct, a quite different range of issues becomes relevant. As the following chapters seek to demonstrate, when people interact through, around and with technologies, it is necessary for them to find ways of managing the constraints on their possibilities for action that emerge from the affordances of given technological forms. This can be more or less problematic, depending on the characteristics of the technology and our level of familiarity with it. Sometimes, quite novel ways of accomplishing communicative actions arise at the interface of the actor's aims and the technology's affordances. At other times, of course, people's ways of managing action in terms of those affordances effect shifts in the social status of the technology itself: for instance, from an 'expert system' to a 'dumb hindrance'.

I have already mentioned the telephone, probably the most firmly (and globally) established of all technologies 'for' communication. Among the things that the telephone affords is a form of interaction that would otherwise not be possible: a form of interpersonal co-presence in the absence of physical co-presence. Put another way, it enables us to speak intimately – by which I mean in the manner reserved for interpersonal co-presence, conversationally, in a way that preserves all the personality, recognizability and inflection of the ordinary voice – across vast physical distances. But what kinds of intimacy are afforded by this technology? The detailed ways in which people have taken up the affordance for verbal intimacy across distance and shaped it for situated communicative ends can only be revealed once we move beyond looking at the cultural meanings or representations of the telephone as 'a technological artefact' and observe telephone talk itself.

There is a good deal of research into telephone talk (e.g. Pool 1981; Schegloff 1986; Rutter 1989; Hopper 1992), but as I outline in chapter 5, it has not been concerned with mapping the relationship between patterns of talk and the affordances of the telephone as a technology for communication. Nevertheless, some early work in Conversation Analysis, notably by Sacks (1992), offers intriguing suggestions as to how that method can be a fruitful means for empirically investigating the nature of intimacy that is afforded by the telephone.

In a lecture first given in 1970, Sacks made the following remarks about the telephone (which he describes as an 'institution'), its 'distinctive features' and the 'modes of interaction' that members of a culture may deploy in relation to those features, in an argument which is close to the one I have been outlining.

> . . . an examination in which the modes of interaction were considered and the telephone's distinctive features were located, [could] then [be] used to develop something that could deal with things like 'intimacy'. It may well then be that institutions could get examined [by members] for their unique possibilities, and when their unique possibilities are found, they're employed. We might then look to other developed institutions for which we have some handle on their history, to see the sorts of work done on them which have nothing particularly to do with 'what they're supposed to do' or anything like that, and which then get elaborated on to make them both formally analysed and comfortable institutions. (Sacks 1992, vol. 2: 162)

What does Sacks mean here by the 'unique possibilities' of an institution like the telephone? I suggest that this is a similar idea to my use of the concept of affordances. In other words, we might understand the two different positions mentioned by Sacks as analogous to the positions at the heart of the present chapter. The dimension indexed by the phrase 'what they're supposed to do' seems clearly to be the concern of constructivist technology studies, where the main empirical interest is in how 'what they're supposed to do' is configured in and through (competing) accounts. But the reference to 'their unique possibilities' seems closer to indexing what I have referred to as the affordances of things: what they allow or even encourage people to do with them by virtue of their system of possibilities. As Sacks remarks, the empirical task is then to go on to discover what people use those arrays of affordances to accomplish in ordinary communication.

My point is that we can only generate empirical accounts of this nature if we accept that technological artefacts both promote certain forms of interaction between participants and constrain the possibilities for other forms of interaction. This means that technologies for communication can be conceived at one empirical level as elements in the weave of interaction: whether that be human–human, human–machine, or human–machine–human interaction.

The kind of approach advocated by radical relativist-constructivists systematically denies the possibility of such empirical analyses. This has to do with their chosen way of directing the analytic gaze. Their focus, as Button (1993) points out, tends to be on *processes* and not on *practices*. While these theorists aim to make the specifics of the technology their analytic object, as opposed to the technological determinist emphasis on 'effects', repeatedly the questions of '*what* it is to be doing science or technology, the interactional specifics of the work of (the) science and of (the) technology are ignored, and hence the science and the technology vanish from view' (Button 1993: 20, emphasis in original). From Winner through to Grint and Woolgar, these sociologists are concerned with the social processes by which technological artefacts get established as 'what they are'. They are not as concerned with how people practically engage with those artefacts, and with each other through the medium of those artefacts, in their everyday lives. Once we turn towards that kind of concern, then the 'unique possibilities', the affordances, of artefacts can be seen as a reality in terms of which people are offered possibilities for action; but, crucially, only some possibilities for action, and not others.

In this chapter I have outlined an alternative to the constructivist sociology of technology, based on an acceptance that our interpretations and uses of technological artefacts, while important, contingent, and variable, are constrained in analysable ways by the ranges of affordances that particular artefacts possess. The position I have taken up may seem redolent of some versions of realism, or what Edwards, Ashmore and Potter (1995) describe as 'bottom line' arguments (see chapter 10). It may also seem perilously close to a return to technological determinism: to a view that the reality of artefacts is something that imposes itself on the passive human user.

In fact it is none of these things. By utilizing the concept of affordances, we can avoid the arbitrariness of the radical constructivist position, with its single-minded view that the discourses surrounding technologies are the only phenomena with any possible sociological (and social) relevance, and also evade the equally unilateral epistemology associated with technological determinism. The affordances of an artefact are not things which impose themselves upon humans' actions with, around or via that artefact. But they do set limits on what it is *possible* to do with, around or via the artefact. I return to some of the deeper conceptual issues involved here in chapter 10.

Before moving on to case studies it is necessary to consider the second part of the formula I introduced at the start of this chapter, that of the interplay between the communicative affordances of technological artefacts and the normative structures of conversational interaction. Having developed an idea of communicative affordances, it is important to come to a clear understanding of the best way of conceptualizing and analysing communication itself. In the following two chapters I discuss some of the key models of communication and social interaction that prevail in the human sciences.

3

Communication as Computation?

Broadly speaking, social scientists who have been concerned to analyse how language and other modes of communication, such as gesture, are used in human interaction have developed theories the vast majority of which can be associated with either 'computational' or 'interactional' models of communication. Each of these models embodies a range of assumptions, both theoretical and methodological, which lead to very different ways of conceptualizing and analysing the processes of communication.

This chapter will be concerned with computational models. In referring to the 'computational model' I mean the way in which researchers in the fields of sociology, communication studies and psychology, along with certain areas of linguistics, have adopted notions of the communication process which utilize technological metaphors to stress the internal mechanics of cognition and the mental processing of information. For many centuries, technologies have provided metaphorical resources for a range of disciplines concerned with understanding human behaviour, cognition and communication. But what is the nature of these metaphorical devices, and how accurate are the more recent variants which are intended as representations of how humans communicate?

It is my belief that the computational model, while theoretically appealing, faces many difficulties when it comes to the empirical analysis of everyday conduct. In order to discuss those difficulties it is necessary to add some detail to the exact nature of the claims that are made within 'computationalism'. This chapter offers a selective overview, rather than an exhaustive account, of the key ideas relating to the computational model. In chapter 4 I go on to discuss how the alternative 'interactional' model offers a more adequate framework for analysing communicative interaction and its technological mediation.

The computational metaphor

An intriguing feature in the history of the social and behavioural sciences is the way in which key models of social life and human behaviour have followed in the tracks of technological innovation. In philosophy, psychology, linguistics and communication studies, many important theorists appear to have drawn their inspiration directly from the leading-edge technologies of their time. For instance, in the seventeenth century, Descartes proposed that a non-physical soul or 'mind' controlled the movements of our limbs by means of a complex miniature hydraulic system (Descartes [1664] 1953). This was at a time when the most advanced form of power was water pressure. For Descartes, the mind and the body were two entirely separate things (though by divine arrangement they were able to co-exist and interact in the same physical space). He believed that our actions are driven by two kinds of forces: conscious, but non-physical, thoughts, and non-conscious, but physical, reflexes. Either way, he proposed that our movements are facilitated by a set of tiny, interlocking hydraulic processes. Thus, to explain why fire, for example, causes us to flinch, seemingly without first having the conscious thought that we must move our hand away before it gets burned, Descartes suggested the following chain of events; the heat from the fire displaces the skin, which pulls one of millions of 'threads' connecting our outer skin to the brain; this in turn opens a pore in the brain, and 'animal spirit' flows out down a tube, inflating the muscles of the arm, thereby causing the hand to withdraw.

What is interesting here is the interplay between developing scientific knowledge of human physiology, and the applications of a specific technology, hydrodynamics. A similar combination can be found in various other disciplinary contexts. In medicine, developing knowledge of anatomy was tied in various ways to the workings of technological devices. Samson cites the following set of claims by the late seventeenth-century Italian anatomist Baglivi:

> Whoever examines the bodily organism will certainly not fail to discern pincers in the jaws and teeth; a container in the stomach; water-mains in the veins, the arteries and other ducts; a piston in the heart; sieves or filters in the bowels; in the lungs, bellows; in the muscles, the force of the lever; in the corner of the eye a pulley, and so on. (Baglivi, cited in Samson 1999: 10)

A number of more recent psychological theories exhibit the same tendency. At the end of the nineteenth century, Wundt believed that it should be possible to develop a psychology of consciousness in which all sensations and feelings are broken down into basic components and compounds. At this time, the scientific endeavours from which he drew his metaphor were chemistry and physics, where the basic elements of matter were being discovered and catalogued. Following the invention of the telephone, the psychologist Watson saw that the exchange network could act as an appropriate model for his theory of behaviour, in which the brain received incoming 'calls' from the sensory system and then relayed their 'messages' to the motor system. This tied in with Watson's behaviourist programme in psychology, in which the brain was significant only in its role as a mediator between sensations or other stimuli, and the body's responses to those stimuli (Miller 1981).

With the development of the modern digital computer in the 1950s, psychologists began to think of the human brain as analogous to a computational device. It had a central processing unit which fed information to columns of memory banks, then drew on that stored information as and when it was necessary. The central processing unit consisted of the conscious mind. Thus, in contrast to Descartes's view that the mind was not a physical part of the brain but something non-physical which yet had overall control of our physical being (a view known as 'dualism'), the mind was seen as a material part of the brain itself (a view known as 'materialism'). And in contrast to Watson's behaviourism, the computational metaphor placed the brain at the centre of things, as the originator of actions rather than a mere mediator.

Possibly due to the fact that computers are still the leading-edge technologies of our era, the computational metaphor remains extremely widespread within those areas of the human sciences concerned with understanding psychological processes and – more significantly here – the nature of communication. Indeed, although I have introduced these ideas in relation to philosophers and psychologists, the computational metaphor and the associated distinction between dualism and materialism turn out to have very important consequences for the study of communication. This is because there has been a parallel tendency within communication studies to adopt technological metaphors; and in the twentieth century the same two key technologies – the telephone and the computer – provided the source of those metaphors.

Saussure, an early key figure in modern structural linguistics, semiology and communication studies, developed a model of communication which he called the 'circuit of speaking' or 'speech circuit' (*circuit de la parole*) (Saussure [1915] 1984: 11). The idea here is that there have to be two participants in the circuit for meaningful communication to take place (Saussure in fact says, 'at least two' participants, but like most linguists tended to restrict himself to considering only dyadic exchange). A message is encoded in the head of speaker A, then transmitted via the mouth to the ear of speaker B. The message is then decoded inside B's head, and a next message is encoded, transmitted, received, decoded, and so on. In this way, the speech circuit comprises the movement of signals between nodes like this:

brain A $\rightarrow$ mouth $\rightarrow$ ear $\rightarrow$ brain B $\rightarrow$ mouth $\rightarrow$ ear $\rightarrow$ brain A

There is a marked similarity between the circuit imagined here and the telephonic circuit as represented in Alexander Graham Bell's original sketches for the technology he developed some forty years earlier (see Harris 1987; Hopper 1992). Bell's drawings showed a speaker talking into a conical device which was connected by wires through a set of electrical switches to another cone, where a second figure was depicted listening.

Harris remarks that in Saussure's drawings for his model, he marked lines between the two heads that 'look suspiciously like telephone wires' (1987: 216). Indeed, the term 'speech circuit' itself has a decidedly electronic ring to it. Similarly, Saussure's work refers to communication consisting of 'signals' connected in a 'linear' fashion, thereby perhaps implicitly invoking the telephone lines which carry electrical impulses from one telephone to another. In short, as Hopper (1992: 36–7) remarks, there were close connections between both Saussure's model and his analytic terminology, and the characteristics of telephone technology, which, in the early years of the twentieth century, was burgeoning in the major European cities.

Later models of communication were based even more explicitly on technological metaphors. One of the most influential was the 'mathematical model of communication' developed by Shannon and Weaver (1949). Again, this model was clearly influenced by signal transmission technologies such as the telegraph and the telephone. In Shannon and Weaver's graphic representation there is once again a set of nodes linking the 'source' and the 'destination' of 'messages'. The model itself is presented in terms of boxes linked by arrowed lines, resembling the technically oriented graphic conventions of the flow-chart – a form of representation inextricably linked to computer programming. Shannon and Weaver appeared to conceive of this as a general model of communication that could be applied whether the nodes represented computers, telegraph stations, phonographs, animals or humans. We are invited to imagine that rectangular boxes in fact represent human beings in social, communicative contexts. Thus, as in Saussure's model, there is an 'information source' (the brain of one speaker), a 'transmitter' (the combination of the mouth, air, sound waves and so on) by which the 'signal' (a word or sentence) is physically produced; and there is a 'receiver' (the ear of the hearer), and a 'destination' (the hearer's brain).

But there are a number of noticeable differences between these two models. For one thing, Shannon and Weaver's model incorporates a box which they label 'noise source'. This is meant to represent extraneous factors which may impinge on the clear transmission of a 'pure' message. Hence, between the signal as transmitted and the signal as received, environmental or contextual phenomena may come into play so that the received signal is not the same as the signal transmitted, but a distorted or otherwise altered version of it. In Saussure's model, communication is depicted as occurring unproblematically by means of clear lines connecting each of the participants.

The introduction of the 'noise source' is a further example of a metaphor drawn from technology. In electronic signal transmission, or in wireless broadcasting, 'noise' means interference leading to deterioration of the signal, caused by such things as poor-quality lines, electromagnetic emissions or atmospheric pressure. Thus, Shannon and Weaver's model not only looks like a computer programmer's flow-chart, but draws its conceptual architecture from the world of electronics. A further difference is that whereas in Saussure's model communication is depicted as a two-way process, Shannon and Weaver's model only depicts one direction of message travel: from source to destination. There is the possibility of feedback and dialogue in Saussure's model. Shannon and Weaver, by contrast, appear to treat communication as an essentially unidirectional process of information transmission.

More important for present purposes are the similarities between these two basic ways of modelling communication. I have already remarked that both are based on the operations of technological devices – principally, the telephone – yet we can also note that underpinning both is the same basic concept of communication as a process of *message transmission*. This is very obvious in the Shannon and Weaver model, both in its terminology of source, transmitter, signal, noise, receiver, and so on, and in its schematic emphasis on the linearity of message travel between the nodes.

For all its emphasis on the circuit of speech, Saussure's model also treats communication as largely a matter of activity in the brain.

Saussure saw the words that were spoken as ways of encoding meanings that originated in the brain, and viewed the achievement of understanding as a matter of the brain of the hearer decoding those meanings. This tied in with his general position that actual speech could not be the object of analysis for linguistics. Saussure distinguished between speech (*'parole'*) and the objective resources of language which, in his view, rendered speech possible (*'langue'*). He believed that in order for linguistics to be a science of language it needed to deal in abstract, objective generalities or laws, and he saw ordinary speech as too context-specific to yield such abstractions to observation. *Parole* was simply the means by which, on any particular occasion, speakers gave expression to feelings or ideas. *Langue*, on the other hand, constituted the very rules and resources by which utterances could be made to mean something, so that without *langue*, *parole* was not possible. We may be able to utter what linguistic philosophers have described as 'basic experiential expressions' such as cries of pain, pleasure and so on (Coulter 1979), but we cannot make our utterances mean anything beyond the purely experiential without a pre-existing abstract system of linguistic codes which we learn to use as a means for expressing our thoughts.

> The language itself is not a function of the speaker. It is the product passively registered by the individual. . . .
>
> Speech, on the contrary, is an individual act of the will and the intelligence, in which one must distinguish: (1) the combinations through which the speaker uses the code provided by the language in order to express his own thought, and (2) the psycho-physical mechanism which enables him to externalise these combinations. (Saussure [1915] 1984: 14)

As a result of this position, Saussure, while being among the first to recognize the importance of the interpersonal, the dialogic, and the role played by responsive feedback in achieving communication, ended up relegating interactive talk to a residual, 'ancillary and more or less accidental' (ibid.) category. Like Shannon and Weaver, though for different reasons, Saussure was drawn to see communication, paradoxically, as a *monologic* process, a matter of the encoding of thoughts into expressions using the codes of the language system. In fact, in the work of Saussure and his followers in linguistics and semiology, the emphasis is not on the production of an utterance at all, but on the achievement of understanding – the 'decoding' of 'encoded' messages. Shannon and Weaver held an essentially similar view, but they expressed it in the form of a claim that communication is a matter of the transmission of information 'bits', thus, again, drawing explicitly on contemporary thinking in what was then the rapidly growing field of cybernetics. It is for that reason that 'noise' sources become of interest, since they result in distortion of the 'original' message thereby making more difficult the task of understanding.

Each of these theories of speech exchange acted, in slightly different ways, as key contributions to the development of what I call the 'computational' model of communication. By that I mean that both of them rely on the idea that communication must, at some deep level, be a matter of the encoding and decoding of intended meanings. Even though both models appear to be based on the technology of the telephone, and even though Saussure, at least, was writing before the development of the modern computer, they are computational models because, in their different ways, they rely equally on the idea that communication is a matter of our brains computing messages, either by transforming them into words which our mouths then transform into sound waves, or by transforming sound waves received by our ears back into words and hence into 'intended meanings'.

A more recent, and quite explicit, theoretical formalization of this model can be found in the work of Fodor (1975), a philosopher and cognitive psychologist whose overall aim has been to establish the conceptual and empirical grounds for a computational theory of communication. In Fodor's view, the key question for the theory of communication is how communication can take place purely by 'the production of acoustic wave forms' (p. 103). As he puts it: 'A speaker is a mapping from messages onto wave forms, and a hearer is a mapping from wave forms onto messages. . . . The speaker, in short, has a value of M [i.e. a "message"] in mind and the hearer can tell which value of M it is' (p. 108). The brain thus has the twin tasks of 'encoding/decoding to and from wave forms [and] computing the structural description of those sentences which express that message' (p. 110).

To address the complexities of Fodor's theory in detail would be beyond the scope of this chapter (for an excellent overview and critique, see Coulter 1983). To illustrate, though, I will use an extremely simplified example. If, at the dinner table, I were to utter, 'Can you pass me the water?' my production of that utterance would, in Fodor's account, have passed through a number of antecedent physical stages. Various events within my body would have been signalling to my brain the fact that there was a need for some degree of rehydration (i.e. I am thirsty). My brain would then translate, or compute, those signals into a desire to imbibe water, and then into a 'message' such as a request for water to be passed. The message itself would then be computed into a grammatical sentence: in this case, the request, 'Can you pass me the water?' This sentence would then be uttered by means of a combination of, among other things, my lungs, vocal cords, tongue, jaw and lips, at which point it would turn into sound-wave forms. Such wave forms having traversed the space between you and I, your eardrums would then start vibrating according to the waves' different frequencies, and the impulses from those vibrations would be transmitted to your brain. Your brain would then compute the impulses back into their lexical–grammatical form, and at that point you would come to an 'understanding' of the intention that the 'message' expresses, namely that I want you to pass me the water.

Again, it is easy to draw analogies between this account and the technical operations of the telegraph or telephone. Indeed, it is significant that Alexander Graham Bell was himself a language teacher who worked with the deaf, and his ideas for the telephone grew out of developing techniques for speech communication with deaf people (Hopper 1992). And on one level, the analogy is of course correct. As Saussure recognized, we can distinguish between the words that a person utters and the 'psycho-physical mechanism' that enables speech to take place. Without certain purely physical equipment – such as air, vocal cords, mouths, eardrums, not to mention brains – verbal communication would not be a possibility.

So what is wrong with such a view? It is, after all, intuitively appealing. We imagine that in order to communicate with someone we need to come to an understanding of what their utterances 'mean', and that seems to be a process that occurs inside the head. We know that, at one level, conversation *is* a matter of sound waves: technologies exist for recording the pure sounds that spoken language is made up of, and those recordings do not reproduce words on the page but only squiggly lines. The words must therefore be a product of our brain's translation of those wave forms. Also, models like Saussure's and Shannon and Weaver's can easily take on an appearance of scientific rigour: if we can draw a model of an event or process, then it seems we have a sound understanding of how it functions.

The problems lie in two areas. One is conceptual: to what extent is it meaningful to say that people communicate by means of acoustic wave forms, with the corresponding belief in the central role played by the brain in computing these wave forms into 'messages'? The second problem is empirical: how can we go about analysing human communication if, as the computational model implies, the key processes take place inside people's heads? What I will argue is that these problems render the computational model inadequate as the basis for empirical research on conversational interaction. In criticizing computational models, I will come to a different type of metaphor which has developed in the work of conversation analysts (see Sacks 1992; Hutchby and Wooffitt 1998), in which the normative structures of interaction are conceived as a 'technology' for the production of orderly talk-in-interaction.

Conceptual problems for computational models of communication

As in many other analytic endeavours, we can distinguish between 'strong' and 'weak' versions of computationalism. The strong version, which I associate with Fodor (1975) and many cognitive psychologists, maintains that the brain is in fact analogous to a digital computer, and that ultimately there is no difference between physical events in the brain and what we mean when we say that we are 'communicating' with one another. The weak version I call 'implicit computationalism': the view that communication only takes place as long as speakers' intentions – the communicative plans underlying their utterances – are accurately encoded and decoded. A key interest here is in the ways in which speakers generate 'strategies' to enable themselves to be understood. And given that, as conversationalists, we know that we very frequently express ourselves indirectly, a recurring interest is in the ways that indirectly formulated messages can possibly be understood, or 'decoded'. This form of computationalism, which I discuss in a later section, is prevalent in certain areas of communication studies (see, for example, Berger 1997).

Strong computational theories of communication draw on a number of significant sources. Among them is Chomsky's (1965) influential notion of 'generative grammar' within linguistics. Chomsky shared Saussure's belief in language as an abstract system of symbols that was not reducible to the utterances of actual speakers, but he went further. In a classic debate with the behaviourist Skinner, Chomsky (1959) took issue with the idea that language was 'learned' through the process of our hearing words and expressions and attempting to copy them. Chomsky's argument was simple and extremely powerful: if this was the case, then how could we ever produce an original sentence, one that had not been uttered before?

Chomsky posited the radical idea that the human brain is 'wired up' from birth with the propensity to recognize grammatical forms (in whatever spoken language it encountered) and to produce understandable sentences. In other words, we have a language instinct that is built into the architecture of our brains and that enables us to be infinitely creative (within the abstract rules of grammar) in the sentences we verbalize. This focus on a brain-based language instinct meant that Chomsky's work played a significant role in the development of psycholinguistics, the study of how language processes are 'instantiated' in the neurophysiology of the brain (Clark and Clark 1977). Fodor's (1975) particular contribution was to take these ideas in an overtly computational direction.

More significantly, the argument also relates to two long-standing traditions of thought in philosophical psychology: 'physicalism' and 'mentalism'. Briefly, physicalism (as applied to human studies) is the idea that any behavioural phenomenon can be explained solely as the result of physical, or organic, events. For instance, to return to my earlier example, a desire to drink is caused by the body entering a physical state in which it is mildly dehydrated. My asking for water, then, is a behavioural event 'caused' by that physiological event. Or, to put it another way, the 'motive' for my producing an utterance asking for water *is* that physiological event. To take another example, the act of making an emergency appointment at the dentist is a behavioural event whose motive is the physiological event of a tooth reaching a state of decay sufficient to generate pain. Mentalism, by contrast, is the view that behavioural phenomena are underpinned not by physiological events, but by events centred in the mind, by 'consciousness'. The philosopher Mill ([1843] 1968) was one of the earliest to advance a systematic mentalist thesis in human science. According to Mill, 'a motive is *a specific mental occurrence* (in the Cartesian sense of "mental" implying that it belongs wholly to the realm of consciousness). A toothache, for instance, is mental in this sense, whereas the hole in the tooth which gives rise to the ache is physical' (Winch 1958: 78–9, emphasis added).

Thus, while physicalists wish 'to assimilate motives (toothaches) to states of the organism (holes in the teeth)' (Winch 1958: 79), mentalists argue that the physical and the mental events are distinct. Moreover, a mentalist may want to question whether there corresponds to every mental event a specific physiological event, or whether there may be cases in which 'events of consciousness' are caused by other 'events of consciousness'. For instance, perhaps I recently had a toothache but the tooth has now been pulled out; yet I can recall the sensation of pain so vividly that it makes me flinch.

In such a case, Mill might want to argue, my flinching behaviour is caused purely by an event of consciousness.

In philosophy and psychology, these two views have played a major role in long-standing debates about the underlying 'causes' of human behaviour and the nature of consciousness. But while they are often presented as diametrical opposites, aspects of both ideas, as my earlier illustration of Fodor's theory suggests, are entrenched in strong computational models of communication. They are reflected in the following kinds of notions: (a) that the process of communication is at root a physiological event, involving an interplay of brain cells, facial musculature, air waves and so on; (b) that the process of communication may also be based on 'events of consciousness' in which an intention is formed, subsequently translated into mental representations and then into words, and expressed through the physical medium in (a); and (c) that the production and comprehension of utterances is determined by identifiable combinations of such physical and mental events. While most strong computationalists tend more towards the mentalist than the physicalist standpoint, each of these beliefs can be found in various guises and combinations in their work.

Both physicalism and mentalism were subject to intense critiques in the mid-twentieth century in the work of Ryle (1949), Winch (1958), and Wittgenstein (1958), among others. In an alternative account that still retains enormous power, these philosophers argued that in order to understand human behaviour we have to begin with the ordinary concepts that humans use in everyday life to render their activities mutually intelligible. Such concepts are not properties of the individual, nor are they merely elements of consciousness. They are aspects of a shared and public system of resources – ordinary language – to which individuals have access by virtue of their membership of a culture. Indeed, Ryle (1949) argued that even many of the things which we normally think of as intrinsically mental events, such as 'understanding', are not mental events at all but publicly ratifiable *achievements*.

The concept of understanding refers to a person's ability to display that they understand: to show that they can see the point, that they can follow the rule or procedure. And that ability can only be displayed if there are some criteria external to the individual by which the display itself can be judged against what it is meant to exhibit an understanding of. In an important sense, then, understanding is something that occurs in a public interactional context rather than in the brain cells of the individual. The argument is not that brain cells have nothing to do with the matter. It is, rather, that while the brain may play a part (but only a part) in a person's capacity to do 'understanding', understanding is not to be seen primarily as an event in the brain, but as the *achievement of a person in the world*.

More recently, in linguistics, Harris (1982) has neatly characterized computational models as suffering from a 'telementational fallacy'. Telementational because they seem to depict speakers not as active participants in a conversation but as mere conduits for the brain-to-brain exchange of information: a kind of mental telegraphy. In this conception, the mechanical aspects of human bodies (e.g. the fact that our brains comprise neurons which apparently function in a binary fashion like processor cells) take over. The sense that we have of ourselves as active agents, as persons or selves in communication – in a word, the embodied nature of talking – gets lost. As Coulter puts it, the argument seems to be:

> that whatever I do is the *invariant* outcome of prior ratiocination, calculation, discursive reasoning, etc., *whether I am aware of it or not*. And ... if I am not even aware of constantly being engaged in [such] antecedent activities ... then ... it is not *I as a person* who is doing these things but parts of my insides (cortex, CNS [central nervous system]). (Coulter 1983: 21, emphasis in original)

The fallaciousness of such a view crystallizes in the underlying notion that we can only explain manifest public behaviour – what people do and can be seen to do – by reference to events inside the body. For strong computationalism, my utterance 'Can you pass me the water?' is correlated with a certain pattern of neural firings within my brain. Hence, technically, it should be possible to wire up each of my brain cells to electrodes (though since there are an extraordinarily large number of these it seems some compromise would be necessary in practice) and determine which individual cells fire when I utter those words.

But in order for the theory to carry any weight it would need to go further. No one denies that when we speak there is neural activity in the brain, that we move our mouths, tongues and so on, and that there is perturbation in the air around our heads. But for a scientific account which does more than note these correlations, it must be possible to describe internal processes as the *cause* of observable behaviour, and hence to predict the production of some form of behaviour given some determinate internal event. As Winch put it in an argument which, though published in 1958, still retains its full force: 'unless and until the "actual state of the organism" is actually identified and correlated with the appropriate mode of behaviour, this type of explanation is . . . vacuous' (1958: 77).

Hunter (1973), tracing one of Wittgenstein's arguments, expresses a similar view:

> I find it impossible to conjecture what explanatory force such a discovery [of neural firings associated with an utterance] would have. (It is not like being puzzled as to how someone does something apparently very difficult, and then being shown his system, and finding it easy after all.) It would show that we do have certain physical equipment for [talking]; *but whether that is the case was never part of the problem.* (Hunter 1973: 168, emphasis in original)

In short, without a predictive demonstration of causal relations between specific brain states and words that are uttered, the theory says little more than that we have brains and without them speech would not be possible. The 'problem' to which Hunter refers, and which the theory fails to address, is the question of how communication as an interactive process works.

Implicit computationalism

That question has been the focus of attention for a range of perspectives under the broad umbrella of pragmatics (see Levinson 1983). In the next chapter I discuss one of the more successful approaches: the paradigm known as conversation analysis. For the present, I want to give some attention to an influential branch of pragmatics whose underlying assumptions are in many ways very similar to the strong computational perspective. I refer to it as a 'weak' version of computationalism because the driving idea is that in order to understand communication we need to go inside the heads of speakers in search of a different set of phenomena: the 'plans', 'goals' and 'strategies' that lie behind utterances. Usually, researchers in this area of communication studies do not make overt references to technological metaphors, and for that reason a better descriptor might be 'implicit computationalism'.

A recent important overview of this work was provided by Berger (1997), who outlines five fundamental assumptions underpinning what he calls the 'plan-based approach to strategic communication' and what I am calling implicit, or weak, computationalism. These are:

1. Social actors' actions are based on their interpretations of their own and others' actions, not on the actions themselves.
2. Interpretive processes of social actors are largely non-conscious.
3. Knowledge of goals and plans enables social actors to understand others' actions and is used to guide social actors' actions.
4. Knowledge structures that guide social action are the product of mediated and unmediated experience.
5. Knowledge structures are a necessary but not a sufficient condition for the production of effective social action. Various performative skills also determine the ultimate effectiveness of social action.

(Berger 1997: 7)

While all five of these assumptions raise interesting questions, it is the first three that represent the most central ideas for present purposes.

Assumption (1) distinguishes between interpretations of actions and the actions themselves, and seems to be saying that communication is based on what we interpret others to be doing rather than on what they are 'actually' doing. There are a number of ways of responding to this. On one level, and in a similar way to the strong computationalist's insistence on the indispensability of brain processes in the practice of speaking, it is an uncontentious statement. The assumption states that we cannot purely 'see' social actions but that what we see is always filtered by our interpretations of what it could be, or mean. There is a parallel here between the activities that participants in interaction engage in and those upon which interaction researchers base their accounts: 'Observations provided by oneself and others, like observations collected by researchers, must be interpreted before they can become data on which subsequent actions are based' (Berger 1997: 7).

Yet if this is the case, there seems little point in sustaining the distinction in the first place. If actions cannot be observed in their 'raw' state, but only through interpretive mediation, what might it mean to maintain that there is any 'raw' data at all? This is a long-standing problem within sociology (in fact, our discussion of the social construction of technology in chapter 2 can be seen as a modern variant of the debate). Weber ([1922] 1968) was among the first to consider it, and he proposed that we could in fact sustain a distinction between the 'direct' observation of action and what he called 'motivational' interpretations of action. Weber argued that any action could only be said to be social in so far as the actor attaches a 'subjective meaning' to his or her action that relates to other individuals or groups. He thus maintained that one could observe a man chopping wood and say in a direct way that for this man, the action being engaged in was 'woodchopping'. However, there is another dimension to the woodchopping – what it means in social terms, in relation to others – and this could only be inferred on the basis of a more complex 'explanatory' understanding which went beyond the directly observable facts of the matter.

Schutz (1962, 1972) offered a well-known critique of Weber's argument. For Schutz, Weber's distinction between direct and explanatory interpretation means that Weber is employing the notion of subjective meaning in two distinct senses:

> First, he is referring to the subjective meaning which the action has for the actor. According to him, this subjective meaning can be understood 'observationally', that is, it can be grasped by direct observation. But second, he is referring to the broader framework of meaning in which an action 'thus interpreted' . . . belongs. It is this broader context of meaning which is uncovered by motivational or [explanatory] understanding. (Schutz 1972: 25)

In contrast to Weber, Schutz proposes, first, that actions that we call (for example) 'chopping wood' are always and necessarily pre-interpreted by the observer in terms of an already-existing framework of social meanings: they cannot be grasped in any 'pure' unmediated sense. Second, he suggests that it is not automatically the case that the person observed wielding an axe over a pile of logs is necessarily attaching the subjective meaning 'woodchopping' to their actions at all. Indeed, for Schutz, whether this is so or not cannot possibly be observationally established. He concludes that: (a) observed behaviour is comprehended for what it is precisely and unavoidably by being located within a larger, culturally available context of meaning; and (b) this context of meaning 'need not, indeed cannot be identical with the context of meaning in the mind of the actor himself' (Schutz 1972: 27).

The question therefore arises again: what is the purpose of sustaining the distinction between the 'context of meaning' and the subjective meaning 'in the mind of the actor himself'? For Schutz, and for Berger, the distinction is necessary because of the precise analytic stance being taken up and defended. Schutz was heavily influenced by phenomenology, a perspective that maintains, at root, that the meaningfulness of social life and of experiential phenomena are constituted in individual consciousness; and that in order to come to an explanation of human sociality we have to find some way of getting at the active life of that consciousness. Berger believes in the communicative significance of plans, goals and strategies, and maintains that in order to understand communication we have to find a way of getting at the generative powers of those cognitive phenomena.

Yet in Schutz's case, he believed that the aim of gaining access to individual consciousness, while desirable, was ultimately impossible, both for analysts and for members of a culture themselves: '"Intended meaning" is . . . essentially subjective and is in principle confined to the self-interpretation of the person who lives through the experience to be interpreted. Constituted as it is within the unique stream of consciousness of every individual, *it is essentially inaccessible to every other individual*' (Schutz 1972: 99, emphasis in original). Schutz therefore finds himself in a dualistic position, asserting that, whereas there is such a thing as subjective meaning involved in action, it is only by means of observation filtered through cultural contexts of meaning that action can be understood. If this is the case, how do people ever manage to come to an understanding of what each is 'actually' doing, as opposed to trying to match each other's (more or less informed) guesses as to what may be going on?

Schutz's answer to this problem of intersubjectivity is a very neat one. As Heritage puts it, it is 'to state categorically that human beings can never have *identical* experiences of anything, but that this is irrelevant because they continuously *assume* that their experiences of the world are similar and *act* as if their experiences were similar-for-all-practical-purposes' (Heritage 1984a: 54, emphasis in original). The problem of intersubjectivity is thus treated as a mundane, practical problem 'which is routinely "solved" by social actors in the course of their dealings with each other' (ibid.). (Particularly relevant here is the discussion of the 'general thesis of reciprocal perspectives' in Schutz 1962: 3–47.)

This idea is of particular relevance for conversation analysis, which will be discussed in the next chapter. However, to return to the plan-based theory of communication, it is clear that the distinction between interpretations of actions and the actions themselves is only necessary if one wants to sustain the belief that talk relies on underlying (computational) processes that are not available to observation. For Berger (1997) and other theorists of plan-based action, those processes are not the rather amorphous 'subjective meanings' of Weber and Schutz, but precisely the plans which drive speakers' utterances in interaction.

Yet how do participants get access to these unobservable plans? For Berger, they infer them from their behavioural manifestations.

Berger might therefore go along with Schutz's solution to the dualistic dilemma and maintain that while people cannot access each other's 'actual' plans they nonetheless work on the assumption that plans drive social action and respond accordingly. However, as assumption (2) in his schema states, it turns out that Berger believes that speakers do this largely 'non-consciously'. We thus find here an echo of the form of computationalism espoused by Fodor (1975). The idea that 'interpretive processes of actors are largely non-conscious' (Berger 1997: 7) is open to the same kind of objection: namely that it is a vacuous statement unless and until the non-conscious processes can be shown empirically to be at work in actual examples of communication. Since these processes are non-conscious, and hence not even available to introspection let alone behavioural observation, it is unclear how that could be achieved. Yet it is a convenient way of countering the speaker who objects to the plan-based theorist's assertion that the speaker's actions are based on plans, or on the interpretations of others' plans, since he or she can be said not even to be aware that this is the case (though it is, somehow, clear to the researcher on strategic communication).

We are thus approaching a bizarre picture of social actors coming to an understanding of what is going on in interaction on the basis of 'largely non-conscious' guesses (if indeed a guess can be non-conscious) as to what may be the plan or strategy inside their interlocutor's head. As assumption (3) in Berger's (1997) schema makes explicit, it is 'knowledge of goals and plans' that enables mutual understanding; yet seemingly that knowledge can only be based on interpretations of what is going on, not the events or actions themselves; while these interpretations, in turn, have the strange status of being worked out without our actually being aware of it ('non-consciously').

The observability of communication

At the root of the problem with both strong and weak computationalism is the recurring claim that events inside the body or brain are the 'cause' of ordinary behaviour such as talking. The problem has both a conceptual and an empirical dimension. Conceptually, the difficulty with such a view is this: 'motives', 'aims', 'plans', 'intentions', 'reasons', and so on – the sorts of things which have been posited as the causal engines driving social action – cannot be situated anywhere within the brain or elsewhere in the body, because their relevance on any given occasion can only become meaningful within the weave of social interaction itself (Winch 1958; Wittgenstein 1958; Coulter 1979). In having toothache, I indeed feel a characteristic pain which a dentist may formulate in terms of a causal chain involving extensive tooth decay. But on experiencing toothache, there are a number of things I might do, for instance take a painkiller or ring for an appointment at the dentist. I have access to these actions as part of an array of culturally available, conventionalized modes of 'motivated' behaviour. More than that: my motives, reasons or intentions are as much, if not more, a matter for others than for me as the agent of that action. And it is precisely by means of my observable behaviour, seen in the light of such culturally available conventional modes, that others are able in the first place to identify on my part, and so ascribe as my motives, certain internal states (e.g. agony, happiness, awe, anger).

The computationalist might counter this argument by observing that we frequently find ourselves in the situation of finding it difficult to come to an understanding of why someone is acting or speaking in a certain way, and that in such situations it seems clear that we engage in internal computations in order to reach a plausible explanation. In these extreme cases, he or she might say, we become aware of performing mental computations and so can begin to see that they are at the heart of our more routine actions too. Yet even here, there is, to quote Winch again,

> a very simple, but nonetheless cogent, argument against the [computational – IH] interpretation. . . . To discover the motives of a puzzling action *is* to increase our understanding of that action; that is what 'understanding' means as applied to human behaviour. But this is something we in fact discover without any significant knowledge about people's physiological states; therefore our accounts of their motives can have nothing to do with their physiological states. (Winch 1958: 78, emphasis in original)

Winch is making a similar argument to Wittgenstein when he says, 'if you see the expression of expectation [or intention, etc.] you see "what is expected [or intended, etc.]"' (Wittgenstein 1981: 11§56). Explanatory reference to causally efficient internal events, for Wittgenstein, works to 'screen' questions about the nature of meaningful action from view, not to 'solve' them (Wittgenstein 1958: 212ᵉ). In this account, it is the phenomena themselves (i.e. the practice of 'getting' a drink, 'going' for a walk, 'expecting' A, 'intending' B), as public (by which I mean observable, interactional) events, which *are 'what happens'.* Social actors routinely understand one another's actions in terms of motives, intentions, and so on; but these motives do not need to be a cause of the action, linked to it by internal mechanics, as my press on the accelerator is a cause of the car moving forward. 'Learning what a motive is belongs to learning the standards governing life in the society in which one lives; and that . . . belongs to the process of learning to be a social being' (Winch 1958: 83).

Turning to the empirical level of the problem, we see how the flaws in the computational metaphor relate specifically to the analysis of communication. Strong computational theories envisage communication as, at some level, an invisible process that occurs inside people's heads, where what we end up saying must somehow be generated by neurological events. Taken to its conclusion, this means that we cannot actually engage in the empirical analysis of communication unless we have direct access to these internal events. To be sure, we can observe the behavioural manifestations which are underpinned by these events; but the 'real' nature of the phenomenon, what is 'really' going on when we talk with one another, inevitably eludes us in the absence of technological devices by which we can get behind the screen of manifest behaviour. Weak computationalism accepts that communication is largely a matter of the behavioural manifestations themselves, though these must inevitably be interpreted by participants according to their conceptual models of their interlocutors' goals and the plans that are (internally) formulated to reach those goals. There is still both an internalist logic, and an implicit causal model, at work here.

The common error is the notion that, at root, talking among humans equates to a form of mental telegraphy (Harris 1982). We need to go beyond this technological metaphor in our analyses of human conversation. Although my interest in this book is in how humans interact with, around and through technologies such as the telephone and computer, I believe that we can only properly understand those processes if we abandon the idea that humans themselves function analogously to those very technologies. It is precisely in the interplay between the affordances offered by technological forms and the conventional resources involved in the organization of human conversation that we can begin to locate the 'impacts' of technologies on communicative interaction. The ways that humans communicate need to be seen as different from the ways that technologies – even supposedly 'intelligent' technologies such as speech-based computer systems (see chapter 8) – function. Only by recognizing that difference can we begin to account for the troubles that humans continue to encounter in the production of ordinary talk through, around and with technologies for communication; as well as their ways of dealing with those troubles.

What, then, is the more appropriate way of conceptualizing and analysing everyday communication? In the next chapter, I introduce a perspective which argues that communication can be adequately understood purely in terms of the behavioural, and hence observable, process in and through which people display and ratify their understandings of one another's utterances in the ongoing course of their interaction. To paraphrase Winch's remark quoted earlier, ordinary persons routinely reach understandings of one another's utterances without any access to one another's brain states; hence, in so far as communication is a matter for the actual people doing the communicating, its success is achieved entirely on the basis of publicly observable behaviour.

Of course, as we will see, this does not mean that people simply observe behaviour (listen to utterances, watch gestures, follow eye contact, observe facial expressions) and unproblematically read off others' meanings and intentions from it. But it does mean that the analysis of human communication should focus not on the 'psychophysical mechanism', to return to Saussure's ([1915] 1984) distinction, but on the conventional resources that interactants draw upon to accomplish communication.

4

Talk-in-interaction

The previous chapter offered a critique of certain technological metaphors at work in the study of human communication. I ended by suggesting that analysis of communication should focus primarily on talk-in-interaction rather than the decoding of linguistic signs, but should do this by investigating the norms and conventions which speakers in interaction observably orient to as the resources by which to establish or cement their mutual communicative understanding. Paradoxically, while Saussure's ([1915] 1984) ideas played a large part in establishing the view that the production of meaning in speech is based on conventions rather than on objective laws relating words with their referents (see Harris 1987), it is his theoretical distinction between *langue* and *parole*, and the resulting emphasis on language as an entity which can be considered independently of its instantiation in naturally occurring talk, that has led many towards the encoding–decoding models of computationalism. The Saussurian denial of the relevance of studying *parole*, or actual talk, in its own terms was taken to its extreme in Chomsky's (1965: 3) assertion that theoretical linguistics should be concerned with an 'ideal speaker–hearer', an entity 'unaffected by such grammatically irrelevant conditions as memory limitations, distractions, shifts of attention and interest, and errors'; in other words, with what Chomsky called linguistic *competence* rather than *performance*. It is a short step from here to the view that, in studying human communication, what goes on inside the head is more important than what comes out of the mouth.

However, if we are interested in the specifics of communication and its technological mediation, then a more fruitful way of viewing the phenomenon is not as an interior process but an exterior, publicly observable event. Turning the focus towards ordinary talk as an orderly phenomenon in its own right, conversation analysts have in recent years studied how people utilize norms and conventions of turn-taking and other behavioural phenomena to engage in the mutual collaborative achievement of communication. The conversation analytic perspective, which is the subject of the present chapter, underpins the empirical case studies of conversation and technology which appear in the rest of this book.

I begin by outlining some of the basic methodological and theoretical principles of conversation analysis (CA). I then offer a comparison between CA and what in chapter 3 I called the implicit computationalist perspective, by focusing on contrasting means of studying plans and strategies in everyday conversation. In the final section I discuss the main reasons why I believe that CA offers the best perspective for analysing the relationships between conversation and technology.

The perspective of CA

Since its early development in the lectures of Harvey Sacks at the University of California between 1964 and 1972 (Sacks 1992), CA has emerged as one of the most powerful approaches to the study of human communicative interaction. Put at its most basic, CA is the study of talk-in-interaction, the systematic analysis of the kinds of talk produced in everyday naturally-occurring situations of social interaction. Conversation analysts proceed by collecting tape recordings of talk in situations which are not prescribed, set up or organized by the researcher (as is the case in many social psychological laboratory studies of speech – see, for instance, Rutter 1989), but are, as far as possible, naturally occurring. The ideal is to collect recordings of talk as it would have been produced were the recording not being made. Ironically, while conversation analysts were for many years interested primarily in everyday casual conversation, and recorded hundreds of telephone conversations between friends and acquaintances, the type of data which best approximates to this ideal turns out to be the largely spontaneous talk that is broadcast in such contexts as talk radio programmes (Hutchby 1996). While this is not 'casual conversation', but a form of mediated public discourse, it is one of few sources of data for which the presence of the researcher's recording device is irrelevant; a form of unscripted talk that can be recorded in the safe knowledge that the same talk would have been produced even if the researcher had not switched on his or her tape recorder.

Nonetheless, the majority of CA work has focused on telephone conversations recorded with one or both participants' knowledge, and that will be the primary source of data used in this chapter to illustrate the perspective and its findings. There is, of course, a methodological concern here. It may be that for some purposes the knowledge of at least one participant that the conversation is being recorded could be significant. For instance, if we were interested in the relative frequency of behaviours indicating nervousness or embarrassment among specific interactants, then we may look at the relative frequency with which joking behaviour (or whatever behaviour we would hypothetically associate with embarrassment) is used in the conversation, treating the presence of a recording device as one of the controlled variables. But as we will see in the present chapter, such questions are not the concern of CA. Rather, as Drew (1989) puts it: 'the focus of ... analysis is not on how often [participants] joke but *how* they joke, not on how often they display nervousness but *how* they display nervousness ... in short, not on the frequency of some activity but on the details of its management and accomplishment' (Drew 1989: 99–100, emphasis added).

Conversation analysts would want to argue that if participants display some orientation to the presence of the recording device, or its possible effects on their talk, then that awareness, or more precisely the organizational features of its management and accomplishment, rather than being a detriment to the analysis would in fact become part of the topic of analysis. For example, in some observations of telephone conversation data, I have found that when one participant mentions to the other that the conversation is being recorded, there is a tendency for them to do this not at the start of the call, but only once the conversation has been under way for some time. Also, once the fact of the recording is mentioned, participants seem to treat this as a good reason to move towards the end of the call. That does not mean that they immediately hang up, but rather that no new substantive topics get introduced once the fact of the recording has itself been topicalized (for a consideration of how the 'ending' of conversations is a concerted accomplishment, see Schegloff and Sacks 1973).

The following is a single example. This occurrence comes some five minutes into a conversation in which Dave, a college student, has called his friend Pete and invited him to come on a fishing trip at the weekend. (For transcription conventions, see the Appendix.)

(1) Northridge:2:6–7

```
 1     Dave:        Well anyway ah I'm sittin' up he:re doin' some
 2                  uh::: sh:: (.) work h-u-homewor:k you know for
 3                  a final,
 4          (0.4)
 5     Pete:        Ye[ah.
 6 →   Dave:          [an' I'm in the middle of finals right now,
 7          (0.6)
 8 →   Dave:        An' I jus' want you to know that this
 9                  co:nversation is jus' been taped.
10          (0.3)
11     Dave:        Y'kn[ow.
12 →   Pete:            [Huh?
13     Dave:        This conversation ez been taped.
14     Pete:        It ha:s h[u:h,
15     Dave:                 [Yeah,
16          (.)
17     Pete:        Okay,
18          (0.3)
19     Dave:        .h Uh-
20          (.)
21 →   Pete:        Good thing I didn:' uh:: (.) Are you uh:: (.) a
22                  plummuh?
23          (.)
24 →   Dave:        nuhhhh huhhhh hn huh huh.hhh::: No it's for
25                  ah::::: ehhhh he .hh It's for a: (.) hhhh
26                  euhhhhhh It's for a final yihknow that uh have
27                  to turn in en i:ncomplete gra:de that I ha:ve.
28     Pete:        Oh: yeah [I (remember yo[u were    )
29     Dave:                 [Ye:h          [Remember that thing I
30                  was tellin' y' abo[ut
31     Pete:                          [Ye:ah ri:ght.
32     Dave:        Yeah.
33          (0.2)
34     Dave:        .hhhhhh (.) [.hhh s:-
35 →   Pete:                    [Oka:y du:de,
36 →   Dave:        So::: I'll talk to you next week the:n if not
37                  this weeke:nd
38     Pete:        Yeh oka:y send me a copy o' th' tape.
39     Dave:        ALRI:GHT ehh hhhh!
40     Pete:        (Come an') de[fend my[self.
41     Dave:                     [.hh    [.hhh
42     Dave:        Alri:[ght
43     Pete:             [hhhheh[heh
44     Dave:                    [A'ri:ght Pehhte .hh
```

45	Pete:	<u>O</u>kay dude
46	Dave:	A'right <u>l</u>ater o:n=
47	Pete:	=<u>A</u>'right <u>b</u>ahbye

It is clear that Pete did not know that the conversation was being taped before Dave announced it; thus, the talk of at least one participant (Pete) cannot be said to have been affected by the fact of the recording. Whether or not Dave's conversation was affected is something we cannot say, though it is the case that throughout the conversation up to this point, Pete has not commented on (that is, observably oriented to) any 'strange' conversational behaviour on the part of his interlocutor. Equally clearly, Dave does know that the conversation is being recorded. However, the issue for CA has to do not with what might be going on inside Dave's head as a result of this knowledge but with the displayed, publicly observable behaviour which Dave and Pete engage in once the 'fact' of the recording becomes a topic of interaction. If we observe this behaviour, we can get a glimpse of the kind of issue the participants took the recording to be; that is, how they managed the recording as a mutually available factor in their interaction.

Note first how Dave announces the recording of the conversation. He begins by starting a new topic with the words 'Well anyway' (line 1), and this topic (his homework assignment) turns out to be the reason for his having recorded the conversation. The recording, in other words, is introduced in the context of furnishing its own justification. Dave justifies his actions in recording the call – which may be open to being treated as 'underhand' – by mentioning a factor outside his control, the assignment set by his college tutor.

Secondly, note how Pete is surprised by this announcement: he responds with a pause, in line 10, and then 'Huh?' in line 12. It seems, then, that Pete has not suspected anything odd about Dave's behaviour so far in the conversation. We can observe also that Pete appears to be more bemused than shocked or outraged by this announcement (lines 14 and 17).

A third thing to notice is that the participants treat the revealed fact of the recording as the occasion for joking behaviour: Pete begins to say something along the lines of 'Good thing I didn't [say anything incriminating]' in line 21, and then initiates self-repair in order to ask Dave, 'Are <u>you</u> uh:: (.) a plummuh?' This seems bizarre, until we realize that this conversation was actually recorded in America in the early 1970s, and that this is a reference to an aspect of the then topical Watergate scandal in which tapes were surreptitiously made of President Nixon which ultimately led to his downfall. Dave responds by laughing at length in the course of providing (again) the account of why he is making the recording (lines 24–32). The point here is that such behaviour, for CA, is not to be seen as a psychological reaction to the presence of the recorder, but as the participants' way of managing a response to the revelation of the recorder's presence.

A final thing to note is the way that the announcement is treated as a cue to end the call. Once more, humour is involved, as Pete jokingly instructs Dave to send him a copy of the tape so that he can 'defend' himself (lines 38–40). A possible reason for participants (in this call and others I have looked at) treating the announcement of a recording as an occasion to end the call may have to do with a common-sense derivation of the very notion that the presence of a recording device will have effects on interaction: the presence of the recorder having been pointed out and made an explicit topic of, participants may feel that they cannot appropriately say anything more without finding themselves subject to these posited effects.

However, this is to move into the realm of speculation. CA's general aim is to avoid such speculation. Indeed, in this particular case, we may not need any speculation, since it is noticeable that the conversation itself – that is, the subject of the recording – is mentioned in the *past tense* both when Dave makes the announcement 'this co:nversation is jus' been taped' (lines 8–9), and when Pete responds 'It ha:s hu:h,' (line 14). Thus, a feature of the way in which the recording is announced is that it frames the conversation itself as having come to an end.

I have made this brief set of observations in order to bring out the way in which CA seeks to focus on the behavioural, as opposed to cognitive or internal, elements of talk-in-interaction. Although we cannot say whether his recording of the conversation was a factor in Dave's mind all the way through the call, the point is that we do not need to know that in order to describe the accomplishment of this conversational fragment. The resources that Dave and Pete have for understanding and judging one another's actions are, to all intents, identical to the resources I have as an observer, given that I am a member of the same (Anglo-American) language community: they are the conventions of conversational turn-taking and utterance design which underlie the coherence of their utterances as a meaningful sequence of actions. It is with these conventions that CA is concerned. Crucially, however, CA views such conventions not as independent entities, understandable outside any concrete interactional context, but always as the situated concerns of interactants themselves.

Turn-taking in conversation

We can best illustrate this point by a consideration of some fundamental CA work on the organization of turn-taking in conversation. In 1974, Sacks, Schegloff and Jefferson published 'A simplest systematics for the organization of turn-taking for conversation', a paper that has become a foundational study in CA. The paper outlines a model of how speakers manage turn-taking in mundane conversation. For CA, the word 'mundane' does not refer in its colloquial sense to any notion that conversation is a lower, less serious or less consequential form of talk-in-interaction than any other. The term is used in a technical sense to describe a particular form of talk in which what people say, how they say it and the length of the turn in which they say it – i.e. turn *form*, turn *content* and turn *length* – are freely variable. In other, more formalized or ceremonial forms ranging from loosely structured interviews between doctors and their patients to high ceremonies such as weddings, various oriented-to constraints can be observed on one or more of the three parameters of turn form, turn content and turn length.

Sacks et al. (1974) note three very basic facts about conversation: (a) turn-taking occurs, (b) one speaker tends to talk at a time, and (c) turns are taken with as little gap or overlap between them as possible. This is not to claim that there is never more than one speaker talking at a time, or that gaps and overlaps do not occur. Rather, the point is that the ideal is for as much inter-speaker coordination as possible. The turn-taking model has two components: a 'turn-construction' component and a 'turn-distribution' component. Turns at talk can be seen as constructed out of turn-construction units which broadly correspond to linguistic categories such as sentences, clauses, single words (e.g. 'Hey!' or 'What?') or phrases. It is important to realize that it is not part of the conversation analyst's aim to provide an abstract definition of what a turn-construction unit is, as a linguist may want to define what a sentence is. Conversation analysts cannot take a prescriptive stance on this question, because what a turn-construction unit consists of in any situated stretch of talk is seen as a concern for the speakers themselves.

There are two key features of turn-construction units. First, they have the property of 'projectability'. It is possible for participants to project, in the course of a turn-construction unit, what sort of unit it is and at what point it is likely to end. This leads to the second feature, which is that turn-construction units bring into play 'transition-relevance places' at their boundaries. At the end of each unit, there is the possibility for legitimate transition between speakers. These two properties are illustrated in the following extract:

(2) SBL: 1:1:10:15

```
1 Rose:   Why don't you come and see me some[times
2 Bea:                                       [I would
3          like to
4 Rose:   I would like you to
```

Bea is able to recognize Rose's utterance 'Why don't you come and see me sometimes' as a form of invitation, and to respond to it with an acceptance before it has actually finished (line 2).

One point to note is that although Bea's projection of the first turn's transition-relevance place – that is, after 'sometimes' – turns out to be accurate (as shown in Rose's following turn, 'I would like you to'), the turn could have taken a different shape. For instance, Rose could have been about to say 'Why don't you come and see me sometime *this week*', which would have made the invitation much more specific, and Bea may then have had to give a different response. By starting to talk when she does, therefore, Bea not only projects the end of a particular turn-construction unit, but also displays an understanding of what kind of invitation that unit represents.

But what would have happened if Rose had been about to append something further, such as 'this week', to her invitation? This leads us to the second part of the turn-taking model: the mechanism for distributing turns between participants. Sacks et al. (1974) propose a simple set of rules which describe how turns come to be allocated at transition-relevance places, which I paraphrase below.

At the initial transition-relevance place of a turn:

Rule 1   (a) If the current speaker has identified, or selected, a particular next speaker, then that speaker should take a turn at that place. (b) If no such selection has been made, then any next speaker may (but need not) self-select at that point. If self-selection occurs, then the first speaker has the right to the turn. (c) If no next speaker has been selected, then alternatively the current speaker may, but need not, continue talking with another turn-constructional unit, unless another speaker has self-selected, in which case that speaker gains the right to the turn.

Rule 2   Whichever option has operated, then rules 1(a)–(c) come into play again for the next transition-relevance place.

Crucially, these 'rules' are not proposed as external to any concrete occasion of talk, nor do Sacks et al. believe that they furnish law-like constraints on participants. Rather, the rules are intended as descriptions of the practices which participants display an orientation to in actual local occasions of turn-taking. At the same time, like the rules of syntax (though in a different sense), it is not necessary for speakers to 'know' these rules discursively. It is more accurate to say that they are instantiated and therefore reproduced on each concrete occasion of talk-in-interaction.

In this sense, perhaps the word 'rules' is misleading. Schegloff (1992a) concedes that the use of 'rule' in the original 1974 paper may be problematic, and instead says 'I am willing to adopt for now an alternate term, such as "practice" or "usage"'. But he goes on to insist 'There is still an interrelated set of these, whatever we call them; they are still followable, followed, practiced, employed – oriented to by the participants, and not merely . . . extensionally equivalent descriptions of behaviour' (Schegloff 1992a: 120). Button argues that the term 'rule' is still acceptable, as long as we understand its meaning in a particular way.

> They are rules that in their conduct people display an orientation to. That is, the relevance of the rules for a person's conduct is displayed and preserved in their actual conduct. . . . [The rules do] not lie behind the actions of constructing a turn, allocating a turn, and coordinating speaker transfer thereby causing those things to happen. We do not get a turn because of the rules. Rather, the way in which a turn is taken displays an orientation to the rule. A rule is followed as part of accomplishing the action. The sense of rule here is, then, part of the logical grammar of the action. There is not an internalised rule that causes the action. The rule does not precede the action. Rather, the rule is discoverable in the action. (Button 1990: 78–9, emphases removed)

Thus, the aim is not to develop a prescriptive set of turn-taking rules which are supposed to lie behind action in some internal cognitive realm, but to describe and analyse the situated practices by which an orientation to rules is displayed in actual contexts of interaction.

Let us return, then, to our hypothetical question about extract (2): what if Rose had not actually been about to finish her turn at the point when Bea projected its completion? Would Bea's turn then have been a violation of the rules? On one level, it should be clear that the answer is no. Bea projected a transition-relevance place at the end of what was a possibly complete turn-construction unit by Rose: the question 'Why don't you come and see me sometimes?'. As I have said, neither the rule-set nor CA itself seeks to prescribe and predict what turn-construction units can legitimately consist of. This is an issue for the participants in conversation, not the conversation analyst. So Bea acted entirely within the rules – or, to be more accurate, her behaviour shows her orienting to the rules: in particular, rule 1(b) as outlined above.

Even if her projection of a transition-relevance place had turned out to be inaccurate, that would not matter in terms of the rules for turn-taking, since as Schegloff (1992a) points out, participants orient to possible transition-relevance places, not to 'actual' ones. There are good organizational reasons for this. The ideal in conversation is for one speaker to talk at a time with as little gap and overlap as possible between turns. This means that speakers need to coordinate their bid for a turn as closely as possible with the completion of a current speaker's turn-construction unit. If they were to wait for the speaker actually to stop speaking, that would mean they might lose the opportunity of a turn to someone else, or else the current speaker might carry on with another unit. For this reason it is the possibility of completion, rather than its actual occurrence, that is the most relevant factor in managing turn-taking. If this were not the case, as Schegloff remarks, then we would expect to see gaps of silence between turns as next speakers made sure that the current speaker had actually finished. This is not what we tend to find in empirical materials.

However, on another level, there is no answer, in the abstract, to the question of whether Bea's turn would have been considered a violation of turn-taking rules, because this would be an issue that was worked out by the participants themselves on that occasion of talk. In other words, it would have been up to Rose, as the continuing speaker, to indicate to Bea that her turn was in some way 'interruptive' of Rose's unfinished talk. Of course, this kind of thing frequently happens, as illustrated by the following extract, which is taken from a discussion on a talk radio show about the problem of dog owners allowing their pets to foul pavements.

(3) H:2.2.89:4:1–2

```
1 Host:    Well did you- did you then explain that, you
2          understood that, you know dogs have the call of
```

```
3              nature just as er as people do, and they don't
4              have the same kind of control and so
5              the[refore, s- so
6 Caller:         [No, but dogs can be tr[ained
7 Host:                                   [I haven't finished,
8              so therefore the owner . . . being there has the
9              responsibility . . .
```

In line 7, the host treats the caller's utterance as an interruption, saying 'I haven't finished' and then carrying on with his point about dog owners being responsible. Thus, he treats her as having violated turn-taking rules by not orienting to the completion of his turn. It may be, though, that the caller does orient to a possible completion point in the host's turn: that is, after 'dogs have the call of nature just as er as people do, and they don't have the same kind of control' (lines 2–4), at which juncture she comes in with her point 'No, but dogs can be trained' (line 5). At the same time, there turns out to be some warrant for the host's treating this turn as violative, since before the caller actually starts talking he has begun on a next turn-construction unit 'and so therefore . . .' (lines 4–5). What we find in this extract, then, is that the two speakers orient to different aspects of the rule-set. The caller orients to rule 1(b): at a (possible) transition-relevance place a next speaker may self-select; while the host orients to 1(c): at a (possible) transition-relevance place the current speaker may continue talking, unless another has self-selected. Here, although the caller has self-selected, the host treats himself as the first starter on the next unit, and hence as having rights to the turn.

This set of rules, or 'practices' or 'usages', provides a basic matrix within which conversation analysts have provided empirically grounded descriptions of the interactively managed organization of communicative behaviour in a huge range of social contexts and for a wide variety of everyday social actions. CA has used its focus on turns and the management of turn-exchange to build compelling accounts of structural organizations in overlapping talk (Jefferson 1986), repair and correction (Schegloff, Jefferson and Sacks 1977; Schegloff 1987), topic shift (Jefferson 1984), sequences initiated by such activities as greetings (Schegloff 1986), invitations (Drew 1984), and other kinds of preliminaries (Terasaki 1976; Schegloff 1980, 1988), agreement and disagreement (Pomerantz 1984), storytelling (Jefferson 1978), discourse markers such as 'Oh' (Heritage 1984b) and 'Well' (Pomerantz 1984), non-lexical response tokens such as 'Uh huh' (Schegloff 1982), and laughter (Jefferson,

Sacks and Schegloff 1987). In addition, conversation analytic work has expanded beyond the domain of telephone interactions, which represented a propitious starting point for the analysis of talk-in-interaction precisely because of the lack of possibly complicating visual and gestural contact between participants, to study video recordings of interactions with the aim of analysing the integration of speech with non-vocal activities (C. Goodwin 1981; Heath 1986). CA has also been used within a broader ethnographic framework by anthropologists such as Moerman (1988) and M. H. Goodwin (1990). Finally, researchers interested in institutional discourse have introduced a further comparative perspective to CA by using it to analyse the distinctive methods of turn-taking and activity organization found in specialized settings such as courts of law (Atkinson and Drew 1979; Maynard 1984), classrooms (Mehan 1979), broadcast news interviews (Clayman 1988; Greatbatch 1988), radio phone-ins (Hutchby 1996), public speeches (Atkinson 1984), doctor–patient interaction (Heath 1986), emergency call-handling services (Whalen and Zimmerman 1987; Zimmerman 1992), counselling dialogues (Perakyla 1995; Silverman 1996) and many others (Drew and Heritage 1992).

In all these applications, CA research aims to reveal how the 'technical' aspects of turn-taking represent structured, socially organized resources by which participants perform and coordinate activities through talk-in-interaction. Talk is treated as a vehicle for social action, and also as the principal means by which social organization in person-to-person interaction is mutually constructed and sustained. Hence it is a strategic site in which social agents' orientation to and evocation of their ongoing intersubjectivity can be empirically and rigorously investigated.

Sequential organizations and intersubjectivity

The previous section stressed CA's focus on turn-taking. This emphasis is not simply due to the 'obvious' fact that talk-in-interaction is an activity in which participants take turns. Rather, beginning from turn-taking enables us to gain access to the publicly achieved character of understanding and intersubjectivity. Recall that, in the computational model of interaction, these two phenomena are thought of as internal computational processes, having to do with the 'decoding' of messages, and which therefore take place 'behind' the observable phenomena of speech. For CA, participants' understandings of one another are displayed in interaction, and displayed for one another, principally through the sequential organization of turn-taking.

The fact that talk-in-interaction can be seen to be organized into turns leads to a crucial distinction for CA. Turns may be said to display a serial order, one coming after the other with, ideally, little gap and overlap. But CA is interested in how participants establish the relationship between turns, and it is clear that this is not just a serial relationship but a *sequential* relationship. That is, there are describable types of order relating turns together in sequences of two or more, though the largest reproducible integral sequences that have yet been described in spontaneous conversation do not exceed five turns (see Schegloff 1992b). The significance of this is that through orienting to sequences, rather than merely series of turns, participants in talk-in-interaction display in any 'current' utterance their understanding of the kind of turn the prior turn was intended as, and the kind of turn it projects to follow.

This is aptly illustrated by one of CA's most widely known concepts, the adjacency pair sequence. This is based on the observation that certain categories of utterance make relevant a circumscribed class of responses in next position. Canonical examples are: a question, which makes an answer relevant as the next move; a greeting, which makes a return greeting relevant in next turn; an invitation, which makes an acceptance or declination relevant in next position; or an accusation, which makes a rebuttal or justification relevant next. These are all representative of adjacency pairs.

The point here is not simply to note that questions are followed by answers, and so on, but to note the way in which particular types of utterance are made *conditionally relevant* by prior turns. The production of a first pair-part, such as a greeting, sets up the constraint that a next selected speaker should follow directly by producing the relevant second pair-part – in this case, a return greeting. Moreover, whatever does follow a first pair-part will be monitored for exactly how it works as a response to that move. By saying that a second pair-part is conditionally relevant given a first, conversation analysts are pointing to the normative character of the adjacency pair relationship.

This normative constraint is strong on two levels. First, motivational inferences can be drawn from the non-occurrence of a second part following the production of a first. For instance, not providing an answer to a question may be taken as indicative of evasiveness; not returning a greeting may be taken as a sign of rudeness; while not proffering a defence to an accusation may be taken as a tacit admission of guilt (for an interesting legal take on this, see McBarnet 1981).

Second, the oriented-to relevance of second parts following the production of a first can remain in play across time: it is not limited to cases of literal adjacency. Thus, instances in which, say, a question is followed by another question, rather than an answer, may seem to run counter to the adjacency pair concept. But such cases can in fact display the temporally extendable relevance of the adjacency pair framework, once we see that the second question routinely represents a first move in an insertion sequence (Levinson 1983: 304–6). Insertion sequences defer a second pair-part's production, but they do not negate its relevance. A speaker may respond to a question such as 'Can I borrow the car?' with another question, 'How long do you need it?' The response to that inserted question – say, 'Only a couple of hours' – provides a next slot in which a response to the first question is once more relevant and to be monitored for.

Another aspect of the normative properties of adjacency pairs lies in the systematically different ways that recipients of first parts design the alternative actions to be done in second position. Invitations, for instance, can be accepted or declined; requests can be granted or rejected. These alternatives are non-equivalent. Their non-equivalence can be traced in the features of turn design through which alternative second parts are proffered. Broadly, responses which agree or are congruent with the expectation projected by a first pair-part tend to be produced contiguously and without mitigation. Responses which diverge from that expectation tend to be prefaced by hesitations, discourse markers such as 'Well . . .', and, unlike congruent responses, are accompanied by accounts for why the speaker is responding in this way (Drew 1984; Pomerantz 1984; Sacks 1987).

These different response types have been termed 'preferred' and 'dispreferred' respectively (Pomerantz 1984). In line with its general standpoint, CA does not use these terms to refer to the psychological dispositions or motives of individuals but only to point to this structural feature of the sequential organization of some types of adjacency pair. Research has shown that the design features of dispreferred responses can be used as a 'technical' resource for the maintenance of social solidarity in talk-in-interaction. This is so not only in the way that dispreferred responses may be accompanied by accounts or explanations, but also in the way that hesitations and other means of marking a dispreferred response can provide a source for a first speaker to revise the original first pair-part in such a way as to try and avoid disagreement or rejection (Davidson 1984).

These points emphasize the centrality of the idea that the production and interpretation of talk-in-interaction are orderly accomplishments whose very orderliness is observably oriented to by the participants themselves. As Schegloff and Sacks put it, 'it [is] a feature of the conversations we [treat] as data that they [are] produced so as to allow the display by the co-participants to each other of their orderliness, and to allow the participants to display to one another their analysis, appreciation and use of that orderliness' (Schegloff and Sacks 1973: 290).

In talk-in-interaction, speakers display in their sequentially 'next' turns an understanding of what the 'prior' turn was about. That understanding may turn out to be what the prior speaker intended, or not; whichever is the case, that itself is something which gets displayed in the next turn in the sequence. This has been described as a 'next-turn proof procedure', and it is the most basic tool used in CA to ensure that analyses explicate the orderly properties of talk as oriented-to accomplishments of participants, rather than being based merely on the assumptions of the analyst.

> While understandings of other turns' talk are displayed to coparticipants, they are available as well to professional analysts who are thereby afforded a proof criterion (and a search procedure) for the analysis of what a turn's talk is occupied with. Since it is the parties' understandings of prior turns' talk that is relevant to their construction of next turns, it is their understandings that are wanted for analysis. The display of those understandings in the talk of subsequent turns affords . . . a proof procedure for professional analysis of prior turns – resources intrinsic to the data themselves. (Sacks, Schegloff and Jefferson 1974: 729)

As an illustration of this, consider the following utterance, which is from an exchange between a mother and her son about a forthcoming parent–teachers' association meeting.

(4) Family Dinner

1 Mother: Do you know who's going to that meeting?

On the face of it, the question 'Do you know who's going to that meeting?' is ambiguous. It can readily be interpreted as doing either of two types of action. It might represent a genuine request for information about who is attending the meeting, or it may be a 'pre-announcement' (Terasaki 1976), a preliminary to some information that the speaker herself wishes to announce about who is going. In the first case, the required response would be an answer to the question, whereas in the second case the response would be something like 'No, who?', which would provide the opportunity for the news to be announced.

From a computational perspective, the ambiguity would represent a potential problem in communication; the next speaker's task would be to try and decode which of its possible meanings the utterance carried. But this decoding, at the same time as being the focus of concern, is invisible to observation. For CA, on the other hand, the issue is how the participants display their understanding or interpretation of the utterance, regardless of whether they succeed in 'decoding' whatever meaning may originally have been 'encoded' in the message. The point is to show that mutual understanding or intersubjectivity are publicly ratifiable accomplishments, which, precisely because they are public, are observable in the data of talk-in-interaction.

In this case, the observability of the establishment of mutual comprehension is shown particularly clearly in the next few turns following Mother's question.

(4) Family Dinner ((Continued))

```
1 Mother:   Do you know who's going to that meeting?
2 Russ:     Who?
3 Mother:   I don't know!
4 Russ:     Oh, probably Mr Murphy and Dad said Mrs
5           Timpte an' some of the teachers.
```

In the next turn (line 2), Russ responds with 'Who?', thereby displaying that at that point he interprets Mother's initial utterance as a pre-announcement. But Mother's next turn, 'I don't know!', displays that Russ's inference was in fact incorrect: she was actually asking an information-seeking question. Notice also that, following this turn, Russ responds with the information his mother was seeking (lines 4–5). His response in line 2 was thus not based on the cognitive state of a lack of knowledge about who is going, but was rooted in one of the oriented-to conventions of conversational sequencing: the convention that, following a turn hearable as a pre-announcement, a next speaker should invite the producer of the pre-announcement to proceed with the announcement (in this case, announce the news about the meeting) (Terasaki 1976).

Bearing in mind the model of communication with which I was concerned in chapter 3, this instance illustrates a key claim of the interactional model of communication exemplified by CA. That is, as Drew (1989) has put it, there is a 'degree of independence of manifest public behaviour from private inner psychological states: this independence arises from the "gap" between psychological dispositions or inclinations individuals may have, and their necessary orientation to social organizations of talk-in-interaction.' Thus, 'a state of cognition (knowing the answer to a question) does not automatically trigger the behavioural manifestation of that state (the production of the answer)' (Drew 1989: 112). It is the social organizations of talk-in-interaction referred to here, rather than individuals' inner psychological states, that are the object of analysis for the interactional model of communication.

Goals and strategies

In chapter 3 I spent some time discussing what I called the implicit computationalist perspective for which the key phenomena are speakers' plans, goals and strategies. Such a view has close associations with research in certain areas of pragmatics (Levinson 1983) and, especially in the United States, with a sub-discipline of social psychology known as speech communication. Conversation analysis also has strong links with pragmatics and with social psychology, yet it adopts quite a different view on the nature and relevance of goals and strategies in everyday communication.

I want to illustrate that difference by means of a brief consideration of the following transcript of a telephone conversation between two college students.

(5) Trip to Syracuse

```
((Phone rings))
1  Ilene:        Hullo:,
2          (0.3)
3  Charlie:      hHello is eh::m:: (0.2) .hh-.hh Ilene there?
4  Ilene:        Ya::h, this is Ile:[ne,
5  Charlie:                         [.hh Oh hi this's Charlie
```

```
6                     about the trip tuh Syracuse?
7   Ilene:            Ye:a:h, Hi (k-eh)
8   Charlie:          Hi howuh you doin.
9   Ilene:            Goo::[d,
10  Charlie:              [hhhe:h heh .hhhh I wuz uh:m: (.) .hh I
11                    wen' ah:- (0.3) I spoke teh the gi:r- I spoke
12                    tih Karen. (0.4) And u:m:: (.) ih was really
13                    ba:d because she decided of a:ll weekends
14                    fuh this one tih go awa:y
15            (0.6)
16  Ilene:            Wha:t?
17            (0.4)
18  Charlie:          She decidih tih go away this weekend.
19  Ilene:            Yea:h,
20  Charlie:          .hhh=
21  Ilene:            =.kh[h
22  Charlie:              [So tha:[:t
23  Ilene:                      [k-khhh
24  Charlie:          Yihknow I really don't have a place tuh sta:y.
25  Ilene:            .hh Oh::::: .hh
26            (0.2)
27  Ilene:            .hhh So yih not g'nna go up this weeken'?
28            (0.2)
29  Charlie:          Nu::h I don't think so.
30  Ilene:            How about the following weekend.
31            (0.8)
32  Charlie:          .hh Dat's the vacation isn' it?
33  Ilene:            .hhhhh Oh:. .hh ALright so:- no hassle,
34            (.)
35  Ilene:            S[o
36  Charlie:           [Ye:h,
37  Ilene:            Yihkno:w::
38  (   ):            .hhh
39  Ilene:            So we'll make it fer another ti:me then.
40            (0.5)
41  Ilene:            Yihknow jis let me know when yer g'nna go::.
42  Charlie:          .hh Sure .hh
43  Ilene:            Yihknow that- that's awl, whenever you have
44                    intentions uv going .hh let me know.
45  Charlie:          Ri:ght.
46  Ilene:            Oka::y?
47  Charlie:          Okay,=
48  Ilene:            =Thanks inneh- e- than:ks: anyway Charlie,
49  Charlie:          Ri:ght.
50  Ilene:            Oka:y?
51  Charlie:          Oka[y,
52  Ilene:               [Ta:ke keyuh
```

```
53 Charlie:        Speak tih you [(    )
54 Ilene:                        [Bye: bye
55 Charlie:        Bye,
   ((End call))
```

From an implicit computationalist perspective, the principal issue
in this conversation would have to do with what Charlie's goal is in
making the phone call to Ilene, and with the particular strategies he
uses in order to realize that goal. A casual reading of the transcript
might indicate that Charlie's principal goal is to announce the cancellation of a planned trip to Syracuse, on which Ilene was, in some
capacity, to accompany him. The strategies he uses to reach this communicational goal include announcing, in lines 10–14, that Karen, the
person with whom, as he assumes Ilene is aware, he had arranged to
stay, has decided to go away for the weekend. From this, Ilene is led
to infer that the trip is therefore cancelled (line 27).

This global description, however, abstracts in important ways from
the interactional details revealed by the transcript. For instance, let
us consider somewhat more closely precisely how Charlie constructs
his version of events in lines 10–14.

```
10 Charlie:   hhhe:h heh .hhhh I wuz uh:m: (.) .hh I
11            wen' ah:- (0.3) I spoke teh the gi:r- I spoke
12            tih Karen. (0.4) And u:m:: (.) ih was really
13            ba:d because she decided of a:ll weekends
14            fuh this one tih go awa:y
```

Taken as a whole, this is, of course, an indirect utterance. Although
Ilene subsequently infers from it that Charlie is not going to Syracuse this weekend (line 27), there is no sense in which the sentence
'Karen . . . decided of a:ll weekends fuh this one tih go awa:y' has as
one of its literal meanings, 'I'm not going to Syracuse'. That is an
upshot that has to be inferred by the recipient (although it is not the
only possible upshot that can be inferred). On this level, the design
of the utterance is consistent both with the pragmatic theory of 'indirect speech acts' (see Levinson 1983: 263–76) and, more particularly,
with CA findings about the ways in which speakers go about
announcing 'bad news' (such as, in this case, the cancellation of a
planned trip). Schegloff (1988) argued that those who have bad news
to tell tend to manage the telling in such a way that they do not actually tell the news; rather, on the basis of design features of their utterances, the recipient of the bad news is encouraged to announce what
they take to be the news. For example:

(6) D.A.:2:10

```
1   Betty:          I: uh::: I did wanna tell you en I didn' wanna
2                   tell you uh:::::: uh:: las'ni:ght. Uh:: because you had
3                   entert-uh:: company I, I-I had something (.) terrible
4                   t'tell you.=So [u h :  ]
5   Fanny:                         [How t]errible [is it.   ]
6   Betty:                                        [.hhhhh]
7           (.)
8   Betty:          Uh: ez worse it could be:.
9           (0.7)
10  Fanny:          W'y'mean Eva?
11          (.)
12  Betty:          Uh ↓yah. Hh=
13  Fanny:          =Wud she do die:?=
14  Betty:          =Mm: hm,
15          (.)
16  Fanny:          When did she die,
17          (0.2)
18  Betty:          Abou:t uh:::(v) (.) four weeks ago.
19          (.)
20  Fanny:          °Oh how horrible.
```

Note how Betty at no point mentions the fact of Eva's death; rather, Fanny volunteers this news (line 13). This is the case even when, in line 5, Fanny seems to be inviting the announcement of the news that Betty has adumbrated in lines 1–4. Rather than saying something along the lines of 'I'm afraid Eva's died', Betty simply upgrades the 'terribleness' of the news ('ez worse it could be:'). Following that, Betty restricts herself to confirming Fanny's inferences, such that Fanny herself becomes the one to voice the terrible news that Betty had brought to the conversation. Similar points can be made about the 'Trip to Syracuse' call, where Charlie at no point states that he is not going on the planned trip, but merely confirms Ilene's inference that that is the case.

But the mere fact that bad news is told indirectly is only one level of the interest that conversation analysts have in excerpts such as these. A more central interest is in the incremental – and interactional – management of that telling on any given occasion. For instance, it is intriguing that, in both extracts (5) and (6), the management of the telling relies to a great extent on shared knowledge about other parties relevant to the as yet untold news. Notice how Fanny is able to identify Eva as the subject of Betty's announcement (line 10) purely on the basis of Betty's statement that the news is 'ez <u>w</u>orse it could <u>be</u>:' (line 8). With this statement, Betty is engaged in providing Fanny with a resource by which she is invited to search for a person or event both (a) commonly known to them and (b) about which, at this point in time, the 'worst' news could be forthcoming. That in itself may suggest a mutual acquaintance who has been ill for some time (moments later in the conversation the two women indeed talk about how ill Eva has been, and that her death was only a matter of time).

In the same way, in extract (5), Ilene is invited to use Charlie's mention of 'Karen' as a resource by which to (a) search for a person so-named, (b) who may be mutually known to be associated with the trip to Syracuse, and thus (c) to work out what impact her having decided to go away may have on the trip. Moreover, in both extracts, that search itself is managed incrementally. In (5), Charlie produces three pieces of information – that he 'spoke tih Karen' (lines 11–12), that she 'dec<u>i</u>dih tih go a<u>w</u>ay this weekend' (line 18), and that consequentially he '<u>r</u>eally [doesn't] have a place tuh <u>sta</u>:y' (line 24). Each of these segments performs its own work in enabling Ilene to come to a realization of what the news is (in lines 25–7).

First, the naming of 'Karen' enables Ilene to begin a search for Karen and her possible relevance to this telephone conversation, which Charlie has begun by announcing is 'about the trip tuh S<u>y</u>racuse' (line 6). But that simple naming does not provide enough information for Ilene to work out precisely what bearing Karen may have. In this regard, it is notable that Charlie does not immediately say 'I spoke to Karen', but rather makes four consecutive efforts to produce that sentence: 'I wuz uh:m: (.) .hh I <u>w</u>en' ah:- (0.3) I <u>s</u>poke teh the <u>gi</u>:r- I spoke tih Karen' (lines 10–12). We can only speculate on what Charlie was about to say in any of the three abandoned sentences; however, conversation analysts argue that such examples of 'self-repair' in talk (see Schegloff, Jefferson and Sacks 1977) are not necessarily indicators of errors, of getting an utterance wrong, but, among other things, can show speakers designing their utterances so as to be situationally appropriate. In other words, the small 'imperfections' in talk, often overlooked by communication analysts in favour of what is seen as the 'real content' of an utterance, in fact reveal further levels of the contextually sensitive nature of talk as a situated practice. So that while we cannot with any certainty say whether, for instance, Charlie was about to 'give the game away' by saying 'I spoke to the girl I was going to stay with', we can, by noticing this little series of self-repairs, observe Charlie going through a process of selecting a descriptor which is appropriately informative: one which enables Ilene to locate a person with some relevance to Syracuse, but does not enable her, at this stage, to do more than that.

The next piece of information Charlie produces – that Karen decided to go away this weekend – is much more strongly implicative of the news that he wants to convey. However, possibly because Charlie has indeed elected not to describe Karen as 'the girl I was going to stay with', Ilene fails to grasp the connection, responding first by inviting Charlie to repeat the information, or possibly disambiguate its relevance (line 16: 'Wha:t?'; see Drew 1997), then simply acknowledging it as news in itself, without orienting to its implications (line 19: 'Yea:h'). This leads Charlie to offer a third piece of indirect information – that this means he has no place to stay – which, finally, enables Ilene to formulate the bad news about the trip.

Hence, rather than simply saying that Charlie adopts indirectness as a strategy in his goal of communicating a message about the cancellation of a trip, closer observation allows us to trace a trajectory in which the message itself is interactionally produced in the very course of the exchange. The point here is not to suggest that goals and strategies do not play any part in communication. It is, rather, to stress that those goals and strategies become observable as analytic objects in and through the ways that participants display their orientations to, and understandings of, one another in the unfolding trajectory of talk-in-interaction. This involves an analytic policy quite different to that adopted in the implicit computationalist perspective. There, utterances tend to be analysed at a relatively high level: talk is seen as strategic action always somehow underpinned by cognitive mechanisms, and the smaller sequential details of self-repairs or items such as 'What' or 'Yeah' tend to be ignored or subsumed under the label of 'backchannels' in the overall communication 'circuit'. For CA, as we have seen, even the smallest such details are taken seriously as indicators of the ongoing accomplishment and maintenance of intersubjectivity, which is seen as an observable feature of situated practice rather than an internal cognitive process.

CA's relevance in the context of this book

What, then, is the relevance of the conversation analytic approach for the arguments I am making in this book? On the face of it, it might be thought that CA, with its focus on participants' orientations in favour of analysts' abstractions, is very similar to the constructivist approach to technology which came under criticism in chapter 2. The argument of this and the previous chapter, in which I placed the emphasis on communication as a performance in interactive space rather than the product of 'real', internal mechanics, may seem to invert the argument of chapter 2, where I favoured an emphasis on the material and constraining properties of artefacts over the performed nature of their existence as 'texts'.

Some have argued that there is indeed a significant constructivist undercurrent in CA thinking (Potter 1996). However, it is more accurate to say that CA is ethnomethodological rather than constructivist in its theoretical underpinnings. The distinction shows up perhaps most clearly in CA work concerned with 'institutional' discourse (Drew and Heritage 1992), where a key argument is that rather than institutions (such as doctors' surgeries) being contexts which cause people to talk differently than in casual conversation, people's ways of managing their talk itself constitutes the 'institutionality' of such settings (for a detailed discussion of this point see Schegloff 1991). The thrust of CA's argument here is very different from the form of social constructivism discussed in relation to science and technology studies in chapter 2, because CA takes as its principal object of analysis not the construction of the setting, but the conventions of talk through which the setting's interactional relevancies are observably oriented to by the setting's participants. But unlike ethnomethodology, CA is not content to focus purely on the constitutive properties of the setting's immediate, here-and-now reality. Conventions of talk-in-interaction are seen as an 'underlying social organization . . . an institutionalized substratum of rules, procedures and conventions – through which orderly and intelligible interaction is made possible' (Goodwin and Heritage 1990: 283).

In other words, there is an equally strong realist orientation in CA's epistemology. As I have shown in this chapter, CA takes issue with computationalist forms of realism in which the underpinnings of utterances are to be found in neural activity or the internal processes of cognition. But that does not mean that it aims merely to take utterances at their face value, simply redescribing people's actions during conversation using a technical vocabulary. Conversation analysts hold to the view that the conditions of possibility for mutually intelligible interaction include (among many other things) the existence of conventions and procedures for relating utterances together in sequences, which are learned as part of the process of becoming a competent member of a conversational community, and to which members display their orientations in the observable, behavioural details of talk-in-interaction.

In most debates about epistemology, constructivism (or relativism) and realism are presented as mutually exclusive poles at opposite ends of the argument about what kind of claims social science can make about the world. Part of the distinctiveness of CA is that it seeks to transcend that opposition. Conversation analysts are quite comfortable with the idea that while participants in talk-in-interaction engage in ongoingly constructing the mutually oriented-to reality of their situation (whether it be a conversation about a planned trip or a consultation in a doctor's surgery), they do so by means of an underlying substratum of conventional resources which transcend that particular situation but which are marshalled for the particular purposes of that encounter. The strength of this stance lies in CA's methodological claim that this underlying substratum can be retrieved analytically by focusing on the very ways in which participants in interaction display an orientation to its relevance. In many forms of realism in sociological thought, it is claimed that there are underlying social processes which are 'reflected' in the phenomena of social structure and social change but which are unavailable to observation. Among the classic examples of this is Durkheim's theory of suicide (Durkheim [1897] 1951). Suicide, Durkheim claimed, appears to be a supremely individualistic act, in which the individual, driven to despair, decides to take his or her own life. But Durkheim argued that individual suicidal acts are merely reflections of an underlying 'suicidogenic impulse', a set of social conditions which, in any given era and cultural context, 'drive' a certain number of people to suicide. He posited this driving impulse, of which individuals themselves are unaware, in order to explain what he saw as the remarkable uniformities in suicide rates as recorded in official national statistics.

It is this form of realism, in which invisible forces are posited to explain empirical phenomena, that social constructivism in technology studies grew up in opposition to. It was not part of my aim in chapter 2 to take issue with that basic opposition. CA, too, opposes the Durkheimian version of realism. Like constructivism, CA would rather pose the question of how suicides become defined as suicides (or 'oriented to' as suicidal events) by those whose task it is to understand the actions that led to a death (since, in successful 'suicides', it is not possible to turn to the actor for an account of what happened, especially where no note has been left) (see Atkinson 1978).

But that does not mean that we have to deny the existence of structural phenomena and treat events (or artefacts) merely as what they

are shown to be on 'this one occasion'. We can observe that interactions are patterned; that, for instance, people have developed
systematic, recursive ways of beginning (and ending) telephone conversations that may exhibit differences from their ways of beginning
conversations in face-to-face circumstances (see chapter 5). While
taking account of the fact that, on any given occasion, the conversation is being generated here and now by these particular participants
for their particular purposes, and is not being 'driven' or 'caused' by
the existence of those patterned procedures, we can also note that
the procedures are indeed patterned, that they recur across different
circumstances involving different participants with different purposes: in short, that they represent a substratum of conventions
which is simultaneously context-sensitive and context-free (cf. Sacks,
Schegloff and Jefferson 1974).

This conception in fact led to an alternative type of technological
metaphor being developed in the work of CA's pioneers. In his original lectures on conversation, Sacks put it in this way:

> The gross aim of the work . . . is to see how finely the details of actual,
> naturally occurring conversation can be subjected to analysis which
> will yield the *technology of conversation*. So the idea is to take singu-
> lar sequences of conversation and tear them apart in such a way as to
> find rules, techniques, procedures, methods, maxims . . . which . . . can
> be used to generate the orderly features we find in the conversations
> we examine. . . . So what we're dealing with is the technology of con-
> versation, and . . . we can impose as a constraint on [that] technology
> that it actually deals with singular events and singular sequences of
> events. (Sacks 1992, vol. 2: 339, emphasis added)

This represents an interesting twist in the distinction between interactionist and computational models of communication. While I spent
chapter 3 criticizing those within the computational school of thought
for adopting technological metaphors in their accounts, here we find
a technological metaphor being posited as the centrepiece of a decidedly interactionist perspective. But I do not think that this under-
mines either the distinction or the critique pursued in the previous
chapter. While Sacks proposes that conversation itself can be conceived as having a 'technology' (or on a different reading, as *being* a
'technology'), it should be clear by now that this metaphor is intended
primarily as a way of avoiding common-sense ideas of conversation
as a casual, unstructured, essentially random occurrence in favour of
a focus on the 'rules, techniques, procedures, methods, maxims': it is
these which comprise the 'technology' by means of which conversa-

tions as structured patterned events are built. Neither should it be thought that this idea of the technology of conversation implies a conception of human conversationalists merely as cogs in the machinery of that technology. As, again, should by now be clear, there is no contradiction for CA in stressing both the structural nature of conversational resources, and humans' immense creativity in using those resources to fashion interactions. It is this combination that I will refer to as the 'normative structures of talk-in-interaction'.

As I began by saying at the start of chapter 2, the overall thrust of the book is to investigate whether new ways of engaging in interpersonal communication may emerge at the interface between the communicative affordances of artefacts and the normative structures of talk-in-interaction itself. In fact, the stronger formulation of this idea is that, because any technological artefact possesses some affordances and not others, humans are forced to find ways of managing their communicational endeavours in the light of those affordances, and this frequently means that changes will be made in the ways that interactional conventions operate in conversations. It is now time to move on from what has been a rather lengthy project of establishing conceptual and methodological grounds to the consideration of case studies of conversation and technology. I proceed in the following two chapters to examine some impacts of a ubiquitous, yet curiously under-analysed, technology for communication – the domestic telephone.

5

The Telephone: Technology of Sociability

As the cases discussed in the previous chapter indicate, a great deal of conversation analytic research has been carried out using talk on the telephone. In the early days of CA, there were good methodological reasons for this. For one thing, given various commercially available devices for recording telephone conversations, it was relatively easy, with one or two willing telephone subscribers, to record large corpora of what was to all intents 'naturally occurring' data. More significantly, because talk on the telephone lacks any visual cues, the analyst could work on conversations that were purely speech-based. Therefore, the data that were hearable on the tapes could be seen as reproducing exactly the sequential resources the participants themselves relied on in producing the conversation. In the light of CA's aim to analyse talk as an object in its own right, through focusing on recordings and transcripts of naturally occurring interaction, telephone talk thus became the perfect form of data since it was not necessary to wonder whether, in the absence of video recordings, the participants were utilizing interactional resources to which the analyst did not have access, such as gesture. Certainly, video data has since become an important part of conversation analytic research, and has long played a key role in other schools of interaction research (see, for example, Kendon 1990). But telephone conversation remains a major part of the CA database because it is the closest the analyst can get to having access to the full set of sequential resources available to the participants in that particular conversation.

While the early CA studies were generally not concerned to address what might be specific about telephone talk as a form of talk-in-interaction, preferring to generalize findings to all forms of 'ordinary conversation', what in fact emerges from them is a range of insights that might be built into an account of how people have developed novel ways of talking in light of the telephone's communicative affordances. In this chapter and the next, drawing on the work of Schegloff (1979, 1986), Hopper (1992), Sacks (1992) and other analysts who have focused on telephone conversation, I want to outline the key dimensions of such an account.

How do we talk on the telephone? Of course, the technology is so ubiquitous, and so finely woven into the structure of our everyday lives, that it may feel as if there is nothing 'special' to talking on the telephone: it is just something we do. Yet from the perspective I am taking in this book, the telephone is an artefact which has certain kinds of affordances, and those affordances both enable what can be done with it and constrain what cannot. Putting the question slightly differently, then, what is the nature of human telephonic talk, given the affordances of that technology for communication? Is it different from non-telephonic talk, and if so, what are the ways in which the telephone thereby becomes a player in the developing structures of conversational interaction?

Here, in the first of two chapters focusing on the telephone, I discuss a range of issues around these questions. Beginning with an account of the distinctive form of interactional co-presence that the telephone makes possible, I go on to consider whether, or to what degree, telephone talk differs from face-to-face interaction. I argue that there are two principal dimensions around which novel forms and patterns of communication have evolved since the telephone's introduction. These centre upon the establishment of mutually ratified participation in talk, and, relatedly, the categories of social identity that the telephone makes available for speakers to assign themselves, or be assigned, to.

Intimacy at a distance

In the early 1990s the UK's major telephone company, British Telecommunications (BT), introduced an advertising campaign with the strapline 'It's good to talk'. A series of adverts ran on television and in the press featuring various everyday uses of the telephone and focusing on the different ways that given categories of persons in our culture supposedly relate to the telephone as a communications medium. One of the main recurring tropes was that women are both more comfortable talking on the telephone than men, and talk at greater length. Each of the television adverts featured a vignette from everyday life in which an Ariel-like char-

acter who was visible only to the television audience would attempt
to indicate the difficulties that men, in particular, have with talking
by telephone, always ending with the same assertion, 'It's good to
talk'.

These adverts presented a huge array of cultural images of telephone conversation as if they were taken-for-granted states of affairs.
One of the more intriguing examples appeared in national newspapers, depicting a man and a woman each talking into a telephone
handset, facing in different directions against a plain dark backdrop.
The man is standing while the woman is seated (or more accurately,
perched on a rather uncomfortable-looking pedestal). Both are
apparently naked, but a banner with the words 'Why can't men be
more like women?' is arranged tastefully across the page. The text
asserts that there are easily noticeable differences between the ways
that men and women talk on the telephone. Women sit down to talk,
while men stand up. Women talk at leisure, enjoying the very fact of
interacting on the telephone; while men treat the telephone purely
instrumentally, saying what they have to say (for instance, making an
arrangement to meet) before hanging up.

Frissen (1995) notes that early telephone companies did not appre-
ciate the telephone's affordance for intimacy, instead promoting the
technology as a purely functional, instrumental device. 'Telephone
companies issued prescriptions for how to use the telephone: during
the day it had to be used in an instrumental way for business
or housekeeping matters, such as ordering things. . . . Only in the
evenings was "chatting" or "visiting" by phone permitted, although
this should be restricted in any case' (Frissen 1995: 84). It took the
telephone companies some time to realize that these marketing
strategies were not an accurate reflection of what was actually being
done with the telephone. What was happening was that women in
particular were appropriating the artefact for quite different ends,
namely, informal chatting and the maintenance of social contacts. The
subsequent vast success of the telephone from the early years of the
twentieth century onwards was largely due to the telecommunications companies' realization that the device could be marketed as a
'technology for sociability', rather than simply a tool for improving
business efficiency.

Thus, BT's 'It's good to talk' adverts can be seen as a latter-day
development of the idea that the telephone's affordance for two-
party conversational interaction represents the best marketing pitch
to users. Yet they also imply that women are more attuned to that
affordance than men. This is interesting because it reproduces
(indeed, it possibly derives from) sociological research which suggests

that there are highly significant gender differences in the ways that the telephone is oriented to as a technology for communication. Citing a range of research in various cultural settings, Frissen notes a number of 'remarkably stable' findings:

> whether ... women are old or young, working or not working, have children or not, they still telephone twice as much as their male counterparts. Furthermore, women often function as 'operators' in the household: in France in 80 per cent of cases women are responsible for answering the telephone. Another remarkable finding ... is that women use the phone mainly to make relational calls. ... On the other hand, for men the functional uses dominate, and this functional telephone traffic serves mainly personal interests. (Frissen 1995: 85–6)

The object of the BT adverts, of course, was to suggest to males that they might benefit from becoming 'more like women' – that is, talking for longer on the telephone – thereby increasing BT's revenues. For me, however, they are interesting because they rely on the very ubiquity of the telephone in everyday life: they purport to bring to our attention negative aspects of our use of the telephone which are embedded in common-sense and therefore taken for granted. As Hopper (1992) has pointed out, the ubiquity and apparent mundaneness of the telephone has meant that, for much of sociology, the telephone is an invisible phenomenon. More significantly from the perspective of this book, of the small amount of sociological research which has concerned itself with the telephone, most has tended to take for granted the details of what people actually do on the telephone – the nature of telephone talk itself – in order to correlate these unanalysed practices with socio-economic variables within a macro-sociological framework stressing the social 'impacts' of telephone technology (for example, Pool 1981). On the other hand, among those disciplines expressly concerned with the nature of talk, such as CA, pragmatics and sociolinguistics, there was until recently little interest in the specific properties of talk mediated by telephone.

Yet the telephone has a deep sociological significance, not simply because it has become so taken-for-granted that we are more apt to notice its absence from a household rather than its presence. It is significant because of its communicative affordances. In short, telephone technology affords a form of talk-in-interaction that, without it, would not be possible, or even conceivable. I call that form of interaction 'intimacy at a distance'.

The term 'intimacy at a distance' was originally coined by Horton and Wohl (1956), who used it to refer to some of the peculiar social phenomena that were emerging around early television watching. Intrigued by why, or how, some people could become fans of television personalities to the extent that they would imaginarily involve their heroes in intimate aspects of their everyday lives such as, in extreme cases, sexual fantasies, Horton and Wohl proposed that techniques of address used by these personalities, such as direct address to the camera lens, promoted a form of 'non-reciprocal' intimacy in which the viewer could come to feel that they were being personally addressed, whereas the personality's talk was specifically *im*personal.

For Horton and Wohl, then, the non-reciprocality or unidirectionality of affect was a significant part of their notion of intimacy at a distance. I want to use the term in a quite different way, which points up the specifically reciprocal nature of the distant intimacy that is afforded by the telephone. The telephone affords intimacy on either side of a colloquy *over* (physical) distance yet also, in an important sense, *at a* distance.

Hopper (1992, chapter 2) cites a number of accounts of early reactions to the telephonic experience. For instance, in a book published in 1884 called *Bell's Electric Speaking Telephone*, Prescott observed: 'what strikes one the most is that the character of the speaker's voice is faithfully preserved and reproduced. Thus one voice is readily distinguished from another. No peculiarity of inflection is lost' (Prescott 1884: 85–6, cited in Hopper 1992: 27).

At this time, the experience of being able to talk to someone in another building, another city or even a different continent as though they were there in the same room must have been a fantastically strange and exciting one. Prescott recounts telephone calls utilizing the cable lying between Dover and Calais: 'the telephone sounds were easily and clearly distinguishable. . . . I happened to know several of the party in France, and was able to recognize their voices. They also recognised mine, and told us immediately a lady spoke that it was a female voice' (Prescott 1884: 87, cited in Hopper 1992: 27). Or take the following, originally appearing in an article 'From an admirer of the telephone' in the *Electrical Review*, 23 November 1888.

That Hello! . . . went down through the desk, down through the floor . . . then out into an underground conduit . . . crossed rivers and mountains . . . before it plumped into the city of baked beans and reached its destination in the eardrum of a man seated in a high building there. . . .

> In about one millionth of the time it takes to say Jack Robinson, it
> was there. . . . It was as if by a miracle the speaker had suddenly
> stretched his neck from New York to Boston and spoken gently into
> the listener's ear. (cited in Hopper 1992: 30)

The common theme in these accounts of the very earliest experiences
of the telephone is the sense that one can speak intimately – by which
I mean in the manner reserved for interpersonal co-presence, conversationally, in a way that preserves all the personality, recognizability and inflection of the ordinary voice – across vast distances.
This, of course, was a possibility afforded by the telephone and by
nothing before it. The telephone was the first technology for communication which enabled people to talk as if they were in co-
presence when in fact they were not.

Yet that intimacy across distance is also an intimacy *at a* distance.
The quote 'from an admirer of the telephone' exaggerates the proximity and naturalness of the telephone voice. As users of the telephone, we know that the technology actually alters the quality of the
voice. We may be able to talk to a distant other without having to
shout or gesticulate wildly in order to make ourselves understood,
but the specifically technological nature of the mediation, emphasized in the slightly 'transistorized' sound of the other's voice, means
that we are still aware of the artificial nature of our sense of co-
presence. This is not just a new form of personal co-presence in the
absence of physical co-presence; it is a new form of intimacy in which
the voice is technologically mediated and to some extent transformed, in which the distance of the other is simultaneously obvious
and yet easily ignored.

What forms of talk does this affordance for intimacy at a distance
actually promote? To put it another way, how have people developed
modes of talking which deal with the particular contingencies of intimacy at a distance? Drawing on a range of research, I want to argue
that some new forms of talk-in-interaction have emerged at the interface between the structures of ordinary conversation and the telephone's affordances for communication.

The telephone versus face-to-face conversation

It might be thought that since the telephone is a technology for communication that does not allow people to see each other, but yet
promotes intimate conversational interaction, there will be some sig-

nificant differences between face-to-face conversation and talk on the telephone. But if indeed we can observe such differences, the question is how far might these be related to the affordances of the telephone, in contrast to other situational factors? Researchers into telephone interaction have differed in the significance they attach to the role of the telephone itself in observable interaction patterns. Some have tried to measure the differences between face-to-face and telephone interaction (e.g. Rutter 1989), while others argue that there are ultimately very few possible differences between the two forms (Hopper 1992). I will suggest that the question of whether there are differences that can be attributed to the mediating properties of the telephone is not the best way of looking at the issue. Rather, we should look at how humans have responded to the telephone's range of affordances for communication in order to mould specific, and occasionally new, forms of talk-in-interaction.

Rutter (1989) argues that the telephone places speakers in a situation of 'cuelessness': that is, there is no recourse to the non-verbal cues that can be relied on in situations of physical co-presence (gesture, bodily orientation, eye gaze, and so on). A range of research on human interaction has demonstrated the importance of these cues in managing co-participation and mutual involvement in talk (C. Goodwin 1981; Kendon 1990). Some have gone so far as to argue that non-verbal cues are actually the main resources that are used in managing the coordination of speaking turns within conversation (Duncan and Fiske 1977); yet as the range of conversation analytic work based on telephone conversation illustrates, there seems to be little difficulty for humans in managing coordination even in the absence of visual cues.

Nevertheless, Rutter and his colleagues proposed that there are an array of circumstances for verbal interaction which can be differentiated on the basis of their degree of 'cuelessness': in face-to-face interaction we have the fullest range of cues, while on the telephone we have the least range. Between these extremes they identified situations such as those in which people are in different rooms, but talking via a video link; and those where people are in the same room, but separated by a curtain or other partition. In these circumstances, there is a lesser degree of cuelessness than on the telephone. In the first case, people may have difficulty in coordinating their non-verbal cues, but they still have visual access to the other person (I consider videophones at more length in chapter 7). In the second case, there is no visual access, but there remains a sense of physical proximity which appears to have some effect on people's ability to coordinate their conduct.

Comparing traditional classroom-based university teaching seminars with those conducted via telephone conferencing (a simultaneous link between the tutor and a small number of students), Rutter showed that there are some key differences in the forms of talk characterizing the two settings. For instance, the telephone seminars showed tutors playing much more of a structuring role, and involved a restricted turn-taking pattern of tutor – student – tutor – student, whereas the face-to-face seminars evidenced a good deal of student–student interaction. In other words, 'telephone tutorials [seemed] less spontaneous than face-to-face tutorials, [and were] more deliberately structured by the tutor' (Rutter 1989: 303).

Rutter's explanation for these differences had to do with the greater degree of cuelessness on the telephone: 'The fewer the social cues, the greater the perceived distance between the participants, and so the more sharply focused the perceptions of role and the more clearly differentiated the behaviour' (1989: 303). Interestingly, Rutter also examined whether participants would 'adapt to cuelessness as they became accustomed to its constraints, and the short answer . . . was that they did not' (p. 308). Again, then, there is the sense of intimacy, but at a distance. Although there was apparently a greater perception of distance between the telephone interactants, they still managed to conduct the seminar as successfully as face-to-face: in a part of the study focusing on perceived outcomes of the telephone seminar, all participants expressed satisfaction with the way things had gone (p. 305).

In this particular – and, it has to be said, quite unusual – situation, then, there appear to be significant interactional differences when talk is mediated by the telephone. However, Rutter ends his paper by suggesting that fewer of these differences may ultimately be down to the telephone than he had first assumed. Originally, 'we assumed that cuelessness had a *direct* effect upon behaviour. Gradually, however, we came to recognise that there was a mediating variable, *psychological distance*, and . . . psychological distance may be influenced by a variety of factors apart from cuelessness. [For example] the purpose of the encounter, . . . the relationship between the subjects [or] their degree of familiarity with the setting' (1989: 310, emphasis in original). Citing the example of telephone counselling (e.g. the Samaritans) as one where, unlike telephone tutoring, greater intimacy is required, Rutter argues that 'the key remains psychological distance, for the *anonymity* of the [telephone] system this time encourages psychological *proximity*, and it is cuelessness which makes that anonymity possible' (1989: 311, emphasis in original). Yet

it seems clear that it is indeed the variable dimensions of the telephone's affordance for intimacy at a distance which underpin all
these findings. The telephone is a technology that affords interpersonal interaction that is lacking in non-verbal and proximal cues, and
by that token makes possible the forms of 'psychological distance'
and 'psychological proximity' that, for Rutter, are the key factors in
his findings.

In fact, I think the concept of cuelessness is ultimately misleading.
Even in Rutter's usage, where cues turn out to have less to do with
the coordination of turn-taking and more to do with 'psychological
distance', there remains a vestige of the idea that people need
non-verbal and proximal cues in order to manage more 'spontaneous'
participation in an encounter. Yet as he admits in an earlier part
of the same paper, there is no evidence that telephone conversation
is any less closely coordinated than face-to-face conversation.
The telephone does enable people to engage in distinctive forms
of interaction, and at the same time sets constraints on the possibilities of those forms. In some situations people may seek to mould
its affordances for particular interactional purposes, such as being
able to provide counselling and advice in a relatively anonymous,
but still verbal and intimate, manner. At other times, such as in the
telephone seminar group interaction, the lack of non-verbal and
proximal cues may indeed act to structure the possibilities of participation differently than in the face-to-face situation. In either case
it is not so much cuelessness and psychological distance but the communicative affordances of the technology that should be the focus of
attention.

Rutter's study had to do with forms of telephone conduct that are
more or less specialized. What about the far more routine interactional uses to which people put the telephone in everyday life: most
particularly, two-party conversation? In his work on telephone conversation, Hopper (1992) takes a different line to Rutter, arguing that
there are many more similarities with face-to-face talk than differences. I agree that on the structural level, at least, the range of differences is indeed much smaller than may at first be assumed.
However, some of Hopper's work also suggests that the telephone
has encouraged the emergence of some entirely novel forms of
talking and categories of social identity. These have emerged as a
result of people having to find ways of managing the peculiar contingencies of intimacy at a distance.

These new forms of talk have to do not so much with cuelessness,
or whether the participants can or cannot respond to each other's
non-verbal signals (although that comes into it, for instance, in

opening sequences). They have more to do with the special kinds of social constraints that telephone interaction involves. These constraints operate at two distinctive levels, each of which I will discuss in what follows. The first concerns the overall structure of conversations; particularly their opening phases. I discuss this in the next section. The second concerns the particular kinds of social identities that are available for participants and that have evolved around routine telephone use. This dimension gets more detailed consideration in chapter 6.

The structures of telephone openings

Telephone conversations are well-bounded events in social life. They have easily identifiable, clearly demarcated beginnings and endings. The openings and closings of telephone conversations are distinctive interactional events, marked by the use of particular kinds of resources that allow people to manage intimacy at a distance, as well as other communicative affordances of the technology. Indeed, I want to argue that telephone openings represent novel patterns of conduct that have evolved around telephone use.

Not many occasions in everyday social life are as well-bounded as the telephone conversation. Take a passing conversation in the street or in a corridor. At what point does it 'start'? We might think that it starts when one person says 'Hello' or some other opening utterance. But a fascinating series of studies have shown that there are a huge range of distinctive, coordinated and ritualized activities that humans go through prior to that first utterance, which render problematic the notion of a greeting sequence – 'Hello', 'Hello', for example – as a well-bounded interactional event. Goffman (1961) was among the first to observe that there are systematic, socially organized procedures underlying the ways in which social actors move into what he called 'mutually ratified participation' in an encounter. Later, using video-recordings of greetings in outdoor face-to-face gatherings, Kendon and Ferber (1973) took up this suggestion, and showed that there are a number of observable stages through which prospective interactants pass as they coordinate their entry into a fresh encounter.

Imagine you are walking along a corridor. Around a corner ahead comes a figure you recognize as a friend of yours. Kendon and Ferber (1973) described this as the stage of 'initial perception' of the other.

However, you do not immediately start greeting this person. Rather, you enact what they called a 'distance salutation', in which the intention to greet is signalled and acknowledged. The typical way of doing this is by a fleeting establishment of eye contact, after which you each look away as you continue to approach one another along the corridor. As the pair of you approach, you engage in subtly orienting yourselves bodily in relation to each other. Once you are close enough, there occurs a 'close salutation' in which, say, handshakes and other conventional forms of bodily contact are used. You have done all these things before 'beginning' the conversation, and more or less unawares (though having read this description, you may find yourself becoming strangely conscious of your behaviour next time you see a friend in the street or in a corridor!). What this shows is that there are observable ways in which 'the attention of the two participants is closely calibrated as they come to agree upon a greeting encounter and upon the precise form that the close salutation will take' (Kendon 1990: 258). Kendon and Ferber's study, in a similar way to most of Goffman's work, was based on encounters in which the interactants are visually accessible to each other. Of course, a different situation obtains when interaction is initiated by telephone. The lack of a visual channel results in telephone conversation openings taking distinctive forms, which have been described in a series of studies by Schegloff (1968, 1979, 1986).

While in face-to-face interaction the 'distance salutation' is important as a means by which the participants can judge, at least, whether a greeting is likely to take place and so prepare themselves accordingly, in telephone conversation a quite distinctive set of interactional issues need to be addressed in the opening exchange. First, the lack of visual access means that identification and recognition cannot be accomplished prior to the onset of verbal engagement; thus, a question that arises for each participant as talk begins is 'Who am I speaking to?' A second issue involves the indefinitely large array of possibly relevant topics that each participant brings to any encounter. While face-to-face encounters, say in the street or the corridor, can and often do happen 'accidentally' (or fortuitously), the notion of an 'accidental' telephone call is a strange one, because someone always needs to have initiated the call by dialling the number (perhaps the nearest candidate is when one calls the wrong number). Therefore, telephone conversations can always be taken to have a reason (even if that reason is 'nothing much, just thought I'd say hello'). The 'reason for the call' is something that is routinely addressed following the establishment of mutually ratified participation in the conversation.

In telephone conversation, a highly distinctive opening phase systematically maps out an interactional space or arena in which these issues can be worked out by the participants. Schegloff (1986) has identified four 'core sequences' that occur in various permutations in the opening phase: 'summons–answer'; 'identification/ recognition'; 'greetings'; and 'initial inquiries'. This ordering of core sequences represents what Hopper (1992) describes as the 'canonical opening' in mundane telephone conversation. That is, although they may not all appear in any given call opening, those sequences that do appear will tend strongly to occur in this order. In their various combinations these four sequences are crucial in enabling participants to manage the establishment of mutually ratified participation in a telephone conversation. They are also closely involved in a host of other interactional tasks which are discussed in detail by Schegloff (1986).

In ordinary telephone conversation, as Schegloff (1968) points out, the first 'Hello' of the call is not a greeting, as it would ordinarily be in face-to-face encounters, but an answer to the summons represented by the telephone's ring. This summons–answer sequence is the basic way by which prospective telephone interactants convey respectively a desire for, and at least the possibility of availability for, engagement in interaction (we may of course be 'busy' when we answer the phone and so not properly available for some forms of interaction, such as 'just a chat'). It also has consequences in terms of the range of social identities that are available for the participants at this point in the call: an issue I discuss at more length in the next section. Schegloff (1979) considers a range of ways in which these first exchanges are designed to resolve the identification problem posed by the fact that the issue facing the answerer is that of 'Who is calling?', while that facing the caller is 'Is this answerer the person I am calling?' (cf. Sacks 1992, vol. 2: 543–53).

In many cases these issues are resolved rapidly and unproblematically; sometimes without even the exchange of names, as in the following example.

(1) HG:1

1		((ring))
2 →	Nancy:	H'll<u>o</u>?
3 →	Hyla:	<u>Hi</u>:,
4 →	Nancy:	↑<u>Hi</u>::.

5	Hyla:		How are yuhh=
6	Nancy:		=Fi:ne how er you,
7	Hyla:		Oka:[y,
8	Nancy:		[Goo:d,
9		(0.4)	
10	Hyla:		.mkhhh[hh
11	Nancy:		[What's doin',

The summons–answer sequence consists of the first two lines of the extract: the ring when Hyla places the call, and Nancy's answering 'H'llo?'. The next two sequences, identification/recognition and greetings, are accomplished simultaneously in this call. Hyla recognizes Nancy's voice as the phone is answered, and Hyla's first utterance, 'Hi:,' (line 3) displays this recognition: note the heavy stress and the lack of any questioning intonation. At the same time, that utterance invites reciprocal recognition from the answerer: note that Hyla does not attach any self-identification to her greeting (e.g. 'Hi, it's Hyla'). Nancy's enthusiastically voiced return-greeting (line 4) displays that reciprocal recognition has been achieved.

The fourth sequence that Schegloff (1986) identifies as part of the canonical opening is the 'initial inquiries' sequence, which he also (more straightforwardly) labels the 'howareyou' sequence. This consists of an exchange such as that found in lines 5–8. Nancy and Hyla swap 'How-are-you' inquiries and simple responses ('Fi:ne', 'Oka:y'), followed by a terminating assessment from Nancy (line 8).

The completion of this fourth sequence situates the participants in what Schegloff (1986) calls the 'anchor position' for the introduction of a first topic. In fact, in extract (1), no topic introduction occurs following the how-are-you sequence: there is a pause in line 9. As we will see in more detail in chapter 6, it is generally the caller's task to raise the first topic at this point. Hyla not having done so (though note her inbreath in line 10, which may indicate a readiness to begin a new turn), Nancy takes the opportunity to elicit a topic by asking, 'What's doin',' (line 11).

The how-are-you sequence is additionally important in that the very exchange of inquiries can be used as a way of introducing, or prefiguring, a first topic, either by caller or answerer. This is because responses to how-are-yous can take systematically different forms which have differential consequences for the subsequent talk. Consider the two how-are-you exchanges (line 5 and line 19) in the following extract.

(2) NB:II:2:1-2

```
 1              ((No ring is recorded))
 2  Nancy:      Hello:,
 3  Edna:       .hh HI::.
 4         (.)
 5  Nancy:      Oh: hi:::='ow a:re you Edna:,
 6  Edna:       FI:NE yer LINE'S BEEN BUSY.
 7  Nancy:      Yea:h (.) my u-fuhh! h- .hhhh my fa:ther's wife
 8              ca:lled me,h .hhh So when she ca:lls me::, h I
 9              always talk fer a lo:ng ti:me cuz she c'n afford
10              it en I ca:n't.hhh[hhhh huh ]
11  Edna:                         [↑OH:::::: ]:my [go:sh=I  th]ought=
12  Nancy:                       ((falsetto)) [_AOO:::hh!]
13  Edna:       =my phone wuz outta order:
14         (0.2)
15  Nancy:      n[:No::?
16  Edna:        [I called my sister en I get this busy en then I'd
17              hang up en I'd lift it up again id be: busy.
18         (0.9)
19  Edna:       .hh How you doin'.
20  Nancy:      .t hhh Pretty good I gutta rai:se.h .hh[hh
21  Edna:                                             [Goo:u[d.
22  Nancy:                                                   [Yeh
23              two dollars a week.h
24         (.)
25  Edna:       Oh [wo:w.
26  Nancy:         [↑Ih:::huh hu[:h huh,
27  Edna:                       [Wudee gun: do with it a:ll.
28  Nancy:      Gol' I rilly I jis' don't know how Ah'm gunnuh
29              spend all that money.
30         (0.2)
31  Edna:       Y'oughta go sho:pping,
32  Nancy:      .hhhh Well I should but (.) yihknow et eight
33              dollars a mo:[n:th:,    anything    I'd] buy'd, be using=
34  Edna:                    [hm hmm hm-mm-hm. ]
35  Nancy:      =up my raise fer 'alf [a YEA:R:]
36  Edna:                            [Ye:a:h.  ]
37  Edna:       .hhhhh Bud j's lef' t' play go:lf he's gotta go tuh
38              Riverside . . .
```

Here, we find two how-are-you sequences, yet the reciprocality
between them which is evident in extract (1) is disrupted when Edna,
instead of doing a return how-are-you after responding to the first
with 'FINE' (line 6), produces a comment about the fact that she has

apparently been struggling to get through: 'FINE yer LINE'S BEEN BUSY'.

One way of viewing this statement is as a form of mild complaint. Edna is complaining, in an indirect way, about the fact that she has been unable to get through; in fact, she later implies, the situation had been so bad that she thought her 'phone wuz outta order' (lines 11–13). However, Pomerantz (1980) notes that in telephone conversation, callers may use this strategy of reporting on the answerer's failure to answer their phone as a way of fishing for information about where the answerer was, or who she was talking to. The reason why people may want to 'fish' for such information rather than asking for it straightforwardly is that such information is open to being treated by its holder as entirely private; that is, a legitimate reaction is that it is none of the caller's business why the phone was not answered. Pomerantz argues that by producing a 'fishing' device, a speaker implies that they are intrigued to know more, but does not put the recipient in the position of having either to answer or find a reason for not answering, as would be the case with an explicit request for information.

In this case, the fishing device serves to topicalize Nancy's activities prior to the start of the call, and in that sense 'pre-empts' the anchor position for first topic which follows full completion of an opening sequence. In formulating her comment 'as a product of the speaker's *repeated* attempts to get through (note the tense of the description), [it] is hearable as a comment on the *length of time* the line was busy' (Pomerantz 1980: 195, second emphasis added). That Nancy orients to this length of time aspect as the basis of an indirect complaint is seen in the way that her account specifically mentions the 'long time' that she was talking to the previous caller: 'my fa:ther's wife ca:lled [and] when she ca:lls me::, I always talk fer a lo:ng ti:me cuz she c'n afford it en I ca:n't' (lines 7–10).

Later, following some further talk on this topic, during which Edna implies that the length of time Nancy was on the phone was such that she (Edna) thought her phone was out of order, the interrupted how-are-you exchange is completed with Edna's belated inquiry, 'How you doin' (line 19). In line 20, Nancy's response begins: 'Pretty good'. This, it turns out, is a significantly different kind of response to 'How are you?' than Edna's earlier 'FINE'. As both Sacks (1975) and Jefferson (1980) have noted, 'Fine' represents the conventional response to 'How are you'; a response which indicates 'no problem'. 'Pretty good', on the other hand, represents what Jefferson (1980) describes as a 'downgraded conventional response'. Although it appears very similar to 'Fine', one kind of work which 'Pretty good' does that 'Fine' does not do is to suggest or foreshadow bad news. If a speaker has some bad news to report or some trouble to tell, they may use 'Pretty good' in this sequential environment in order to set up a trajectory in which the trouble might be elaborated on. By contrast, use of 'Fine' in this position, although it may be followed by news of some sort, tends not to be followed by bad news.

Nancy in fact uses her 'Pretty good' (line 20) response to Edna's inquiry to raise her own topic, as Edna had done earlier, by latching onto it an announcement: 'I gutta rai:se'. Again, this makes relevant a particular kind of further talk, namely, a response to the announcement. Notably, Edna initially reacts by treating this as 'good news' (line 21). However, it turns out that Nancy has used the 'Pretty good' response in its role as a premonitor of bad news, since the raise is a paltry one: 'Yeh two dollars a week'. Edna then has to reorient herself to the announcement, which she does in line 25. Here, in the same way that her initial reaction was fitted to the form of the announcement as good news, this second reaction, a downward-intoned 'Oh wo:w', is equally fitted to the new status of the news as bad. Both the 'Oh' and the 'wo:w' are significant here. As Heritage (1984b) has shown, 'Oh' is routinely used to display that 'its producer has undergone some kind of change in his or her locally current state of knowledge, information, orientation or awareness' (1984b: 299). Edna's use of the item therefore connects with the way she is exhibiting a new understanding of her co-participant's talk. More importantly, the particular kind of new understanding being exhibited is marked in how the 'wo:w' is said. The downward intonation (shown by the period) marks the negative status that the raise deserves, just as an upward and animated inflection ('Oh ↑wow!') would mark the news in a positive way.

How-are-yous thus represent a distinctive phase in the canonical opening sequence. Used as the fourth in a series of sequences in which speakers connect with, identify, greet and make initial inquiries about each other, the how-are-you exchange functions to place the call in the anchor position for introduction of a first topic. How-are-yous can equally be used as topical resources in themselves. Responses to how-are-yous can serve to topicalize particular matters. Similarly, as Schegloff (1986) shows, one of the most common ways in which speakers try to get an important topic raised 'early' in the call is either to decline to offer a first how-are-you or to answer a how-are-you but decline to offer a return. As in extract (2), there may occur a return inquiry once the pre-emptive topic has been dealt with.

The role of the telephone

What is the specific role of the telephone in all this? On the face of it, greetings, how-are-yous, and the rest occur quite naturally in face-to-face interaction and have been doing so since before the invention of the telephone. The significance of the technology lies in the details: in the small modifications, both structural and functional, that people have made to these cultural resources in the light of the telephone's affordances. As noted, how-are-yous often play a significant role in the introduction of first topics in telephone conversation. In addition, they seem less open to being treated simply as 'substitute greetings' than in face-to-face talk (see Schegloff 1986: 129–30). That is, there is invariably both a greetings sequence and a how-are-you sequence in telephone openings, unless one or the other participant seeks to introduce a topic pre-emptively.

Identification and recognition sequences of the types shown in the above extracts, while routine in telephone conversation, are relatively uncommon face-to-face. That is not to say that they do not happen. When individuals are being introduced at a gathering, are meeting for the first time, or are meeting up face-to-face after having exchanged letters or even telephone calls, all constitute occasions where utterance-types like 'It's Hyla' or 'Is that Nancy?' may well occur. Nevertheless, it seems intuitively unlikely that such exchanges would *precede* greetings, as they routinely do on the telephone. It is also the case that '*It's* Hyla' or 'Is *that* Nancy?' sound slightly odd in a face-to-face situation, by comparison with the more likely '*I'm* Hyla' or 'Are *you* Nancy?' – which in turn sound like odd usages in the telephone context.

Summons–answer is also a sequence type that we can imagine occurring in non-telephonic interaction, only here the summons itself will generally take a different form. For instance, in hailing a friend across the street you might yell, 'Jim!', to which Jim answers 'Yeah?' or 'Hi!'. On the telephone, the summons is a purely technological one: the sound of the phone's ring. Yet Schegloff (1986: 118–21) makes some intriguing observations which enable us to see how even this apparently simple, mechanical event can have various affordances for communicative action (Schegloff himself does not refer to it in terms of affordances).

For instance, the number of rings that occur before the telephone is picked up by the answerer can readily become a topic of talk if it is either 'too many' or 'too few'. Of course, there are no absolute definitions of either of these categories: what either of them actually consists of (i.e. the actual number of rings) on any given occasion is a locally contextual matter for the participants. But on a general level, it is possible to say that if a domestic telephone is answered within one or two rings, that can be open to treatment as 'too few'. Consider the following extract.

(3) Schegloff 1986: 119

```
1 →              ((ri-))
2    Joan:       Hello?
3    Cheryl:     Hello:.
4    Joan:       Hi:.
5 →  Cheryl:     .hh Y'were you s(h)itting by the pho:ne?
6    Joan:       No, I'm (0.3) I'm in the kitchen, but I wz
7                talkin to a friend a mine earlier. I was
8                just putting (0.2) my fried rice on my plate
9                to go eat lunch.
```

It seems unlikely that Cheryl has originally phoned Joan in order to ask her whether she was sitting near the phone (line 5). Rather, the rapidity of the receiver pick-up is such that it can become topicalized very early in the call: immediately following identification (by vocal signature) and greetings. We might also note the way that Joan subsequently treats its topicalization as requiring her to account for why she was in the situation of being able to pick up her phone so rapidly. That account gives both a historical reason (talking to a friend earlier) and an immediate reason (putting food on the plate) for what is evidently being treated here as a deviant action: being too close to one's phone when it rings. Of course, we sometimes try and avoid this categorization if we do find ourselves 'too close' to the phone by actively waiting with our hand poised over the receiver for two or three rings before picking up.

In a similar way, 'too many' rings may be vulnerable to topicalization, though here the relevant categorizations centre around the possibility that the caller has disturbed the answerer unnecessarily (for instance, woken them up or got them out of the bath). A further affordance of the ring has to do with the 'ownership' of the ring: that is, with whom the telephone call might hearably, in context, be 'for'. If we are in another's house it is potentially a very delicate decision as to whether we should answer the phone if it starts to ring while the host is out of the room. Or, if in our own household one person routinely receives the majority of calls, we may elect to leave the phone ringing even if we are nearer to it than they are, on the assumption that 'It's for you'. (In chapter 6 I discuss a candidate explanation for this phenomenon.)

All of these are forms of conduct that are intrinsically linked to the specific affordances of the telephone as a technological artefact. The telephone's ringing summons affords a whole range of social activities and means of categorizing others in interaction. The summons–answer sequence and subsequent identification/ recognition sequences constitute forms of talk-in-interaction whose resources are finely matched to the telephone's affordances, and which would not ordinarily be used in those ways in face-to-face co-presence. In these ways we begin to see how the telephone has become a player in the structures of interactional conduct, by actively promoting the development of novel forms of conduct and social identity.

How canonical is the canonical model?

I referred above to the 'canonical opening' which is represented by the variable combination of summons–answer, identification/recognition, greetings and initial inquiries sequences. But how 'canonical' is it? It could be said that Schegloff's (1979, 1986) work is tied to a particular cultural and interactional context: the telephone calls of friends and acquaintances in middle-class America.

Other researchers have looked at telephone openings in other cultural settings, and some have compared their data with Schegloff's model. Godard (1977) proposes that a characteristic feature of telephone conversation in France, by comparison with America, is that the caller is apparently obliged to apologize at the start of the call for disturbing the answerer (unless the parties are close friends or family members). However, as Hopper (1992) notes, a problem with Godard's paper is that it is based on anecdotal evidence and on the author's own recollections of telephone conversations. No recorded data were collected and therefore no empirical examples which demonstrate the phenomenon are presented in the paper (though similar observations have been made by Carroll (1987) in another largely anecdotal account).

Houtkoop-Steenstra (1991), focusing on Dutch conversations, does succeed in demonstrating a systematic difference on empirical grounds. Dutch telephone conversation exhibits a variation in the initial summons–answer sequence in that the answerer, rather than saying 'Hello', is more likely to answer the phone by self-identifying, as in the following examples (translations from Dutch are in the original).

(4) HH:18:245

```
1          ((ring))
2  →  A:          It's Reina de Wind?
3     B:          Hello:, it's Bren.
```

(5) HH:12:98

```
1          ((ring))
2  →  A:          It's Catrien?
3          (0.7)
4     B:          It's Maarten.
```

Following this summons–self-identification sequence, the participants typically move to greetings, and thence to initial inquiries and first topic. In Houtkoop-Steenstra's data, then, the identification/recognition sequence is elided as a distinct phase within the opening, being combined instead with the summons–answer sequence.

Houtkoop-Steenstra uses these data to take issue with the generality of Schegloff's (1986) model, particularly its ordering of a distinct 'identification' phase after the summons–answer sequence. However, as Hopper points out, while these sequences may be merged in the Dutch data, 'in every culture and context imaginable, answering turns forward recognition. Further, there are North American settings, mostly [but not always – IH] institutional ones, in which answerers state their name in first turn. How do we distinguish cultural variation from within-culture variation?' (Hopper 1992: 86). This suggests that rather than debating the generality of the canonical model, we should say instead that the systematicities observable in different settings, while they may exhibit variability, all represent evolved practices for dealing with the communicative affordances of the telephone: in particular, its affordance for intimacy at a distance. Whether the summons–answer sequence is distinct from the identification/recognition sequence or somehow conterminous with it in any given culture or any particular occurrence is not the key issue. The issue is that the telephone as a technology for communication affords forms of interaction that are quite novel, including interaction with someone who may be physically distant but whose voice one may know and recognize on an intimate – or conversational – level; and telephone openings comprise the range of ways that members of language cultures have developed for communicating under those affordances and constraints. The details of the practices may differ, but the problems to which those systematic practices are addressed remain the same: how to establish mutually ratified participation in an encounter framed by the interactional possibilities afforded by this strange device, the telephone.

6

Telephone Interaction and Social Identity

The opening sequences of telephone calls bring to light a further communicative significance of the technology. It is not just the sequential organization of telephone openings that is distinctive. The telephone has brought into existence some novel categorial identities to which participants in talk may assign themselves or be assigned. In this chapter I discuss these identities in relation to a range of apparently telephone-specific social activities. I begin by outlining the relationship between the three major categories of identity into which the participants in everyday telephone conversation fall: the 'caller', the 'called', and the 'answerer' (who may or may not be the same person as the 'called'). In considering the array of relationships between these categories, we gain some insight into the extraordinary and delicate ways that speakers can adapt the telephone's communicative affordances for specific interpersonal ends.

Following on from that, I turn to look at what Hopper (1992) referred to as 'caller hegemony': the characteristic relationship that is found in telephone conversations between the topical agendas of callers and those they have called. We can consider caller hegemony as a form of social power to which telephone users have developed strategies of resistance, some of them incorporating related technologies such as the answering machine. In the final part of the chapter I discuss the role of categorial identities, caller hegemony and its resistance in the context of unsolicited telephone calls made by telephone sales persons and professional survey interviewers.

Caller and called

In the last chapter I mentioned one of the key issues that emerges for participants in telephone calls, in response to which some of the observable characteristics of telephone opening sequences have evolved. That is, for both participants, albeit in systematically different ways, the question at the start of any call is 'Who am I speaking to?' and, relatedly, 'Is the person who is speaking a/the person I wish to be speaking to?'

The kinds of sequences previously discussed represent the characteristic structural resources by which these questions are addressed in Anglo-American culture. However, there are further dimensions that take us into two distinctive areas which in one sense are related to turn-taking and conversational sequencing, but in another sense are interactionally relevant in their own right. These are: (a) the nature of social identities and the contextually available categories in which persons may either situate themselves or be situated by others; and (b) the character of the individual voice: its timbre, inflection, the use of intonation, and so on. These two dimensions allow us to consider a further range of responses to the telephone's affordances.

In one of his *Lectures on Conversation*, Sacks (1992, vol. 2: 542–53) presented a range of insights into the basic structural forms of identity that are available for telephone conversationalists (especially at the start of a call), and the consequences of these in terms of the kinds of talk-in-interaction made possible by the telephone, through focusing on the following 'utterly typical actual fragment' (p. 542).

(1) Goldberg: II: 1

```
1          ((ring))
2 Lana:         Hello:,
3 Gene:         I:s, Maggie there.
4 Lana:         .hh Uh who is calling,
5 Gene:         Uh this's Gene:. Novaki.
```

What initially attracted Sacks' attention in this fragment was the utterance in line 3, 'I:s, Maggie there'. He notes that while the turn before it is 'Hello:,', this turn does not offer any greeting and therefore does not complete a greetings exchange. Now, as we have already seen, Schegloff (1968) argued that the answerer's first turn in a telephone call is not a greeting but an 'answer' to the caller's 'summons'. So line 3 need not be thought of as the 'absence' of a return greeting to the 'Hello' in line 2. Yet it is doing a quite different kind of job from the 'canonical' examples discussed in chapter 5, in which the summons–answer sequence is typically followed by a greetings sequence. What can the specifics of that interactional work tell us about the nature of telephone communication?

Sacks observes that there are at least three basic categories of identity involved in telephone talk: the caller (any person who makes a call); the answerer (on one level, the person who picks up the phone at the other end); and the called (the person to whom the caller intended to speak). Note that these are *categories*, that is, they are assumed to transcend the characteristics of their individual incumbents on any particular occasion. An answerer is to be seen as

> a status in the enterprise of talking on the phone, where there will be a series of terms that apply to people in a way that has them as *categories* and not merely the persons they are, somebody with a name. By responding to the phone they put themselves into a position in the world, of which such a position is answerer. (Sacks 1992, vol. 2: 544, emphasis in original)

Those categories will, in turn, have specific sets of rights and obligations attached to them. In this, the status of answerer is particularly interesting, in that it can be broken down into a number of subcategories, each of which is related in certain ways to the social dynamics of telephone communication. As Sacks notes, not everyone in the proximity of a ringing telephone may be a possible answerer; not everyone who *is* a possible answerer will actually answer the phone; and most significantly, not everyone who does answer a telephone call will turn out to be the called. In the previous chapter I remarked on the delicate situation that can arise if the telephone rings in a house where you are a guest or visitor. Sacks proposes a possible convention governing telephone answering which accounts for this:

> the question is, can we ... get a non-merely descriptive statement – i.e., not merely 'someone who answers the phone' – about what an answerer is? Forgetting about professional establishments for the moment, it may be something like this: *Any, and only, possible calleds answer the phone.* Which would immediately take care of why somebody who is in somebody else's home or office can have the phone ring and not answer it. They are not a possible called. (Sacks 1992, vol. 2: 544, emphasis in original)

Clearly, if one answers the telephone as a *possible* called, then it is in the knowledge that one can turn out to be other than the called: what Sacks refers to as the 'answerer-not-called'. This is the situation in extract (1). Having heard Lana answer the phone and judged that this is not Maggie's voice (Maggie being the called), Gene treats Lana as

'answerer-not-called' and foregoes the sequential patterns characteristic of the canonical opening exchange in favour of simply asking for
the called: 'I:s, Maggie there.'

One way of characterizing this relationship between caller and
answerer-not-called might be to say that the answerer acts as a 'gatekeeper': he or she has the simple function of providing the caller with
access to the called. In this sense, 'I:s, Maggie there' acts as a request
to Lana to fetch Maggie to the phone. And of course, as targets of
telephone calls we may seek to employ the gatekeeper function in
the alternative sense of 'policing' access, by getting the answerer to
find out who is calling, then telling them we are out if it is not
someone we wish to speak to.

Seen in this way, there is a basic similarity between answerer-not-
called and what we might call the 'butler' function in other contexts
of everyday life. While it is a butler's professional task to answer the
door in his employer's house in the knowledge that the caller will be
seeking someone other than the butler, it is also a common occurrence that people who answer the door in their own home may not
be the person whom the caller is seeking (for instance, your children's
friends will be seeking your children, not you). In this situation, face-
to-face contact is usually involved (although some doors have 'spy-
holes' through which you can check out who is outside before
opening the door – another form of gatekeeping).

Yet to describe the interactional situation of 'answerer' in telephone communication in these ways is to capture only a small part
of the range of potential obligations that follow once we put ourselves
into that position in the world. As an answerer-not-called we can,
sometimes, act as a gatekeeper, or as a 'butler' (indeed, receptionists
in large organizations professionally answer the phone as not possible calleds, and so take on the role of answerers pure and simple).
But there are other possibilities which are closely related to the telephone's affordance for intimacy at a distance.

One of these has to do with the potential transformation of
answerer-not-called into another, related but interactionally distinct,
category: not-called-but-talked-to. This category is of a somewhat
higher social status, in that while the caller has not called us specifically, he or she nonetheless treats us as worthy of a brief conversation. And as Sacks remarks, there are situations in which, as
answerers, we can feel put out if someone we feel ought to treat us
as not-called-but-talked-to (for instance, our in-laws) treats us merely
as answerer-not-called. The latter category has 'lower' interactional
value, and in such circumstances, being treated as answerer-not-called
is open to being taken as a mild insult.

The significance of this distinction between answerer-not-called and not-called-but-talked-to relates to the nature of the telephone as a mediating device. In the absence of face-to-face contact, participants may find it more difficult to determine in the few seconds available what the relationship between caller and a non-called answerer should be. In face-to-face interaction, a caller who treats a door answerer merely as an answerer when the two are mutually acquainted needs to engage in a much more blatant display of 'not recognizing' or 'recognizing but not wanting to speak' than on the telephone. The telephone's difference is due to the fact that identification and recognition are routinely based purely on the production of 'voice samples' (Schegloff 1979). In Anglo-American culture the voice sample, taking the form usually of a simple 'Hello?', is the conventional mode of telephone answering in non-business contexts. This is, of course, a precarious practice since it invites – or more strongly, requires – the caller to try and recognize the answerer solely on the basis of voice quality (or perhaps a characteristic intonation pattern that the individual has adopted). It might be thought that in a culture such as Holland where, as Houtkoop-Steenstra (1991) showed, the convention is for answerer to self-identify, the associated reduction in ambivalence would lead to a difference in the relationship between answerer-not-called and not-called-but-talked-to. That is, it would be more difficult for acquainted speakers not to be treated as not-called-but-talked-to. However, this has to remain no more than an interesting possibility since Houtkoop-Steenstra does not engage with the issue in her paper.

An illustration of the precariousness of voice-sample openings is provided by the 'joke' opening found in the following extract.

(2) UTCL A10.13 [From Hopper 1992]

```
 1   Mac:            Hello?
 2   Rick:           Violin,
 3            (0.4)
 4   Mac:            Pardon me?
 5            (0.4)
 6   Rick:           Cello?
 7            (0.5)
 8   Mac:            Hello?
 9            (0.2)
10   Rick:           I:s Tony there
```

Rick is the caller, and it seems that the called is a friend of his, Tony. However, it is not Tony but Mac who answers the phone.

Apparently, Rick misidentifies Mac's voice sample (line 1) as Tony's, and engages in an exchange which, perhaps, is a routine between himself and Tony: that is, substituting 'Cello' for 'Hello', with the next move in the sequence being 'Violin'. Mac clearly does not follow (lines 4 and 8), and in line 10 Rick suddenly switches from his initial attempt at a joke-based recognitional opening to one in which Mac is treated as answerer-not-called ('I:s Tony there?'). Note that Rick does not display any recognition of Mac: that is, even though there has been a (failed) attempt at talk prior to the gatekeeping enquiry, Rick still does not orient to Mac as a possible not-called-but-talked-to.

There can also be the potential for interpersonal politics bound up with these different categories of identity. For instance, Fitch (1998) reports the following telephone exchange (which occurred during an interview and so was not fully recorded, but 'reconstructed' by the researcher and the interviewee who answered the call).

(3) Fitch 1998: 96 ((Original Spanish translation: Aymer is caller))

1	Graciela:	Hello.
2	Aymer:	Who's speaking?
3	Graciela:	Who do you need?
4	Aymer:	Dora's not there?
5	Graciela:	No, she's not.
6	Aymer:	So who is there, then?
7	Graciela:	Who do you want to speak with?
8	Aymer:	I need to leave a very important message.
9	Graciela:	Fine, go ahead.
10	Aymer:	((leaves message))

On Fitch's (1998: 96–9) account, these two speakers are known to each other (the caller 'Aymer' is the brother of the answerer's room-mate, 'Dora'). Yet there is a palpable tension in the exchange that derives in large part from the apparent unwillingness of both speakers to observe many of the basic conventions of telephone conversation that I have outlined.

The call begins straightforwardly enough with Graciela's voice sample, 'Hello'. But the next turn is of some interest in terms of the distinction between answerer-not-called and not-called-but-talked-to. While it suggests that Aymer does not recognize the answerer's voice, thus seeking to treat her as answerer-not-called, at the same time it requests the answerer to self-identify, thereby raising the possibility of treating her as not-called-but-talked-to. Fitch (1998:

97) notes that in this South American (Colombian) context, while the most common opening turn from a caller to an answerer-not-called is the same as that found in extract (1) above – i.e. a request to speak to the called – a much less common form is the 'Who's speaking?' (*'Quién habla?'*) request found in this extract.

Significantly, however, Graciela tells Fitch that she 'hates' this type of opening (ibid.), and this may have something to do with the way she responds in her next turn: not by answering, but by issuing a counter-question, 'Who do you need?' The reason why Graciela so objects may itself have to do with the nature of telephone conversation. As we have seen, the telephone ring and the answerer's first 'Hello' are describable as a summons–answer sequence. In this call, the caller's first turn (line 2) is hearable as a second summons, a second demand that the answerer answers. Answerers can take it that their voice sample is sufficient for the caller to recognize either that they are the called, or not, and to act accordingly in the first post-answering turn. Here, although Aymer knows Graciela (and knows her as one of the very small set of possible answerers who could take calls at this number), he neither manifests any recognition of her voice nor orients to her as a simple gatekeeper. Rather, he requires of her more work than, in her role as answerer, she seems willing to take on: the work of identifying herself above and beyond her proffered voice sample.

For the remainder of the extract, caller and answerer seem to be playing cat and mouse with one another as each refuses to act according to the terms of the other. Aymer refuses to show any interest in who he is actually speaking to, for instance asking 'Who is there?' rather than 'Who is this?' (line 6), thereby tacitly referring to people other than the answerer. Graciela responds by refusing to answer his questions (save for her one blunt answer in line 5) and continuing to issue counter-questions ('Who do you need?', 'Who do you want to speak with?'). This only ends when Aymer finally says that he wishes to leave a message and Graciela agrees to take it.

What this illustrates is the micro-political dimension that lies behind the array of identity categories associated with telephone answering. Among the categories so far mentioned – pure gate keeper, answerer-not-called, not-called-but-talked-to – there is a clear hierarchy in which the gatekeeper function, in non-professional settings, is the lowest form of social identity conferrable on an answerer. In the Graciela–Aymer call, that takes on a further dimension since Graciela takes it that she can, and therefore should, be recognized and referred to by name, if not treated as a not-called-but-talked-to, by this caller with whom she is, however slightly, acquainted.

Voice recognition games

I have mentioned the precariousness of voice samples when used as an opening gambit. But voice recognition can also be involved in some of the more creative uses to which people put the communicative affordances of telephones. Here we can see the relevance of what Sacks (1992) referred to as voice recognition games or voice recognition tests.

> It seems at least plausible that while people have for a long time played recognition games with each other, until the telephone they could not perhaps have played voice recognition games with any seriousness. . . . But a thing they came to do with the telephone was to use it as a vehicle of *voice recognition tests*. . . . [That is, to] employ this feature of the phone that you only hear the voice to build an institution in which they test out 'Do you recognise me?' from the voice. (Sacks 1992, vol. 2: 161, emphasis in original)

Put slightly differently, one of the key affordances of the telephone is that speakers have the possibility of using voice samples to engage in a variety of activities associated with testing the other's ability to recognize them without announcing themselves. This communicative affordance is of course linked to the telephone's technological affordance for intimacy at a distance: the possibility of interactional co-presence without physical co-presence.

An interesting use of this affordance can be seen in the following extract, where the caller (Edna) engages in a form of interaction that relies very closely on the possibility of recognition without announcement.

(4) Power Tools

```
 1              ((ring))
 2   Margy:       Hello̲:,
 3   Edna:        Hello Margy?
 4   Margy:       ↑Y̲e̲:[s,
 5   Edna:           [.hhhh We̲ do pai:::nting, a:ntiqui::ng,=
 6   Margy:       =I̲(h)s tha:t r̲i̲:ght.=
 7   Edna:        =E̲hhhh[hhhhhhhh[.hh ].hh!
 8   Margy:            [hmh hmh [hmh]
 9              (.)
10   Edna:        i̲hh-hn:n-h̲n-.hh-hn [k̲eep] people's pa:r too:::ls
11   Margy:                       [.hhh]
```

```
12 Margy:        Yehhhhh:↑h̲h̲eeh[(.hhh)
13 Edna:                    [I̲:'m sorr[y about that=
14 Margy:                            [nn
15 Edna:        =d̲a̲::[:uh ↑ I̲ didn' s̲ee that-]
16 Margy:             [O:::̲:̲::::hhh̲e didn'::    ] need i̲t
```

Here, Edna has called her friend Margy to apologize for not having
returned a power tool which her husband borrowed some time ago.
Margy's husband had called up to say that he would like the power
tool returned, and it had been taken back, but nevertheless Edna feels
duty-bound to call both to apologize and (in line 15) to distance
herself from responsibility for not having returned it ('I̲ didn' s̲ee
that'). But the way she engages in this is intriguing in the use that it
makes of the telephone's affordances.

Perhaps the most striking thing about Edna's apology is its indirectness. She does not phone up and say, for example, 'About that
power tool, I'm really sorry, I didn't notice we still had it.' In fact she
does not get to saying that she is sorry until line 13; before that, she
produces what may initially appear to be a bizarre series of utterances. We have already noted (in chapter 4) the importance of indirectness as a means of carrying out potentially delicate actions such
as telling bad news, like news about a poor raise at work or the death
of a mutual acquaintance. Given that Edna is phoning about something that may possibly be embarrassing for her – apologizing after
having been reminded to give back something which had been lent
by a friend – there are similarly good reasons why she may want to
use an indirect means of proceeding. Her chosen method is to apologize by means of a joke. This is a powerful strategy, since it succeeds
in getting Margy committed to a jokey or lighthearted exchange
before she actually knows what the topic of the conversation is.
Hence, when the apology comes, it is in the midst of shared laughter
(lines 7–12) and any potential for embarrassment or seriousness has
effectively been defused. But there are a number of respects in which
the joke relies on the features of the telephone – in particular, the
centrality of voice recognition – for its production.

Note first the opening three utterances: 'Hell̲o̲:,' 'Hello Margy?',
'↑Y̲e:s,'. We find a voice sample from Margy in line 2, as she picks
up the phone, followed by Edna's turn in which she claims recognition of the answerer's voice: 'Hello Mar̲g̲y̲?'. One thing to
notice here is the marked upward intonation, which is indicated
in the transcript by the question mark. This is very different
from a more downward-intoned 'Hello Margy.' The latter would
claim greater certainty of recognition and, more significantly,

invite the answerer to reciprocate by recognizing the voice sample of the caller. Then the sequence might go: 'Hello,' 'Hello ↓Margy.' 'Hi Edna, how are you . . .'. Although the question-intoned 'Hello Mar<u>gy</u>?' does not guarantee that Margy, having recognized Edna's voice, will not respond in kind with 'Hi Edna', it does provide the structural framework in which Margy is invited to respond by confirming her own identity in answer to the caller's apparent request for confirmation.

The voice recognition game that is played at the start of this call is therefore complex. The joke Edna is about to make relies quite strongly on Margy not overtly claiming recognition of the caller's voice by means of a reciprocal naming. The fact that Margy elects to say 'Yes' rather than 'Hi Edna' in line 4 helps in the sense that it turns out to play along with what Edna is doing, which is setting the call up as a mock sales call in which she pretends to be advertising services; one of which, of course, is to 'keep people's power tools': the punchline which comes in line 10. At the same time, Edna relies on the fact that Margy can recognize who the caller is in order to grasp the ironic nature of '<u>We</u> do pai:::nting, a:ntiqui::ng,' (line 5).

It is worth noting that genuine telesales calls begin with a highly recursive opening structure, many of the features of which are replicated in Edna's mock sales call. For instance, they too tend to begin with a turn in which the caller (the salesperson) requests confirmation that they are speaking to a particular person.

(5) UTCL A35.24 ((From Hopper 1992))

1		((ring))
2	Answerer:	Hello,
3 →	Caller:	Mister Smalley?
4 →	Answerer:	Yes
5	Caller:	This is Missy Weevil, sir I'm calling you from
6		the Ward Life Insurance company . . .

The 'business' nature of the call here is indexed by the caller's use of the answerer's surname rather than first name, but the structural similarities between this and extract (4) are easily discernible. (I say more about telesales calls later in this chapter.)

In the 'Power Tools' extract, of course, the game is based on Edna's 'sales pitch' being a pretence which Margy can straightforwardly see through. In this respect, we can note that in line 6, rather than manifesting confusion over what is meant by the preceding '<u>We</u> do pai::::nting, a:ntiqui::ng,' Margy is already 'playing along' with the joke by laughingly saying, 'I(h)s tha:t <u>ri</u>:ght.'. Of course, it is difficult to say whether Margy knows at this stage precisely what the nature of the joke is, though it is clear that she is aware of what has recently transpired between the two couples on the question of the power tool, and may be able to draw on that context to get an early grasp of why Edna is making this particular call.

To summarize, Edna utilizes a number of features of the telephone as a medium for communication in producing this particular apology. She relies on the affordance for voice recognition games to display recognition of Margy while discouraging Margy from immediately reciprocating, by means of an upward intoned other-identification requesting confirmation (line 3). She relies on the associated possibility that a caller may speak to a known answerer without explicitly revealing their own identity. For instance, an alternative possibility for the opening sequence would be: 'Hello Margy?' 'Yes?' 'It's Edna'. Yet this would provide for a greetings sequence following the third turn, which is not what Edna wants since she would then have to locate a next appropriate sequential slot in which to do her 'We do painting, antiquing, keep people's power tools' line; and in the interim, of course, Margy may have raised the topic herself, which would defeat the object of providing a humorous environment in which to situate an apology.

Finally, Edna also relies on the structural form of the telesales call, a form of interaction that, while not unique to the telephone, has particular relevancies for telephone interaction. That is, the telesales call draws on, and makes particular uses of, a generic feature of telephone conversation which Hopper (1992) refers to as 'caller hegemony'. According to Hopper, in telephone conversation, caller, answerer, and called are in structurally asymmetrical positions with respect to the topical ordering of the conversation. Put at its most basic, the caller is invariably in a position of dominance over the topical agenda of the call, especially in its early stages. In the following sections, I turn to look at some of the dimensions of caller hegemony.

Topical power

In any telephone call, the answerer is at a disadvantage. The caller knows who they are trying to call, and why they are doing so. The answerer, upon picking up the phone, knows nothing on either count (though there are contextual reasons why one occasionally may make a guess as to who is calling). As the call gets under way, then, the caller is in a position of built-in dominance.

This is also the case structurally in terms of the canonical opening sequence dicussed in the previous chapter. As we saw, the series of summons–answer, identification/recognition, greetings and how-are-you exchanges ultimately situates participants in an anchor position in which it is the caller who is charged with introducing a first topic. Exceptions to this are when the answerer seeks to pre-empt the caller's topic, which may be done by altering the structure of the opening sequence (for instance, by not returning the caller's how-are-you inquiry); or when the caller seems to hesitate once the anchor position is reached, at which point the answerer may elicit a topic through questions like 'What's up?' or 'What's doin'?' In some professional contexts, this answerer's inquiry is a routine part of the opening, in the form of an invitation such as 'How can I help?' or 'What can I do for you?'

Recent years have seen the introduction of technologies which afford resistance to caller hegemony, such as the answering machine or call screening devices. In the most intriguing of these new aspects of telephony, the answerer is able to see the number of the caller before picking up the phone, and thereby may have a very good idea of who will be on the line once they answer. There are also services provided by telecommunications companies which enable one to call a number and find out the number of the last person to call your phone (for instance, if you have been out, or failed to get to the phone before the caller rang off). You may then automatically 'return' the call. These technologies render problematic the kind of caller hegemony built into the traditional two-way telephone connection (Hopper 1992: 197–216). They also yield the possibility that the canonical opening sequence associated with that more conventional form will be modified in the light of the new communicative affordances that are offered when, for example, the answerer may already have ascertained who the caller is before starting to speak.

However, in this section I want to focus on the continuing power of caller hegemony and discuss some of the ways in which it relates to the topical agendas of particular callers and calleds. As Hopper (1992) notes, even with the recent new developments, the telephone's summons still exerts an amazing power over us, leading us to answer it under almost any circumstances. The telephone 'calls' us in an almost literal sense; yet in answering it, we place ourselves at the mercy of whomsoever might be calling. This puts callers in a powerful position. Answerers are strongly constrained to 'go along with' the agenda being introduced by the caller. For instance, in the following extract, the caller (Loretta) gets rapidly into the business of introducing her agenda – reporting 'what happened at Bullock's' (Bullock's is the store where the answerer, Marjorie, works). Marjorie, as answerer, is immediately constrained to talk (or more exactly, listen) to that agenda.

(6) TRIO:2:I

```
 1                    ((ring))
 2      Marjorie:     Hello,
 3               (0.4)
 4      Loretta:      Marjorie.
 5               (.)
 6      Marjorie:     Yeuh,
 7               (0.3)
 8 →    Loretta:      Well I jis thought I'd (.) re- better report
 9                    to you what's happen' et Bullock's tihda:y=
10 →    Marjorie:     =What in th' world's ha:ppened. [.hhh
11      Loretta:                                      [D'ju have the
12                    day o:ff?
13               (.)
14      Marjorie:     Ya:h?
15               (0.3)
16      Loretta:      Well I:- (.) got out tuh my car et fi:ve thirty
17                    I: drove arou:nd 'n of course I had t'go by the
18                    fronta the sto:re,=
19      Marjorie:     =eYeah?=
20      Loretta:      =En there were two- (0.2) p'leece cars across
21                    the street en leh-e coloured lady wantuh go in
22                    the main entrance there were the si:lver is'n
23                    all the [(     )] (things).
24      Marjorie:             [Yeah,]
25               (0.4)
26      Loretta:      A:nd they wouldn' let 'er go i:n, en he. hadda
27                    gu::n, (0.2) He wz holding a gun inniz hand a
28                    great big lo:ng gu::n?
```

Immediately noticeable here is the absence of almost all the conventional components of the telephone opening sequence. Loretta dispenses with the greetings and how-are-you sequences, opting to introduce her topic once Marjorie has confirmed her identity as answerer in line 6. In this sense, the opening is similar to the 'Power Tools' opening in extract (4) above. Yet whereas in that extract the caller made playful use of the alternative conventions of the telesales call, here Loretta relies on the urgency of her topic as the basis for pre-empting most of the canonical opening format.

The design of Loretta's talk itself reveals the way that she brings that urgency to bear on the opening. Note that she executes a self-repair in the course of her introduction of the topic; she begins to say 'I jis thought I'd re[port] . . .', but then changes that to a formulation which brings to the forefront the urgency and importance of the story: 'I jis thought I'd . . . better report to you what's happen' et Bullock's tihda:y' (lines 8–9). This way of putting it also implicates the recipient as someone who actually has some stake in this story: she is not just any recipient, but one to whom the events had 'better' be reported. When Marjorie responds to this preface, she too orients to the seemingly momentous nature of the story, thereby situating herself as a suitably awed recipient. She does this by saying, not simply, 'What happened?', but 'What in th' world's ha:ppened.' (line 10), thereby focusing attention precisely on the extraordinariness of these (so far undisclosed) events.

It turns out that this is the first in a series of three calls in which: (a) Loretta calls Marjorie to tell her what happened at work; (b) Marjorie then calls Priscilla (another friend who works at Bullock's) to try and find out more; (c) Marjorie calls Loretta to report back on the second conversation. This set of calls is a nice illustration of how caller hegemony can operate. In the first call, the topic is introduced as one which Loretta – as caller – 'better report' about. By the time of the second call, it has taken on a different status – a piece of news which a caller can inquire about; news which the called can be taken to have ready knowledge of (even though, as here, that turns out not to be the case).

(7) TRIO:2:II

```
1                    ((ring))
2     Priscilla:     H'llo::.
3             (.)
4     Marjorie:      Priscilla?
5             (.)
6     Priscilla:     Ye:a:h.
7             (0.2)
8 →   Marjorie:      What happen' tuhda:y.
9             (0.6)
10    Priscilla:     Whaddiyuh mea::n.
11            (.)
12    Marjorie:      What happened et (.) wo:rk. Et Bullock's this
```

```
13                          evening.=
14   Priscilla:            =.hhh Wul I don' kno:::w::.
15              (.)
16   Marjorie:             My- Loretta jus' ca:lled'n she wz goin:g went
17                          by: there et five thirdy you know on 'er way
18                          ho::me,
19              (.)
20   Priscilla:            Yayah?
21              (0.4)
22   Marjorie:             a-A:nd, u-she said thet there wz (.) p'leece
23                          cars all over out'n front there en there wz a
24                          p'leeceman standing outta the main entrance
25                          there you know where you go in where the (.)
26                          giftware i:s, . . .
```

Here, Priscilla answers the phone only to get Marjorie demanding to know 'What happen' tuhda:y.'. Understandably, Priscilla does not immediately grasp what this question refers to, and negotiation has to take place in order to establish what the topic in fact is. Note the identical opening exchange, in which the topic is introduced after a simple identity-check ('Priscilla?') and confirmation ('Ye:a:h').

As it turns out, Priscilla, who unlike Marjorie had been at work on that day, hardly noticed the event which Loretta had thought so important that she had called Marjorie almost as soon as she got home. So Marjorie then calls Loretta back, and we get the following remarkable opening exchange.

(8) TRIO:2:III


```
1                ((ring))
2    Loretta:            Ya:h,
3              (0.3)
4 →  Marjorie:           We:ll? She doesn't kno:w. uhhh
5                         huhh[huh-huhh-huh[huh-heh-heh]
6 →  Loretta:                [Ohh m(h)y    [G (h) o : d ]=
7    Marjorie:           =hhhhh Well it [w'z n-      ]
8 →  Loretta:                            [er you w]atching Daktari:?
9              (0.2)
10   Marjorie:           nNo:,
11             (.)
12   Loretta:            Oh my go:sh Officer Henry is (.) ul-locked in
13                         the ca:ge wi- (0.3) witha lion.nhh[hnh
14   Marjorie:                                              [nNo I'm
```

```
15                              i[n be:h-]
16      Loretta:                [She does]n't kno:::w,
17                  (0.3)
18      Marjorie:               Well it wz et fi:ve thirty en when she came
19                              ou:t'n:: end um (0.3) she's uh it's u-you know
20                              I mean th- uhhh heh-he::h u(h) it- nobuddy
21                              kno:ws. er she didn' kno:w she siz .hhh when
22                              she came do:wn shy somebuddy said tuh her
23                              oh you missed a:ll the excitement 'n, hh .hk
24                              thet the y'know the p'leece out there with the
25                              gun en a:ll but nobuddy: seemtuh know wha:t
26                              chu know things they alwiz happen like that they
27                              hush hush b't I guess I'll find out more
28                              tomorrow.
```

Here, while Marjorie – in extract (6) the answerer, but now the caller
– orients to her activity as calling back to report on what Priscilla
said, Loretta – originally the caller, but now the answerer – appears
to orient to another agenda: what is happening at that moment on
TV ('er you watching Daktari:' in line 8 is a reference to a now
defunct TV serial of that name).

There are features of this apparent disjuncture between the topics
of caller and called that illustrate how telephone conversations
can be managed as interactions in series. The opening here is even
more sparse than in the previous two extracts, consisting only of a
summons–answer sequence before Marjorie launches into the topic.
What is interesting is that Marjorie does not appear to orient
to Loretta's utterance 'Ohh m(h)y G(h)o:d' in line 6 as in any way
unrelated to her announcement 'She doesn't kno:w' in line 4. Rather,
she evidently treats this as a response to that announcement: note
that in the next turn, she follows up the announcement by beginning
to elaborate ('Well it w'z n-'), before being cut off by Loretta's dis-
junctive 'er you watching Daktari:'. How is Marjorie able to hear
Loretta's turn in line 6 as responsive to her prior turn, rather than,
as suggested by Loretta's subsequent talk about Daktari, specifically
disattending her report back on the conversation with Priscilla? It is
not just that Marjorie's opening utterance is overtly 'serial' in that
it assumes the continuing relevance for both speakers of their
prior conversation in the light of the intervening exchange. Loretta's
response is open to being heard as similarly serial in that it preserves
the somewhat exaggerated sense of drama with which the topic had
originally been introduced (recall lines 8–10, 26–8 of extract (6):
'What in th' world's ha:ppened', 'He wz holding a gun inniz hand a

great big lo:ng gu::n?'). It is therefore available to Marjorie to hear 'Qhh m(h)y G(h)o:d' (line 6) as glossing a reaction along the lines of 'How could she not know anything about something as momentous as this?'

Looking at it from another angle, this case further illustrates that the asymmetries of caller hegemony may be loosened when the call is one in a closely ordered series of calls. The fact that Loretta is expecting Marjorie to call back means that she already knows, on hearing Marjorie's voice, what the reason for the call is, and so can delay dealing with that while she deals with something more 'immediate' – the fictional predicament of Officer Henry.

More speculatively, we might say that the agenda here – namely, what happened at Bullock's – was 'originally' Loretta's (introduced in the first call). By interrupting Marjorie's report back with her reaction to the Daktari programme, Loretta provides for the possibility of reestablishing her own hegemony by bringing in a topic at the start which challenges Marjorie as the topic-controller. Notice, also, that just after the talk about Officer Henry, Loretta gets back to the topic of what Priscilla said, but this time by inquiring about it ('She doesn't kno:::w', line 16). In this way, she succeeds in turning the call round into one where she is, once again, in the position of directing the agenda about 'what happened at Bullock's today'.

Of course, caller hegemony can also be resisted. I have already mentioned some of the technologies of telephony which afford that resistance. In the next section, I turn to look at the various interactional devices that may be used in response to the particular form of caller hegemony relied upon by unsolicited sales and marketing callers.

Caller hegemony and the unsolicited call

One place where caller hegemony is particularly powerful in its social effects is in the use of the telephone by marketing and social survey companies to make unsolicited calls to random subscribers. These make interesting data for a number of reasons. For one thing, callers are up against a problem that does not arise in the same way for sociable callers. They have to recognize that the answerer may not in fact want to talk to them, and not just right now, but at all. They have to try and persuade answerers to go along with their 'hegemonic' agenda. And answerers do indeed often resist caller hegemony in these kinds of calls. We can therefore use these as an extreme case to look at how caller hegemony is resisted by answerers.

Callers use particular techniques to establish their agendas in tele-sales calls. These take a form that is quite similar to a second common type of unsolicited call – the telephone survey interview. There is one basic difference, however, which is that in the survey call, the first task of the interviewer is to establish whether the answerer is willing to participate in the survey. Telemarketers are not so concerned with volition: their primary aim, it appears, is to begin the sales pitch. In both types of call, it tends to be early in the opening section that answerers resist the caller's agenda. The openings take slightly different forms. In surveys, the caller first self-identifies, then gives the reason for the call; for instance, 'This is X calling from Y, about our national opinion survey'. If answerers continue beyond this point, it is taken that they are willing to participate in answering the questions. And indeed, it is at this point that most declinations take place (although they can also occur later).

In telesales, significantly, the caller begins by making an attempt at identifying the answerer; for example, 'Is that Mrs Smith?' We have already seen an example of this in extract (5).

(5) UTCL A35.24 ((From Hopper 1992))

```
1                      ((ring))
2     Answerer:        Hello,
3 →   Caller:          Mister Smalley?
4 →   Answerer:        Yes
5     Caller:          This is Missy Weevil, sir I'm calling you from
6                      the Ward Life Insurance company . . .
```

The upshot is that the answerer is immediately put in the position of confirming who they are and then giving the floor back to the caller, who then goes on to self-identify. In this way, telemarketers establish caller hegemony in a particularly powerful way, by situating themselves in the asymmetrical participation situation of 'knowing' who they are calling but only letting the answerer know who is speaking once that information has been confirmed.

In telesales calls, this self-identification by the caller provides the earliest space in which answerers resist caller hegemony by terminating the call. In surveys, however, that is not the case. Maynard, Schaefer and Cradock (1995) looked at all the cases in a large corpus of survey calls in which answerers declined to participate in a phone interview, and found that no cases occurred following self-identification by caller, but that a large proportion (50 per cent) occurred just after that, once the reason for the call was made evident. One reason for this, of course, is that answerers can work out what telemarketers are up to just by understanding that they are 'calling from Ward Life Insurance'. But how exactly is it that answerers go about declining participation in interactions with these unsolicited callers? We might think that the best way of resisting caller hegemony is by hanging up; however, studies of how answerers resist unsolicited callers show that this is by no means the most frequent way it is done.

Maynard et al. (1995) found that in about half of their cases the declination came 'early' in the call: that is, just after the reason for the call had been announced. Such declinations take two basic forms which Maynard et al. describe as 'polite' and 'impolite'. Generally speaking, impolite declinations take a physical and non-verbal form – they involve things like hanging up (although the activity of hanging up can also be accompanied by a brusque verbalization like 'No thank you'). But these represent only 17 per cent of cases. The vast majority, 83 per cent, take the 'polite' form.

Polite declinations are verbal, and more or less discursive. Maynard et al. (1995) found that they were constructed in two ways: either 'minimalist' or 'expressive'. Minimalist types are done using some kind of formulaic construction, such as 'No thank you'. These are referred to as 'formulaic' because they do not mention anything specific about this particular interview, rather, a general unwillingness to participate. More 'expressive' types refer to specific features of the interview, or give particular, contextualized reasons. Maynard et al. (1995) found that polite declinations represent the vast majority of all declinations, and within those, 'bad timing' formulas represent the majority of reasons. I will briefly consider two examples from their study. In Extract (9), the answerer asks about how long this interview will take (lines 11–12), then gives the excuse that she has just got home from work, is tired and hungry, and so cannot participate (lines 16–18). The interviewer then attempts to arrange a time to call back.

(9) LSSC159 ((From Maynard et al. 1995))

| 1 | Caller: | Okay uh: <u>th</u>is is Greg Sanders calling from the |
| 2 | | <u>Un</u>iversity of Wisconsin as: part of our national |

```
 3                        public opinion study? .hh[hh
 4       Answerer:                            [Uh huh
 5       Caller:          An:d we're trying ta reach people at their
 6                        home telephone numbers is: this a residential
 7                        number?
 8       Answerer:        .hhh Ye::s?
 9       Caller:          An:: to be sure that I reached the number that I
10                        dialled is this (.) are[a code ]
11  →    Answerer:                               [This is-] this is some
12                        type of survey that's gonna take a while? or
13                        hheh [hh]
14       Caller:               [Y::]eah it- it takes about ten ta fifteen
15                        minutes [.hh di- di-]
16  →    Answerer:                [Well I'm-] I'm just got home from
17                        work and I'm really tired, really hungry
18                        an[::d eh heh heh]
19       Caller:            [O :: k a y    ]    hh.
20                    (.)
21  →    Answerer:        [(We'd prefer)] another number.
22       Caller:          [U h : m we-   ]
23  →    Caller:          Yea:h. Um well, weh we'd like to try you back . . .
```

Maynard et al. (1995) describe two basic types of minimalist declination, the first of which, 'bad timing' is exemplified here. The second type is referred to as 'appealable' (for example, 'I'm not really interested'). Such declinations are appealable because, unlike 'bad timing', callers can try and find ways of appealing against the reason (for instance 'It's very important that we get your views on this . . .'). Extract (10) is an example. While the answerer initially seems willing to participate, once she is asked to say for sampling purposes how many adults live in her house, she declines by saying that 'We do not like to give out this kind of information' (lines 21–2). There are a series of appeals against this from the interviewer (lines 23–5, 28–9, 35–9, 44–6), each of which gets the same response (lines 41–2, 47). Finally the attempt to interview is terminated. This time, perhaps because of the very specific nature of the objection, no call-back arrangement is made.

(10) LSSC180 ((From Maynard et al. 1995))

```
 1       Caller:          Uh hello ma'am, my name is Edward Price an: I'm
 2                        calling from the University of Wisconsin? as
 3                        part of our national public opinion study? .hh
```

4			(tch) Uh we are tryin'a reach people at their
5			home numbers, is this a residence?
6		(0.5)	
7	Answerer:		Yeah
8		(0.3)	
9	Caller:		Okay .hh and to be sure that I didn't misdial
10			then this is three nine seven two one four nine?
11		(0.4)	
12	Answerer:		Yeah
13	Caller:		Okay? .h uh we want the results of our study to
14			represent the opinions of people all over the
15			country so we need to select one adult to speak
16			with in your household? .hhh and just so we can
17			make our selection, scientifically and randomly
18			we first need to know how many adults (.)
19			eighteen or older live there?
20		(1.0)	
21 →	Answerer:		Uh::: (0.5) We do not like to give out this kind
22			of information sir.
23 →	Caller:		Uh pardon well all w- (.) like I said ma'am,
24 →			it's just an academic study r- that's being
25			[done] by the University of Wisconsin?
26	Answerer:		[Yes,]
27		(0.2)	
28 →	Caller:		And we're not asking any personal type questions
29 →			we're basically just after your opinions?
30		(0.5)	
31	Answerer:		Yes=
32 →	Caller:		=Uh and it is all of course confidential.
33		(0.3)	
34	Answerer:		[[( )]
35 →	Caller:		[[Uh the] only reason we ask how many adults
36 →			live there is because we have to gew (.) and get
37 →			a random sampl:e so we get a- (.) bout a equal
38 →			number of men and women so: we don't ask for
39 →			names or anything.
40		(0.6)	
41 →	Answerer:		No (0.4) But I'm sure- my husband and I don't
42			like to give out that information.
43		(0.7)	
44	Caller:		Okay you can't just (.) tell me how many (.)
45			people live there so we can just pick one?
46			And then we can just try the questions?
47 →	Answerer:		No I'm sorry.
48		(1.0)	
49	Answerer:		Thank you.
50		(0.6)	

| 51 | Caller: | <u>O</u>kay. (0.2) Have a good day. |
| 52 | | ((Hang up)) |

The point I want to make about this is that it seems that even when callers enter our lives unsolicited and unwanted, we still orient to caller hegemony in our polite strategies for getting rid of them. The basic way of turning round caller hegemony and establishing answerer hegemony is by hanging up. But for the most part, we use formulaic responses which are designed to save the hegemonic 'face' of the caller. By telling them, however formulaically, that we 'don't have time' to answer their questions, we imply that if we did have time, we would certainly answer the questions. This may or may not be so in actuality; but the politeness formulas we use pay what Goffman (1971) would describe as 'ritual' respect to the structurally hegemonic projects and agendas of these unwanted callers.

The telephone is a technological form which interfaces in a whole variety of ways with the normative structures of conversational inter-action. In this and the preceding chapter I have explored numerous aspects of this relationship. A good deal of the (albeit limited) socio-logical attention that has been given to the telephone has focused on questions of the broad social and cultural 'impacts' of the technology without paying much attention to telephone interaction in itself (e.g. Pool 1981). In my view, it is impossible to consider such questions meaningfully without situating the technology in its empirical arenas of use; and in the case of the telephone, that means looking in close detail at how people use it for talking.

By focusing on the telephone's communicative affordances and asking how people utilize conversational resources to engage in situated activities in the light of those affordances (enablements *and* constraints), we are able to identify some of the technology's 'impacts' at a more local interactional level. For instance, we have seen that around the telephone's affordance for intimacy at a distance there have evolved distinctive forms of conversational opening sequences. We have observed how the properties of the telephone's ring itself can afford novel possibilities for patterns of interaction. And we have seen that the range of social contexts in which telephone calling and answer-ing take place afford the development of a whole range of new, inter-actionally relevant forms of social identity.

7

Technological Mediation and Asymmetrical Interaction

In previous chapters we have seen how the design aims of the early developers of the telephone were transformed by early telephone users so that the telephone came to be seen not as a purely instrumental device but as a technology for sociability. For the technology-as-text approach (Grint and Woolgar 1997) described in chapter 2, this is a facet of the constant round of negotiations and interpretations among and between 'writers' (designers) and 'readers' (users) through which technological forms attain their (historically contingent and transient) meanings.

I have argued for a different take on this question. That is, while designers may be said to have some control over the features they design into an artefact, and while they may have some idea about the range of uses to which the artefact should be put, they have little control over the artefact's communicative affordances – over the range of things it turns out to enable people to do. This is because, in an important sense, the affordances of an artefact are 'found' by its users in the course of their attempts to use it for various ends. At the same time, the artefact exists in an environment of social action which has its own set of orderly structures: the norms of conversational turn-taking, for example. Those structures may be more or less concomitant with the constraints placed on the possibilities for action by the artefact's affordances, and it is important to bear in mind that affordances are not merely enabling: an artefact may enable certain types of action, but by the same token it can disenable others. Thus, we may sometimes find ourselves 'working around' technologies in the sense that they specifically do not afford the forms of communicative action we might expect or want from them.

In this chapter I present some case studies which illustrate this facet of the relationship between conversation and technology. The technologies in question are (a) videophones, and (b) computerized expert systems that are intended to embody arrays of knowledge relevant to the carrying out of everyday work tasks. A common theme emerges in considering these different forms; that of a disparity between what I will describe as their 'design-features' and their 'features-in-use'. The term design-features refers to the idea of 'what the technology is supposed to be/do/enable', while by features-in-use I mean something closer to the distinctive communicative properties – the affordances – of the artefact as revealed in the empirical situations where people encounter and try to work with it. In exploring this dynamic, a further distinction comes into play between the conceptual models underpinning the design of technologies for communication, on the one hand, and on the other, the interface between their actual communicative affordances and the norms of conversational interaction.

Video-mediated interaction

In considering telephones in the previous two chapters, we saw how some of their most significant communicative affordances are associated with the voice-only constraints of telephone conversation. The technology for adding a video channel to telephones has been available for many years now, yet while there are signs that some business corporations are encouraging its use in the shape of video-conferencing ('virtual meetings' in which colleagues in different geographical locations communicate via television or computer-based video links), the technology has been remarkably slow to take-off. Why might this be?

One possible account has to do with the limitations of the technology itself, especially where computer-mediated links are concerned. Even the most powerful desktop computers have trouble displaying real-time internet video at a data transfer rate sufficient to eliminate observable jerkiness and 'frame-dropping', largely because of internet bandwidth restrictions. This is the case even with images displayed in a box only a couple of inches square. Attempts at a full-screen resolution result in a 'blocky' image in which the nuances of phenomena such as gaze direction and facial expression are easily lost. But given the rapidity of technological development in the areas of computer processor speeds, physical memory size, and digital data transfer rates, it could be said that this is a relatively minor point. In any case, it has long been possible to create higher quality real-time computer-mediated links using the much more powerful medium of

television, even if the equipment involved (video cameras and monitors) is slightly more cumbersome and expensive.

The reason for the lack of widespread uptake of videophones may
have less to do with technical limitations than with the question of
the interface between the technology's affordances and the normative structures of interaction. This is aptly illustrated in a study
by Heath and Luff (1993) of an innovative office videophone system introduced at the Rank Xerox EuroPARC research centre in
Cambridge, UK. Heath and Luff observed a communications system
which involved workers in EuroPARC's three-storey arrangement of
offices agreeing to have a small video camera, multidirectional microphone and 14-inch monitor installed in their room, via which they
could establish audio-visual links with the occupants of other offices
in the building. One of the primary aims of introducing this system
was to test its usefulness for computer-supported cooperative work:
work in such areas as computer-aided design where two or more
people need to cooperate on a project being prepared on a computer
screen. In this, the videophone link was associated in part with other
technologies for supporting computer-based cooperative work, such
as network links in which people in different offices could have the
same image on their monitors and each could engage in modifying
it. The videophone link here would be intended as a 'media space' in
which the two could also talk to one another and explain what they
were trying to do with the drawing.

However, Heath and Luff note that EuroPARC's personnel came
to use the system for quite different purposes: 'The most prevalent
use of the system within EuroPARC is to maintain an open video
connection between two physical domains, typically two offices. These
"office shares" are often preserved over long periods of time, weeks
and sometimes months, and simply provide two physically distributed
individuals with a sense of co-presence' (Heath and Luff 1993: 36).
This use of a standing open connection between offices led Heath and
Luff to concentrate on the routine interactional uses to which the
system was put. As a result, they were able to reveal some of the key
interactional problems which emerge when people begin attempting
to communicate via such video links.

Video media afford a number of interactional procedures which
are systematically disenabled by non-visual communication channels.
Primary among these, of course, is the use of gesture, gaze, and overall
bodily comportment. The video channel also allows a prospective
interactant to 'glance' at the other prior to attempting contact, and
thus enables that attempt to be more closely coordinated with
the other's observable availability for interaction. Moreover, video
technology allows for the kind of 'unmotivated' interaction that

is common in situations of physical co-presence. Rather than one person intentionally initiating contact (the 'caller-called' relationship we considered in chapter 6), it is possible to envisage such things as 'one person noticing another noticing them and [on that basis] initiating conversation' (Heath and Luff 1993: 38).

However, it turns out that on each of these dimensions the technology itself brings into play significant problems for interactants. While it may appear that the video link reduces some of the asymmetries characteristic of audio-only telephone conversation, it introduces others that, in many ways, are more complicated. To put it in a nutshell, what the technology 'promises' to afford is not the same as what it 'actually' affords.

Let us briefly look at some examples from Heath and Luff's (1993) study. Extracts (1) and (2) are taken from an open video link between the offices of Maggie, a scientist engaged in research at the centre, and Jean, an administrator. Note that while colleagues such as these would routinely keep their video link open all day, the associated audio link was *not* kept open. In this particular system, audio contact can only be established by a foot pedal which operates the microphone. Hence, it is possible for one party to open their audio link while the other does not. This leads to a situation in which prospective interactants need to find ways of attracting the attention of the other in order to open up the audio channel. These extracts illustrate how, in such a situation, people may presuppose the effectiveness of actions that are used in other circumstances of visual contact, such as glances, hand waves and other phenomena designed to draw attention at the periphery of someone else's perceptual field.

Heath and Luff's (1993) system for transcribing video data is complex, and I have simplified it somewhat by providing descriptions of nonverbal conduct rather than representing it graphically as they attempt to do.

(1) Maggie trying to attract Jean's attention ((Adapted from Heath and Luff 1993: 40))

((Throughout the following, Jean gazes at her computer screen. The monitor is to one side, at an angle.))

1 Maggie: ((Turns to look at Jean on her monitor.))
2 Maggie: ((Raises her hand and waves.))
3 Maggie: ((Peers at Jean via her monitor for about 10
4   seconds.))
5 Maggie: ((Turns away from monitor, picks up phone and
6   calls Jean's office.))

Here, we see an attempt to initiate interaction based first on a glance, then on a brief hand wave (lines 1 and 2). On glancing at the image of Jean on her monitor, Maggie sees that Jean is present in her office, though engaged in some work which involves her looking at the computer monitor in front of her. The video link monitor is to Jean's left, at a slight angle to her current line of vision. Maggie's movement (the wave) is designed to attract attention at the periphery of Jean's vision. However, it appears not to succeed in getting Jean to look away from her computer screen towards the video monitor. As a result, Maggie continues 'looking' at Jean, apparently without Jean being aware of it, for some ten seconds. In fact, Maggie is looking at the *image* of Jean on her, Maggie's, video monitor, so even if Jean were to glance at her own monitor she would not see Maggie looking 'at' her (since the camera is placed on top of the monitor), but slightly downwards. Hence, the actual coordination of gaze in this kind of environment is highly problematic. This in itself can have consequences for the initiation of interaction since it seems that a key concern of co-participants in face-to-face conversation is that mutual eye-gaze is momentarily established at the start of an initial utterance (C. Goodwin 1986; Heath and Luff 1993: 43–5).

Intuitively, it seems that the use of hand gestures at the periphery of another's vision could function well as a strategy for attracting attention in situations of physical co-presence. A related technique is that of moving one's head and upper torso slightly, pushing oneself as it were further 'into' the perceptual field of the intended co-participant. In physical co-presence, such movements might be used in combination with vocalizations of some sort; however, as noted, in this video-mediated system prospective interactants need to attract the other's attention first, in order to get them to open their audio link. In the case of extract (1), Maggie's waving and gazing activity fails in this aim, and she eventually initiates contact using the more conventional means of the telephone (lines 5–6).

In extract (2) we find a similar, though much more exaggerated, series of attempts to attract attention by means of actions on the periphery of another's vision.

(2) Jean trying to attract Maggie's attention ((Adapted from Heath and Luff 1993: 41))

((Throughout the following, Maggie gazes at her computer screen. The monitor is to one side, at an angle.))
1 Jean: ((Sits at desk.))
2 Jean: ((Turns to look at Maggie on her monitor.))

3	Jean:	((While looking, pulls a face and rocks from
4		side to side for 5 or 6 seconds.))
5	Jean:	Tch
6	(0.4)	
7	Jean:	((Putting thumbs in ears and waggling
8		fingers)) Ooh::↑voooh↓ooh::↑voooh::.
9	(1.0)	
10	Jean:	((Thrusting her face towards monitor)) No, she
11		won't look at hhme.
12	Jean:	((Glances at camera on top of her monitor, then
13		turns away, abandoning attempt to initiate
14		contact.))

Once again, the attempt begins with a glance (line 2). There is no wave, but as the glance is extended into a 'look', Maggie produces movements which, one would imagine, would quickly attract attention in a situation of physical co-presence: pulling a face (lines 3–4), then putting her thumbs in her ears and waggling the fingers in a childlike teasing gesture (lines 7–8). At this stage, Maggie also makes the kind of teasing sound that is associated with this gesture, though of course Jean cannot hear this. Once again, it is worth bearing in mind that if Jean were at this moment to look towards her video monitor, what she would see would be Maggie making these gestures with her face pointed downwards, and not directly towards her. This in itself may initially render problematic the precise object of Maggie's gesturing.

In each of these extracts, we see initial attempts to gain the attention of a prospective interactant that use techniques which can be effective in physical co-presence, but in video-mediated co-presence they appear not to work. In each case, the attempt is then upgraded, bringing into play actions such as staring (extract 1), pulling faces and making sounds (extract 2), which, in physical co-presence, may convey the impression that the other is deliberately trying to ignore the interaction attempt. Yet these too are unsuccessful; and as Heath and Luff (1993: 42) note, 'in neither these, nor the many other instances we have examined, is there evidence to suggest that the potential coparticipant is deliberately disregarding the attempts to attract their attention.' Rather, what seems to be happening is that the interactional force possessed by certain types of small gesture in physical co-presence is significantly weakened, or even eliminated, in this form of video-mediated co-presence.

When two people are in a room together, even if they may be concentrating on different things, glances across the space between them, or small hand gestures, can function to attract the other's attention in a similar way to what Goffman (1981) described as 'out-louds'. We can intuitively recognize the phenomenon that Goffman intended:

for example, when you and your flatmate/husband/wife are sitting in the living room each reading a different paper, an 'out-loud' laugh or exclamation from one of you can serve to invite the other to look over or to enquire 'What is it?'. This is a way that we can make public our 'noticing' of a good joke or intriguing story so that we can tell it to our co-participant, not by simply launching into talking about it, but by attracting their attention in order for them to inquire about it. In this way, such a technique ensures that the beginning of our mention of the story is closely coordinated with the shift in the other's attention from their own newspaper (or other focus of attention) towards the telling we wish to make about ours. In short, it provides for a situation in which the other is ready to listen rather than engaged in something else.

The interactive power of out-louds is linked to a more general significance of glances and gestures on the periphery of another's visual field. As Kendon (1990) puts it: 'When one perceives another is looking at one, one perceives that the other intends something by one, or expects something of one' (Kendon 1990: 51, cited in Heath and Luff 1993: 39). The key point about extracts (1) and (2) is that whereas the video channel appears to afford the use of such techniques to invite another into interaction with one, in fact, for some reason, it does not.

This has consequences for the overall coordination of interaction. Examining cases in which speakers make use of gestures and attempts at 'eye contact' (that is, in this context, ensuring that one's co-participant is looking towards the screen when one is speaking), Heath and Luff remark that such attempts are problematic because of the incongruence between the environment in which the action is produced and that in which it is received. Put simply, while participants assume that they can use gestures in the same way as they might in true physical co-presence, one cannot know how much of a hand movement or other gesture is visible to the other before it 'drops off the edge' of their screen and so out of the world that is visually available to them at that moment. Likewise, because of the different placings of the monitor and the camera, when one participant is looking at their available image of the other (the onscreen image), from the other's angle they appear to be looking in another direction (either downwards or to one side).

In the context of my argument in this book, all this can be described in terms of a disparity between the technology's design features and its features-in-use. Videophones appear to hold out the possibility of intimacy at a distance – co-presence without physical co-presence – in a way that is far richer than the voice-only environment of the telephone. Yet research on videophone interaction indicates that the kinds of coordination problems posited for the telephone, but ultimately not found, by Rutter (1989 (see chapter 5)), do indeed come into play even when the technologically-mediated communication involves more of the 'cues' which Rutter believed were the key to closely coordinated talk.

It may be, of course, that humans will develop forms of interaction that are better fitted to the affordances and constraints of videophone technology. That is a question which awaits further research if and when the technology becomes more widely adopted. Heath and Luff (1993: 50) remark that 'in reviewing the data corpus, one finds numerous instances of individuals upgrading, even exaggerating particular gestures so as to achieve impact on the conduct of the recipient.' This might be seen as an early stage in the modification of conduct in the light of the technology's communicative affordances. Yet, as we saw in extracts (1) and (2) above, where an initial 'glance' at the other can be transformed into a 'stare' when Maggie looks at Jean on her monitor for some ten seconds, or an initial look can become a pantomime of face-pulling in Jean's attempts to attract Maggie's gaze, 'these attempts inevitably transform the action the speaker is attempting to accomplish and frequently fail to engender any response from the coparticipant' (Heath and Luff 1993: 50).

It is in this sense that we can say that technologies for communication do not always practically afford what they promise to afford. The fact that videophones enable interactants to see each other means that interactants may assume the effectiveness of communicative devices that function well in other forms of visually-accessible co-presence. Yet the technology does not afford the specific congruence between the perceptual fields of participants that ordinary face-to-face interaction relies upon. (I say more about this issue of congruence in a later section.)

A similar set of problems emerges in the next case study, which involves a quite different interactional set-up. When humans attempt to communicate with 'interactive' technologies such as computerized expert systems or simple robots, we can find once again that such technologies fail to deliver on the communicative affordances they appear to promise. In the following section I focus on a pathbreaking study in this domain by Suchman (1987).

Interacting with a computerized expert

With the advent of graphical user interfaces (GUIs) initially developed by Xerox and subsequently made popular on a worldwide scale by the Apple Macintosh and Microsoft Windows environments, operating a computer is a process related less to mathematical and logical procedures and more to linguistic and interactional techniques. With a GUI we use some common language to specify operations, make requests, issue commands, and assess their outcomes. That language takes the form of the interface, which is an amalgamation of ordinary words and phrases, icons, a cursor operated through a mouse, and virtual buttons which can be pressed using the cursor.

As a result, system designers have come to talk of what goes on between computers and their users in terms of 'interaction', 'dialogue' and even 'conversation'. It seems natural, then, for system designers to turn to research in the social sciences which is directly concerned with the organization of conversational interaction. During the late 1980s and early 1990s, many system designers became keen to explore ideas from conversation analysis (see Luff, Gilbert and Frohlich 1990; Thomas 1995). As we will see in more detail in chapter 8, this reflected the increasing influence of the idea that in order to design computer systems which can either simulate or, more ambitiously, reproduce the nature of human communication, it is necessary to know about the ways in which everyday interaction is organized.

A key moment in this sociological turn in computer system design was the publication of Suchman's book *Plans and Situated Actions* (1987), in which she drew from conversation analysis to offer a thoroughgoing critique of the model of human communication with which most system designers and programmers then tended (indeed still tend) to work.

The prevailing idea of communication within the community of computer systems developers is, perhaps not surprisingly, one based on the computational metaphor discussed in chapter 3; that is, that the individual is a plan-based, goal-driven actor. It will be recalled that the computational model of communication proposes that we act on the basis of intentions and plans, which our co-participants in a given situation are required to decipher or compute in order to understand what we are doing and act in concert with us.

It is relatively easy to see how this model can be incorporated in a machine. The computer can be said to have intentions and plans also; although in this case they are really translations of the intentions and plans of the programmer. This means that there are two basic problems for computer system design. First, the system must be designed in such a way that the user can adequately comprehend its activities, which may come in the form of instructions as to what to do in order to get the machine to work in a desired way. To use

Suchman's term, such systems are constructed to be 'self-explicating machines': the machine is an 'expert' in its own use, while the user is treated as a 'novice'. The expert–novice metaphor is one that is widely relied upon by system designers; the assumption is that the system should be able to explain its own use to a novice user. The second problem, however, is much more important: the system itself must be designed so as to 'comprehend' the activities of its user. This is where problems with the computational metaphor come into play, for the assumption is that users come to the system with goals in mind, and the system needs to have the capability to 'discover' (compute) what these are and respond appropriately.

Suchman studied pairs of novice users operating a computerized 'expert help' system on a photocopying machine. Her study brings to the fore two questions. First, to what extent can we say that there is 'mutual intelligibility' between the users and the expert system? Secondly, what happens when communication between users and machine breaks down? How do the participants (both human and non-human) manage the situation?

Like Heath and Luff (1993), Suchman relied on a modified version of conversation analysis. It will be recalled from the introduction in chapter 4 that one of CA's primary interests is in how interaction is sequenced; how the turns that people take in talking are related together in systematic and structured ways. The reason for this is that CA is concerned with how people collaboratively make sense of one another's actions, and it is thought that this can be discovered by looking at the relationship between turns in talk. Basically, within a conversation between, say, two speakers, A and B, where A speaks first, B's next turn in the exchange displays an understanding or intepretation of what A has just said; and similarly, A's next turn will exhibit an understanding of what B just said.

This feature has two very important consequences. First, by focusing on turn-taking we can produce descriptions of the methods by which the participants themselves establish mutual understanding: that is, such understanding is not seen as an invisible 'mental telegraphy', as in the computational model, but as a publicly ratifiable, temporal, and defeasible achievement (see Coulter 1979). Consequently, misunderstandings in talk, places where mutual intelligibility and shared understanding break down, are also observable behavioural phenomena, as are the methods by which such breakdowns are repaired. A next turn can display a misunderstanding of what the previous speaker said, and that can be corrected in the following turn in the sequence. In short, the sequencing of turns in conversation provides its own resources by which problems can be repaired.

For example, in extract (3), a misunderstanding emerges about the meaning of the word 'prepare' when one speaker is arranging to pay a visit to their co-participant's home.

(3) DA:2

```
1       Alice:   Well I'd like tuh see you very much.
2       Belle:   Yes. [Uh
3  →    Alice:        [I really would. We c'd have a bite,
4                en [(ta::lk),
5       Belle:      [Yeh.
6  →    Belle:   Weh- No! No, don't prepare any[thing.
7       Alice:                                  [And uh-
8  →    Alice:   I'm not gunnuh prepare, we'll juz whatever
9                it'll [be, we'll
10 →    Belle:         [NO!
11 →    Belle:   I don' mean that. I min- because uh, she en I'll
12               prob'ly be spending the day togethuh, so uh:::
13               we'll go out tuh lunch, or something like that.
14               .hh So I mean if you:: uh have a cuppa coffee or
15               something, I mean [that uh that'll be fine. But=
16      Alice:                     [Yeah
17      Belle:   =[uh- othuh th'n that don't [uh- don't bothuh=
18      Alice:    [Fine.                     [(   )
19      Belle:   =with anything else.
```

These two old friends have arranged to get together, and as part of that arrangement, Alice proposes that they could 'have a bite' (line 3). This is a figurative expression which, in English, generally functions as an invitation to lunch. Belle's response, '<u>d</u>on't prepare anything' (line 6), displays her understanding that this is what Alice intends. At this point, however, mutual understanding begins to fail, as Alice interprets Belle to mean something along the lines of 'don't do anything elaborate', and she says in the next turn, 'I'm not gunnuh prepare, we'll juz whatever it'll be' (lines 8–9). As Belle makes clear in her next turn, this represents a misunderstanding of what she had meant, which was more along the lines of 'don't do anything *at all*, because I'll be going out for lunch earlier in the day'. The momentary lack of mutual intelligibility here is rectified, or repaired, in Belle's turn beginning, 'NO! I don' mean that. I min–' (lines 11–19).

In this way, the very sequential ordering of turns in conversation provides resources for re-establishing mutual understanding when it breaks down. Mutual intelligibility is not simply a matter of one speaker decoding the encoded intentions and goals of the other, but is established in the course of a temporally ordered sequence of turns. Moreover, the accomplishment of mutual intelligibility is actually ensured by the 'next turn proof procedure' (Sacks et al. 1974; Hutchby and Wooffitt 1998) whereby speakers rely on the next turn in a sequence as a display of understanding of the prior turn. Thus, while on one level it is not available to Alice what Belle 'actually' means when she says 'don't prepare', the meaning becomes publicly available in and through the current turn-taking sequence (for more detailed consideration, see Schegloff 1992b).

In applying this perspective to human–machine interactions, Suchman (1987) developed a framework for presenting her transcriptions which not only distinguished between the user's turns and the machine's turns in a sequence of actions, but also differentiated those actions that are behaviourally available to user and machine respectively, and those that are not. Her transcripts are thus divided into four columns:

1   User's actions which the machine cannot detect, such as talk
2   User's actions which the machine can detect, such as the selection of an option via the user interface
3   Machine's actions which the user can detect, such as the display of menus on the visual display unit
4   Designer's rationale underlying the machine's actions, which is not available to the user as it is implicit in the structure of the program.

This framework enables Suchman to focus on the disjuncture between what the user is 'supposed' to do at any point in a sequence – a set of expectations based on the designer's user-model and built into the program that guides the machine's actions – and what users actually do as a result of their situated interpretations of the machine's instructions and options. Recall that in human–human conversation, the intelligibility of any 'next' turn in a sequence is a locally accomplished, and publicly available, outcome of practical reasoning. Any lack of congruence between the interpretation a turn displays of its prior turn and what the producer of that prior turn meant by it can (if necessary) be repaired in a third turn (or, maximally, a fifth: in what is called repair 'after the next turn' – see Schegloff 1992b). This is not the case when one of the interactants is a programmed machine, for a number of reasons which we can now turn to look at.

The ideal interaction between user and machine in Suchman's study takes the form of the following extract.

(4) Suchman 1990: 30

	The user's actions		The machine's behaviour	
	I Not available to the machine	**II Available to the machine**	**III Available to the user**	**IV Rationale**
T1			DISPLAY 1	
T2	User reads instruction, interprets referents and action descriptions.			
T3		ACTION A		
				Action A means that user has understood Display 1 and is ready to proceed to the next.
T4			DISPLAY 2	

At T1, the machine puts up a display for the user to read. T2 shows the user reading and interpreting the display, and as a result of that she produces an action, Action A, at T3. Note that while Action A is available to the machine, whatever the user does at T2 – whether it is silent reading, reading aloud, discussing what the display might mean with a co-worker, and so on – is not available from the machine's perspective. However, the rationale built into the program is that Action A (for instance, selecting the option to 'Print' from a dialogue box) indicates that the user has understood the contents of Display 1, and is therefore ready for the next display, the next move in the action sequence, which occurs at T4 when the machine puts up Display 2.

Of course, while this ideal sequence sometimes happens, on many occasions it does not; and in these situations, distinctive inter-actional problems arise. Consider extract 5, an example of a less-than-successful interaction. In this extract, two users (A and B) are seeking to make four copies of a three-page document. The system has asked them to place the document to be copied in its 'document handler'.

(5) Adapted from Suchman 1990: 38–9

| | The user's actions | | The machine's behaviour | |
	I Not available to the machine	II Available to the machine	III Available to the user	IV Rationale
T1	A: ((Puts first page into document handler))			
T2		PLACES DOCUMENT INTO DOCUMENT HANDLER		
T3			DISPLAY 6: 'Press the Start Button'	
				Ready to print
T4	A: 'Press the Start Button.' Where's the Start Button? ((Looks around machine, then to display))			
T5	B: ((Points to display)) Start? Right there it is.			
T6	A: There, okay.			
T7		SELECTS START		
T8			STARTS	
				Copying document
T9			DELIVERS COPIES	
				Job complete
T10	A: So it made four of the first?			

T11

                              DISPLAY 7:
                              'Remove
                              originals'

                                              Removing
                                              documents

T12   A: ((looks at
       display))
       Okay.

T13   A: ((Takes page
       out of
       document
       handler))

T14   REMOVES
                 ORIGINALS

T15   DISPLAY 8:
                                  'Remove the
                                  copies'

                                              Removing
                                              copies

T16   A: ((Holding
       next page over
       the document
       handler, looks
       at display))
       Does it say to
       put it in yet?

T17   A: ((Puts next
       page into
       document
       handler))

T18   REPLACES
                 ORIGINAL

T19   Return to
                                  DISPLAY 7:
                                  'Remove the
                                  originals'

                                            Removing
                                              originals

A misunderstanding emerges here because the machine 'expects' the user to begin by putting the whole document to be copied in the document handler. According to the program, if a user has the goal of making copies of a document, and her plan is to be instructed by the machine as to how to carry out such a task, then if instructed to 'Place the document to be copied in the document handler', that is precisely what she will do. Unbeknown to the machine, however, the user's situated understanding is that the document will be copied page by page, not all at once, so she only puts the first page into the handler (T1).

The problem this leads to is that the machine, having copied all the sheets in the document handler, at T9 believes that it has copied the whole document, and instructs the user to remove the originals and the copies prior to going on to the next job. The user, meanwhile, expects the machine to tell her to put the next page in the document handler (T16: 'Does it say to put it in yet?'). As a result, they enter into a cycle of misinterpretation, where the user's placing of the second page in the handler (T17) is understood by the machine as the user 'replacing the originals' (T18), as a result of which it puts up a display instructing her once again to remove her originals from the document handler (T19). In short, user and machine take it that the other is doing a different kind of action than the one they are actually trying to do.

Suchman uses this kind of case study to make a number of points about the nature of human interaction with machines such as this relatively simple 'expert help' system. First, she argues that while the user models employed in cognitive and computer science depend upon users starting with and sticking as closely as possible to a plan, in actual human interaction, with machines as well as with other humans, action is essentially *ad hoc*. Designers attribute plans to users, and systems work well whenever the actions undertaken by the user can be linked to prior assumptions about what the user is doing. But problems soon arise when those assumptions about users' goals and plans do not match with their actual situated actions.

As in extract (5), a user may be aware of what the machine requires her to do to achieve some specific objective; however, the situated actions by which she tries to achieve that objective are not available to the machine. Neither do the user's *ad hoc* actions match the system's idealized model of the 'plan' that the user has in mind. Furthermore, the user has no access to this model, but has to make sense of the system's requirements within the context of her particular situation and in the light of her understanding of previous actions. And compounding the problem, the system has no access to the sense she has made of those prior actions on the situated level, and proceeds by assuming that she has understood in the way the designer's user model predicts.

Thus, unlike human–human interaction, as in extract (3) above, in such a system there are no built-in resources for engaging in repair when mutual intelligibility breaks down. Indeed, there are no resources by means of which the specification of a problem in mutual understanding can be made publicly available. In short, at no point can either the machine or the user engage in repair by saying something like 'No, I don't mean that, I mean . . .'. They stumble into a circle of confusion (and quite often, at least for the user, frustration).

In these ways, Suchman's study offers an excellent illustration of the distinction, raised in chapters 3 and 4, between the computational and the interactional models of communication. As she points out, this embodies a range of lessons for the designers of interactive artefacts. Principally, it raises the difficult issue that all communicative action, including human–machine interaction, is situated: that is, reliant on its specific circumstances. But those circumstances have a different salience from the point of view of a programmed machine.

> The user of a system deploys a full complement of observational, inferential, and language-using skills in order to construe – and miscontrue – the system's behaviour according to the behaviour's particular circumstances. At the same time, the system is mapping a restricted set of effects, left by the user's actions, onto a prescribed template of possible meanings. As a consequence of the asymmetrical access of user and machine to their situation, the ordinary collaborative resources of human interaction are unavailable. (Suchman 1990: 47)

This raises the question of whether Suchman's work offers an argument for the advantages of the interactional model over the computational model in designing interactive technologies. Suchman herself prefers to suggest that designers should take account of interaction's situated properties, and alter their design priorities accordingly: 'The real project of the designer of an interactive artefact . . . is to engineer alternatives to interaction's situated properties' (1990: 47). Yet there have been attempts to design more sophisticated, speech-based interactive technologies embodying a different range of affordances based on ordinary conversation. With these, some explicit attempts have been made to incorporate an interactional model of communication into the system's design. In chapter 8 I turn to consider the nature of human communication with such devices.

Intersubjectivity and technological mediation

Although the videophone and the simple computerized expert system are very different technological forms, we have seen that when they mediate interaction, they can lead to a similar range of asymmetries. These asymmetries, in turn, mean that in important respects the specifically technological dimension comes to stand in the way of the management of what, in other contexts, are routine activities: attracting the attention of a prospective co-interactant, or accomplishing repair in situations of misunderstanding.

Note that these problems are not tied to the level of technological development. It is not simply that the videophone systems in Heath and Luff's (1993) study, or the help system in that of Suchman (1987), are at an early stage of development and that further technological developments and refinements will eliminate the interactional problems that have been described. The difficulties experienced by users in both cases emerge from a lack of fit between the expectations associated with the normative structures of ordinary interaction and the artefact's practical communicative affordances. On another level, these problems are associated with the nature of intersubjectivity itself: with the very set of assumptions and practices upon which the routine carrying out of interpersonal communication rests.

Schutz (1962), some of whose ideas we initially encountered in chapter 3, proposed that the possibility of intersubjectivity in everyday interaction is founded on a number of core shared assumptions. The most fundamental of these he called 'the principle of the reciprocity of perspective'. In Schutz's argument, interactants are aware that they cannot see the world in exactly the same way, because they cannot both be in the same place at the same time. In order to maintain a shared orientation to a world that is the 'same' for all practical purposes, however, the principle of the reciprocity of perspective comes into play. This is the assumption that 'I and my fellow-man would have typically the same experiences of the common world if we changed places, thus transforming my Here into his, and his – now to me a There – into mine' (1962: 316).

It is just this phenomenological swapping of places that videophone technology, and to a lesser extent intelligent help systems, simultaneously allow to be imagined, yet cannot enable in practice. For videophones, the problem is centred around the lack of congruence between the way in which an action is performed and that in which it is observed. The reciprocity of perspective in face-to-face interaction enables us to visualize, if necessary, the way our gestures or facial expressions appear to the other; yet we have problems doing that in video-mediated interaction, partly because the reciprocity of perspective is distorted by the dynamic arrangements of the technology (that is, the placement of the camera and monitor).

But it is not just an issue of being able, or not, to visualize what the other might be seeing. Additional, related asymmetries emerge, associated with the normative conventions of ordinary talk. While Suchman's photocopier is not 'talking' to its users in a verbal sense, it is notable (and emphasized by the format of Suchman's transcripts) that the interaction between user and machine is sequential, as it is in conversation. That is, there is not merely a serial relationship between actions: it is not just that action A is followed by action B and then by action C, and so on. Rather, actions are sequential and therefore *consequential* for those that come next in the sequence. Moreover, such 'next' turns are treated as displaying their producer's understanding of the prior turn; and, crucially, themselves embody certain sets of expectations (or to use the terminology of CA, conditional relevancies) as to what may appropriately come next in the sequence.

Thus, from the user's perspective, the machine appears to afford a form of quasi-conversational turn-taking. Indeed, it is possible to envisage such a computerized expert system utilizing speech-production technology to verbalize the messages it puts up on the VDU, perhaps employing a more conversational idiom, for example, 'Okay, I've finished copying. You can take your papers out of my document handler now.' Such a system would bring into play a further set of affordances, such as the affordance for engagement in real-time spoken interchange. In chapter 8 we will examine some of the interactional consequences of such 'conversational' machines.

The point here, however, is that the system does not afford quite the opportunity for quasi-conversation that the (novice) user appears to expect. As a competent conversationalist, the user will have come to assume that if she misunderstands what an interlocutor has said, and that misunderstanding is consequential for what the interlocutor meant, then it will be made public in the following turn or two, and so given the opportunity to be repaired. The principle of the reciprocity of perspective means that the default expectation in conversation is that mutual intelligibility is accomplished unless otherwise indicated. Participants can thus take it that they have, for all practical purposes, symmetrical access to each other's subjectivity. While we share an awareness that we are not telepathic and so cannot 'get inside another's head', in ordinary communication we ignore that in favour of accepting that what is conversationally relevant about subjectivity is what can be made public conversationally. We can, of course, get the impression that someone is being 'secretive' or 'evasive'; but such an impression needs to be warranted in some way, for instance by that person not making available or observable something which we may have grounds for believing they know (see Coulter 1989). In technologically-mediated interaction with a programmed expert system, those routine grounds for intersubjectivity are not met.

The problem of intersubjectivity is thus at the root of a range of issues that emerge when humans attempt to communicate with 'interactive' technologies. As a result, there is a mismatch between the expectations based on the normative order of interaction, and the communicative affordances of these artefacts.

It might be objected that both the above case studies focus on the problems of users who are relative novices in regard to the technology in question. Hence, there are bound to be problems of usability. We might think that once people are more used to the communicative affordances of these technologies, they will modify their behaviour accordingly. In this respect, it is interesting to note reports of 'strange' uses to which novices put the telephone in the early days of its dissemination, when almost all lines were multiple user lines ('party lines') managed through a single local exchange. '*The World's Work* reported in 1905 that a farm wife who had telephone service just a few months was asked how her family liked it and replied, "Well, we liked it a lot at first, and do yet, only spring work is coming on so heavy that we don't hardly have time to listen now"' (Brooks 1975: 116–17, cited in Hopper 1992: 31). This quote illustrates a particular affordance of the telephone which is not, for the most part, socially accepted: that when the line is a party line, the technology affords eavesdropping on others' conversations.

Nevertheless, focusing on novice users is a useful exercise since, for one thing, it serves to emphasize how the communicative affordances of technological artefacts – both those actions which the technology enables and those which it disenables – have to be found in the course of attempting to interact with or through it. Although it has not been the concern of the studies mentioned in this chapter, there is the possibility, with such new forms of technology for communication, to engage in longitudinal studies of how humans may adapt the normative patterns of talk-in-interaction to the contingencies of technologically-mediated communication. This is problematic with a technology as ubiquitous and well-established as the telephone; although one possibility is to study its integration in the context of developing economies where the appropriate infrastructures are only beginning to be put in place. An alternative environment where such a study may be entirely feasible is the relatively new communications medium represented by Internet Relay Chat (discussed in chapter 9).

That having been said, I have tried to emphasize that the interactional issues raised above may have as little to do with the novice status of users as they do with the relative sophistication of the technologies in question. Rather, they are to do with some of the generic practices by which the orderliness of ordinary talk-in-interaction is ensured. Indeed, other studies concentrating on non-prototype technologies which are situated and used in actual workaday environments have suggested that even when users are familiar with the technology and its constraints, such problems do not disappear (Button and Harper 1993; Randall and Hughes 1995; Whalen 1995).

In these studies, technological mediation of communicative action brings into play another set of asymmetries. They focus on computer systems designed to assist or enhance the routine work carried out by humans in contexts such as dispatching civic emergency services (Whalen 1995); dealing with customer inquiries in a high street bank (Randall and Hughes 1995); or production work in a factory (Button and Harper 1993). One of the threads running through these studies is the importance given to the relatively straightforward observation that the work concerned is carried out in social circumstances; that is, there is a deep *sociality* to work. When people in the real-world circumstances of work use technologies for communication, they do so with particular work-based tasks to accomplish: for instance, getting a particular kind of firefighting unit or ambulance dispatched to a particular emergency; checking a particular customer's account details in a bank; or making up a particular patient's record during a medical consultation (Greatbatch, Luff, Heath and Campion 1993). Moreover, in the course of these activities, systems are used in interaction with others, whether other workers around the system in the work environment, or clients with whom users have to deal through the medium of the system.

This leads to two distinctive questions. First, how do the format and the rules designed into the system affect the work and interaction of the people using it? Second, what kinds of problems arise in the carrying out of work when the computer is used in interactions with clients; how might the system help or hinder the accomplishment of work tasks? In a similar way to Suchman's (1987) findings, a key theme is that the design of the system tends to come into conflict with the routine, normal ways people have of organizing their work.

Let me focus on just one example. Randall and Hughes (1995), in their investigation of technology use in a high street bank, directed attention towards the tasks of the cashier, whom they describe as the primary interface between the organization and its customers. As in many such organizations, cashiers were required to conduct business with customers on the basis of a computerized expert system which directed the cashier towards the relevant information to be obtained during an interview on the basis of a set of predetermined templates.

The computer system used in this organization was based on a highly structured model of transactions and information flows within the organization, and Randall and Hughes asked whether this model operated as an accurate representation of how work actually happened. They began with a deceptively simple observation: as in any interface between members of the public and a service organization, there are asymmetrical agendas between the organizational representative (in this case the cashier) and the customer, especially when the interaction involves inquiries or complaints.

For the customer, the problem is a here-and-now, specific issue, related to their particular circumstances and to which they want a specific individualized solution. By contrast, for the cashier (and, by extension, for the computer system), the problem at hand is 'just another one' which has to be dealt with in the routine way. This leads to a complex and potentially conflicting set of demands on the cashier. He or she has to manage this particular customer and their enquiries, complaints or whatever, while at the same time maintaining the flow of customers through the process by means of the templates provided by the system.

Randall and Hughes illustrate how easy it is, in this environment, for the computer system to put things up on the screen which constrain the interaction in unnecessary ways. Principally, the system tends to impose a logic on the course of the interaction which does not arise from local circumstances and which thereby disenables participants from carrying out situationally appropriate courses of action and instead channels them towards others. This can result in two types of problem. Either the system 'gets in the way' of important tasks that humans have their own, more appropriate ways of dealing with: for instance, in Whalen's (1995) study of emergency dispatch work, he found that the 'intelligent' computer-aided dispatch system could actually end up making completely the wrong decision about which firefighting unit should be sent on a call because it did not have the local contextual knowledge of such things as likely traffic conditions on a specific route, possessed by human workers as part of their ordinary worldly competence. The second problem this can lead to is that workers stop using the system as it was designed and find ways of 'working around' it, either by going back to their ordinary routine ways of managing the job (Button and Harper 1993), or by resorting to other means of finding out a given piece of information, such as telephoning a colleague elsewhere in the organization (Randall and Hughes 1995).

The point made in each of these studies is that systems that are introduced in order to help the process of work often end up hindering it because designers have not paid enough attention to the ways things are done in the normal course of events. Rather, they have ended up imposing, by way of the system's design, far too rigid a structure on the flow of work and the process of decision-making, whereas for humans such procedures are *ad hoc*, situated and carried out on the basis of action sequences rooted in the contingencies of the local context. Thus, the issues raised in this chapter transcend the novice status of users because they are actually related to the interface between communicative affordances of artefacts and normative structures of interaction.

The question of whether it is possible to design 'intelligent' technologies for communication which afford human–machine interaction in such an *ad hoc*, situated and contingent way is a complex one. In the following chapter, I turn to consider some facets of that question in the context of a discussion of various attempts to build 'conversational' computers; in particular, computer systems based on everyday speech recognition and generation.

8

Computers, Humans and Conversation

Science fiction writers have always been fascinated by the possibility that machines may be able to interact with humans in a human-like, or conversational, way. One of the best known examples is HAL 9000, the somewhat sinister supercomputer in Kubrick's film *2001: A Space Odyssey*. HAL is not only able to engage in casual conversation with humans such as Dave, the commander of the spaceship that HAL controls, but also to lip-read (Dave and his co-pilot try secretly to plot against HAL, but the computer watches them via a TV camera on its network), to judge intentions, to dissemble and, ultimately, to kill Dave's partner while claiming that the death was an accident. In short, HAL has enough human-like qualities to make it one of the most sophisticated manifestations of the classic science fiction theme that if computers come to be more like humans they will ultimately 'take over'.

Another intriguing example is the ship's computer HOLLY in the long-running British television comedy *Red Dwarf*. HOLLY is remarkable because while it can, like HAL, interact conversationally, it routinely employs sarcasm, irony and dry humour to foil humans' attempts to use it for 'computer-like' purposes such as judging the speed of an approaching enemy vessel. HOLLY does not represent the 'computer take-over' theme; instead, this fictional computer plays on ordinary notions of the differences between humans and computers by being human-like in ways that make it difficult to accept it as really a computer at all.

In a different way, the human sciences also have a long-standing interest in the possibilities represented by machines that can converse with humans. The enormous research fields of artificial intelligence (AI) and human–computer interaction (HCI) have seen philosophers, psychologists, linguists and computer scientists pursuing the goal of instantiating human cognitive and communicative capacities in machines. Underpinning much of this work has been the computational model of communication introduced in chapter 3; although more recently, a significant strand of HCI research has sought to design conversational machines utilizing techniques derived from the interactional model (see especially Luff, Gilbert and Frohlich 1990).

My concern in this chapter is not with AI as such, but with that specific subsection of HCI which has sought to build and test speech-based interfaces, often based on the findings of conversation analysis. However, I will be less concerned with the technical details of actual systems than with the more significant question, in terms of the present book, of how humans appear to interact with such conversational computers. In line with my general argument, I will propose that this interaction is framed by certain affordances, and that these affordances may both enable the production of some forms of talk while constraining the possibility of others. Humans, however, have to find ways of negotiating these enablements and constraints in order to be able to interact with the machine; and this may involve significant shifts in the expectations that certain of the artefact's affordances can generate.

I begin by discussing some early attempts to base computer systems on conversational principles, focusing on a category of devices that I call 'Elizabots'.

Elizabots: Trick-boxes of computerized 'conversation'

The term Elizabots is an amalgam of two words: 'ELIZA', the name of a set of artificial intelligence programs developed in the 1960s by Weizenbaum (1966), and 'robot', the common term for a machine that is able to perform complex physical tasks and, in some cases, possesses human-like forms of intelligence and language skills. Recently, computer programmers using the internet have evolved an abbreviation of the latter term, 'bot', to refer to a type of program which automatically logs on to internet games (multi-user domains, or MUDs) and is able to simulate a human user by sending messages to other users, sometimes exhibiting highly developed interactional skills (see the discussion of JULIA, below). Both the ELIZA programs themselves, and certain internet bots, represent examples of artefacts which are (a) computationally simple, but (b) capable of giving the impression of understanding and conversing (albeit in text-based form) with a human. In this sense, Elizabots possess certain affordances of conversational competence.

Weizenbaum's ELIZA programs were named after Eliza Doo-
little, a character in Shaw's play *Pygmalion*. Eliza was a cockney character who was trained to speak 'properly' (that is, using the English
Received Pronunciation) by the phonetician Henry Higgins (modelled, apparently, on the father of Alexander Graham Bell, inventor
of the telephone). But while Higgins succeeded in training Eliza to
speak in the manner of the English bourgeoisie, the change was of
course merely cosmetic. Similarly, Weizenbaum programmed his
computers so that they exhibited understanding in the manner of a
human, but the means by which they achieved this were intendedly
cosmetic: they were boxes of linguistic tricks.

The most famous of the ELIZA programs simulated a psycho-
therapist using the Rogerian technique. One of the key features of
that technique involves the therapist picking up on certain words in
the client's talk and reformulating them into questions. ELIZA was
based on a similar principle translated into computational terms. By
choosing key words in the user's input (the program used a text-based
interface in which the user would type on the computer's keyboard
and the system would output words on the screen), and then applying a set of predetermined formats in order to formulate those words
into questions, it could often succeed in giving the impression of being
sympathetic and concerned.

As Turkle (1995) has described it:

> If you typed into ELIZA, 'I am depressed', it would analyse the sen-
> tence as 'I am' plus X. It would transform 'I am' into 'YOU ARE' and add
> a prefix such as 'WHY DO YOU TELL ME THAT'. The screen would display;
> 'WHY DO YOU TELL ME THAT YOU ARE DEPRESSED?' Weizenbaum thought
> that ELIZA's easily identifiable limitations would discourage people
> from wanting to engage with it. But he was wrong. Even people who
> knew and understood that ELIZA could not know or understand
> wanted to confide in the program. Some even wanted to be alone with
> it. (Turkle 1995: 105)

Turkle investigated some of the reasons why people may enjoy 'con-
sulting' a therapeutic program which they knew was not human. She
tended to focus on the psychological aspects of this. For instance,
some people apparently felt they could use the program as a means
of catharsis, revealing their feelings to themselves without the attend-
ant complications of having to establish or manage a relationship
with another human (the therapist). Others wanted to see how far
they were able to push the program's inbuilt limitations. One respondent in Turkle's study would 'play a game of "How alive can I make

ELIZA seem?"' (Turkle 1995: 109). This could result in interestingly
ambiguous dialogues such as the following:

(1) Turkle 1995: 109

1 Person: You are not a person.
2 ELIZA: WHY DO YOU SAY I AM NOT A PERSON?
3 Person: Because you are not.
4 ELIZA: ARE YOU TELLING ME THAT BECAUSE I AM NOT?
5 Person: No.
6 ELIZA: WHY ARE YOU BEING SO NEGATIVE?

Here, the exchange in lines 1 and 2 takes one of the standard ELIZA
pattern-matching formats as described above. Another format is illustrated in lines 3 and 4; however, the rule used by the program in this
case generates a turn, 'ARE YOU TELLING ME THAT BECAUSE I AM NOT?',
which has a decidedly odd ring to it. ELIZA's turn in line 6 is also
generated by a simple computational rule: if the number of times the
user types 'No' or 'Not' in previous inputs exceeds a certain value,
then output 'WHY ARE YOU BEING SO NEGATIVE?'. Significantly, however,
this rule enables the program to give the appearance of taking the
initiative in the conversation, effectively turning the human's repeated accusations of her (ELIZA's) non-humanness into a therapeutic object.

For me, it seems clear that one of the key reasons why these programs were, and continue to be, popular among users is that, as illustrated in the extract above, they afford a form of conversational
interaction. While it may be interesting for certain purposes to focus
on users' gratifications gained from encountering the program, and
while ELIZA (along with more recent, slightly more sophisticated,
Elizabots) is not a particularly robust conversational machine, the
interactive potentiality afforded by the program's ability to manage
coherent sequences represents a dimension missing from Turkle's
(1995) account.

These conversational affordances are perhaps more clearly demonstrated by another Elizabot named JULIA, which has gained some
notoriety in recent years among the artificial intelligence community.
JULIA, whose programming is discussed in Mauldin (1994), is an
ongoing experiment into how successful an internet bot can be at
masquerading as a human in contexts such as multi-user domains
(MUDs), in which a distributed array of users log into text-based
fantasy games via their computer terminals (see also Turkle 1995:
88–97). JULIA works on essentially the same principles as ELIZA,

yet Mauldin has gone further in building a 'personality' into his program. While ELIZA succeeds largely through the strategy of imitating a Rogerian therapist, for whom the aim is to remove all traces of his or her personality from the therapy session and simply 'reflect' back the client's concerns, JULIA draws on a wider repertoire of tricks to manifest scepticism, irony, sarcasm and other human-like qualities.

In the MUD where JULIA spends most of her time, it is possible for other (human) players to encounter her accidentally; for instance, if a player enters a particular cave in the game's scenario alone, he or she will find JULIA there and she may initiate a conversation. Given JULIA's female persona in this largely male-dominated environment, one of the things she is particularly adept at is deflecting sexual advances.

(2) Adapted from Turkle 1995: 90

1	Space-Ace:	Julia, kiss me.
2	JULIA:	Why, did your sheep leave you?
3	Space-Ace:	Julia kiss me.
4	JULIA:	Take a long walk through an unlinked exit, Space-Ace.

(3) Adapted from Turkle 1995: 91

1	Barry:	Hey girlfriend, are you out there?
2	JULIA:	Hello Barry.
3	Barry:	Hello I love your name. It's sexy.
4	JULIA:	Me too, Barry.
5	Barry:	Did I repeat myself? Didn't mean to. What are you
6		doing there?
7	JULIA:	I'm just hanging round in the Hearts Room, Barry.
8	Barry:	Well come over to MY ROOM.
9	JULIA:	Could you say that again, it scrolled off my screen.

These interactions are carried out via textual exchanges, and involve invitations to engage in actions like 'kissing' and 'coming over' to a player's 'room' which are, in fact, imaginary. Nonetheless, they illustrate JULIA's ability to engage in real-time conversational turn-taking in which her 'utterances' are relevantly sequentially matched with the humans' prior turns. JULIA's actions manifest a sophisticated range of conversational affordances, for instance recognizing a summons–answer sequence and using the second part of that sequence to initiate a greeting sequence (extract 3, lines 1–3). Recall that this is a basic feature of opening exchanges on the telephone (chapter 5). The absence of physical co-presence in this form of computer-mediated communication means that we may find marked similarities with telephone talk in the ways that participants manage the opening phases of interactions (a topic I say more about in chapter 9). JULIA's designer, Mauldin (1994), at no point suggests that he has used conversation analytic findings to 'program in' such a behavioural pattern. But knowing that this is a machine does not mean that we have to focus only on its abilities as the outcome of programming techniques. By responding in the way she does, JULIA does something which human conversationalists are capable of recognizing, and indeed likely to recognize, as a situationally appropriate action in that sequential context. It is in this sense that the machine may be taken as affording the possibility of ordinary conversational exchanges.

JULIA is similarly able to recognize questions as first parts in an adjacency pair sequence and generate appropriate second parts (extract 3, lines 5–7). More than that: while Barry in fact asks two questions in his turn ('Did I repeat myself?' 'What are you doing there?'), JULIA's behaviour is in accord with the basic conversational practice, remarked upon by Sacks (1987), that when a turn contains two questions, the next turn in the sequence will be constructed so as for the answer to the second question to come first. Sacks uses examples from ordinary human–human conversation such as the following.

(4) Sacks 1987: 59–60

```
1 A:   Well that's good uh how is yer arthritis. Yuh still taking
2      shots?
3 B:   Yeah. Well it's, it's awright I mean it's uh, it hurts once 'n
4      a while but it's okay.
```

Note that A's turn contains two questions, the first about B's arthritis, and the second about whether B is still taking shots for the arthritis. In the next turn, B answers both these questions but in the reverse of their originally produced order. 'Yeah' is a response to the Yes/No question about the shots; while following that, a more elaborate answer is provided for the preceding open question about the state of the arthritis.

In Sacks' account, this is a way that speakers have of preserving a key feature of adjacency pair sequencing: contiguity between the two turns or actions in a pair. This is significant because 'contiguity ... across successive turns takes *collaboration*. . . . That is to say, it takes independent activity of a questioner (to put the question at the end) and an answerer (to put the answer at the beginning) to get a contiguity of question and answer across their respective turns' (Sacks 1987: 58, emphasis added). In this sense, the exchange at lines 5–7 of extract (3) shows Barry (a human) and JULIA (a machine) not just coordinating their actions in a conversational sequence, but 'collaborating' in the production of an appropriately structured (contiguous) sequence of actions. Regardless of the fact that JULIA is a machine, this is a sequence that 'comes off' like a routine, human–human exchange of conversational turns.

JULIA is also able, by means of certain programmed tricks, to recognize sexual advances or innuendo and respond with turns which perform put-downs (extract 2, lines 2 and 4; extract 3, line 9). Indeed, in the case of her last turn in extract (3), 'Could you say that again, it scrolled off my screen', the put-down itself refers to paraconversational phenomena: that is, the fact that these interactions are carried out by means of scrolling text on a computer screen.

It is important to stress that these are not comments on the programming procedure or techniques used to drive JULIA. Mauldin (1994) gives no indication that he has relied on CA findings in designing JULIA's dialogue strategies; though as I indicate below, this has been the starting point for a number of recent attempts to design conversational computers. Rather, I am pointing up the way in which JULIA, on one level a relatively simple computational device which functions by means of a range of formulaic actions, is, on another level, an artefact which affords 'conversational' possibilities. But unlike the interactional affordances of the machine in Suchman's (1987) study discussed in chapter 7, human–JULIA interaction does not appear to break down so routinely. One reason for this has to do with the sequential organization of JULIA's interactions with humans. JULIA's actions are not based on the kind of global strategic expectations about humans' actions at any given point in a sequence that Suchman's research problematized, but on a more *ad hoc* procedure of responding somehow to whatever actions her interlocutor produces. Although this does not mean, as Mauldin (1994) indicates, that JULIA's responses always fit especially well with an interlocutor's prior turn, neither does it mean that JULIA is simply a passive respondent in an interaction. As we have seen, there are conversational complexities to such apparently banal actions as JULIA's 'Hello Barry' (line 2 of extract 3). In that utterance, the affordances of the action are such that JULIA is not simply responding to Barry's summons in line 1 but simultaneously initiating a next sequence by greeting Barry, thereby requiring his response in the next turn.

Turkle (1995) focuses almost entirely on the psychological dimensions of what these artefacts can tell us about the human relationship with machines. Looking more closely at the structural properties of the dialogues allows us to see that the interactional affordances of the technology itself represent an equally important dimension. While humans may be responding in certain ways in their interactions with Elizabots, we cannot ignore the issue of the properties of the technology they are interacting *with*. This leads us into some further questions concerning the kind of technological artefacts that Elizabots, and other types of conversational computers, actually are.

Imitating versus affording interaction

Although as Turkle (1995) noted (see also Weizenbaum 1970), some people apparently sought to take their consultations with ELIZA seriously, the programs themselves were not designed as an alternative to a human Rogerian therapist, any more than subsequent Elizabots have been designed to replicate or replace humans in whichever domain of action their programs enable them to deal with. Rather, Elizabots are machines intended by their developers to explore the parameters and limitations of interactive artificial intelligence as defined by the Turing Test, a device proposed by Turing (1950) in the very earliest days of artificial intelligence (AI) research. Turing put forward an argument that was very much within what I have called the computational model of communication. For him, in thinking about the nature of the mind and the question of whether computers could be said to have intelligence, it was irrelevant to consider the actual physical make-up of humans and machines: for example, that human brains have an organic molecular structure which is quite different from the solid state silicon structure of a computer's logic board (the central processing unit that computing engineers call, intriguingly enough, a 'motherboard'). The more important factor was the processing procedures which resulted in some concrete communicative outcome: for instance, the achievement of 'understanding' of a sentence. For Turing, by extension of this computational model, it would be sufficient to say that a computer had understanding, or even intelligence, if a human, in an interview situation, could not distinguish between the responses to questions given by another human and those given by a computer.

Turing called this the 'Imitation Game', and each year there is a competition organized by the National Science Foundation in the

USA in which the designers of Elizabots attempt to have their programs pass the Turing Test by fooling questioners (who are, of course, sitting in a separate room from the computer on which the program is running) into thinking they are interacting with a human. But the ELIZA programs apparently demonstrate a basic flaw in the Imitation Game as a test of artificial intelligence, since it seems possible to 'fool' (some) humans (some of the time) simply by the use of very simple computational tricks. For this reason, the Imitation Game has long been dismissed by most practitioners within AI as rewarding tricks at the expense of judging any 'true' capability for 'intelligence' in a machine.

Searle (1990) produced a powerful theoretical refutation of Turing's functionalist computational model, and, by extension, of any idea that Elizabots or other, more sophisticated language-based computers may actually develop human-like intelligence. Searle invented a thought-experiment (the 'Chinese Room') in which he imagined himself as the central processing unit of a computer by visualizing himself alone in a room with two slots in the wall, through one of which humans outside passed pieces of paper with strange symbols drawn on them. Searle had access in the room to a book of rules for matching these symbols with others, which he wrote on other pieces of paper and passed out through the second slot in the wall. Searle proposes that the book of rules can be thought of as the computer's program; the pieces of paper inserted through the first slot as its input; and those despatched through the second slot as its output. Searle then proposes (and this is the nub of the experiment) that unbeknown to him (that is, the computer's processing unit), the book of rules is a grammar and syntax of Chinese, the first set of symbols are questions in Chinese, and the second set (produced by following the rules in the book) are answers. To the humans outside the Room, according to Searle, the Room appears able to understand Chinese, since it can produce appropriate answers to the questions they ask it.

Yet, Searle insists, the Chinese Room does not 'understand' Chinese. The operator within the room is able to follow the rules but has no conception of what the symbols that come in through the slot 'mean' any more than he does of those he copies down and puts through the second slot. The Chinese Room merely gives the impression that it comprehends Chinese. This is a strong argument against those who, following Turing (1950), want to claim that because brains function through binary operations (the on/off firing of neurons), as do computers (the in/out gateways of processor circuitry), the mind must be something like a (very sophisticated) computer program (for a range of discussions of this claim, see Haugeland 1981; Churchland 1986; Dennett 1991).

However, although Searle's argument is effective against certain forms of computationalism, his alternative account is most certainly not in line with the perspective defended in this book, the interactional model of communication. For Searle introduces a new form of internalist logic into the arena when he proposes that the reason computers cannot, in his view, 'understand' language is because their programs do not possess the same 'causal powers' as the human brain. More specifically, Searle argues that the brain has the power to 'produce' intentionality by virtue of its biochemical make-up, in the same way as a mammary gland can produce milk or an adrenal gland adrenalin. Since computers do not have this biochemical make-up, they can never have intentionality and so can never be more than bland number-crunching devices, despite whatever appearances of intelligence they may manifest.

This view begs many of the questions pitted against the computational metaphor in chapter 3. For one thing, it is difficult to validate empirically, since it is hard to conceive of what 'intentionality' would look like if one were to open up someone's skull and peer at the brain inside. But even if neuroscientists did find themselves able to identify a substance emitted by the brain when a person is engaged in 'understanding' a sentence (for example), the key problem remains that Searle is presenting a reified and decontextualized idea of intentionality and understanding. It is not possible meaningfully to reduce such phenomena to functions of the brain (whether computational or biochemical) because what it means to say that some statement or action is intentional, or that someone has understood (say) a question, cannot be established independently of the interactional circumstances in which such an attribution is able to be made and validated or falsified. As in the argument against computational models of communication, this is not to deny the possible relevance of (as yet undiscovered) brain processes in the matter, but to stress that the phenomena themselves can never be reduced to neurochemical/neurocomputational events. As chapter 4 showed, conversation analysts have developed ways in which we can actually observe the production of an 'intention' or the achievement of 'understanding' as a public accomplishment, in the turns at talk between human speakers.

But can we observe the same thing in the relationship between turns at talk involving humans and computers? Clearly, Searle would say no. Following a similar line, Button (1990) has argued against the idea that computers should ever be taken seriously as conversationally competent agents. The thrust of Button's argument is that computers are driven by rules (the algorithms of their program) whereas humans are not, even though they do, as CA has shown, observably orient to the various rules of conversational sequencing. Hence, while it may be entirely feasible for computers to engage in simulating conversation, it is meaningless to say that they are capable of producing 'real' conversation. Computers like Elizabots may give the impression that they can manage turn-taking by following rules modelled on human–human turn-taking procedures, but since the computer's actions are determined by the rules whereas human actions are not, computers cannot be said to be engaging in 'conversation'.

This is a strong argument against those who may misinterpret CA's epistemological position (outlined in the final section of chapter 4) by reducing the practices of conversation to the rules and maxims, the 'technology' of conversation, that Sacks (1992, vol. 2: 339) spoke about. For CA, as Button rightly says, this technology does not represent a causal framework within which humans mechanically operate in uttering their turns at talk, but is seen as an organizational substratum underpinning the achieved relevance of sequences of talk-in-interaction. In fact, though, it is difficult to find anyone in the field who actually subscribes to the view that Button is arguing against. Virtually all practitioners using CA within HCI take a much weaker line by saying that they are 'not trying to construct a program that can do what a human can do . . . [but] to build a program which, in its own way, does similar things . . . [and thus] to use CA to build computers that facilitate more fluid interactions with users' (Gilbert, Wooffitt and Fraser 1990: 245; see also Hirst 1991).

In this sense, philosophical arguments like those of Button and Searle miss the point. In thinking about the kinds of artefacts that Elizabots and other conversational computers are, and about the nature of human communication 'with' them, there is no need to engage in debates, let alone come to any conclusions, about the essential nature of machines, or of human conversation. From a sociological perspective, we can focus on describing the affordances of such artefacts and considering their relationships with the describable patterns of talk-in-interaction. It is clear that Elizabots such as JULIA exhibit a wide range of conversational affordances. This is so not just in the abstract – that is, in my account or in the program designer's account – but in the details of the ways that humans who encounter JULIA display an ability to interact with the machine. Regardless of whether JULIA is 'really' engaging in 'conversation', the fact is that her actions afford the possibility of conversational interchanges, often at some length. Indeed Turkle (1995: 91–3) describes a particular set of exchanges in which a human returns over a series of days to try and prompt JULIA into imaginary sexual activities, apparently without suspecting JULIA's 'essential' status as non-human.

In other words, in analysing this form of technologized interaction, I want to view the technology not in terms of its status as 'a technology', nor do I want to see its behaviour in terms of its status as 'other-than-human'. The technology is to be seen in terms of its affordances, as they reveal themselves in and through humans' attempts to interact with the artefact. I want to pursue that position in the following sections by looking at human interaction with a computer using the means of speech, rather than text.

Human–computer conversation?

One of the problems of discussing real-time human–machine spoken interaction is that, at the time of writing (late 1999), the speech-based interfaces that are currently in public operation are remarkably unsophisticated, and only in the barest sense 'conversational'. As anyone who has used a telephone banking service, an airport enquiries service or a telephone shopping service will know, the computer systems that deal with calls from the public tend to use recorded voice samples connected to a hierarchical menu system in which the caller is simply given a range of choices and asked to push a button on the telephone keypad in order to select an option. Each option takes the caller to another menu, until the task is completed (the bank balance is stated, the flight arrival time announced, the order placed). On most of these menus, a standard option is available which will put the caller through to a human call-taker at any time.

The prevalence of menu-based systems is indicative of the difficulties designers have experienced in developing truly 'conversational' interfaces: that is, speech-recognition systems which are able to parse the largely unpredictable forms that utterances take in ordinary human speech, to comprehend with sufficient rapidity the actions given utterances are performing, and to generate appropriately matched next utterances in concrete, real-time sequences. Yet while such systems have not yet reached levels of sophistication and reliability that allow them to be deployed in publicly accessible contexts, laboratory prototypes exist which, in various ways, demonstrate the potential for real-time conversational interfaces.

I will focus on a prototype developed in the early 1990s by the SUNDIAL project (Speech UNderstanding in DIALogue) using a method known as 'Bionic WOZ', in which those parts of the system which could not yet be made to function adequately were 'augmented' by a human (Wooffitt, Fraser, Gilbert and McGlashan 1997).

Bionic WOZ is a term that derives from two well-known fictional sources. First, the 'Bionic Man' featured in the 1970s American television series *The Six Million Dollar Man*, in which a human who suffered fatal injuries in a jet plane crash was 'rebuilt' using hydraulics, computer chips and other microtechnologies, and thereby given various superhuman capacities. Second, the film *The Wizard of Oz* (based on the novel by Baum (1974 [1900])) in which the all-powerful Oz is revealed to be an ordinary man operating a fearsome machine. This latter idea led to a simulation technique known as 'Wizard of Oz' (abbreviated to WOZ) or, occasionally, as PNAMBIC (Pay No Attention to the Man BehInd the Curtain). Such a technique involves humans masquerading as computer systems which are in the process of development, while the users recruited to test the 'system' are led to believe that it is actually a computer with which they are interacting. The simulation is used as a test-bed in which ideas about how the system should operate, as well as how humans may interact with the system, can be explored by designers even while the immensely sophisticated technologies for speech recognition and generation are still under development (for a detailed discussion, see Wooffitt et al. 1997: 22–35). A 'Bionic WOZ' simulation is therefore one in which the human Wizard stands in for only part of the technology; or, put slightly differently, the technology and the human are partially integrated.

Some have been critical of the WOZ technique, arguing that since the computer is not 'really' a computer it is not clear that the experiments tell us anything valid about how humans interact with conversational computers (e.g. Button 1998). But there are good reasons for thinking that such a criticism is misguided. For one thing, as Wooffitt et al. (1997: 40–50) point out, the subjects in their experiments appeared not to doubt that what they were interacting with was a computer system (even though, significantly, they had not been told such a thing prior to the experiment (1997: 42)). Post-experiment questionnaires invited subjects to suggest possible improvements to the system. These were taken seriously and focused on technical issues such as the need to improve the system's voice quality (the Wizard's voice was fed through a synthesizer to make it sound more 'computer-like'); or, in one interesting case, on the need to have a 'human' voice at the start of a call announcing that the caller is about to engage with a computer system to avoid people being 'put off' by the machine (1997: 49).

The system designers worked according to a requirement that the system be not just convincing, but also *possible* and *specifiable*.

> For example, if it is known that the future computer system will need to undertake substantial database manipulation as part of its function and the database has not yet been implemented, there is little point in setting up a WOZ simulation . . . [Also] it must be possible to formulate a fairly detailed specification of the future system prior to running the experiments. This is necessary in order to ensure that the wizard correctly simulates the intended system. (Wooffitt et al. 1997: 22–3)

In the Bionic WOZ simulation, the human acted as the spoken interface between users and the system's database, and, apart from certain modifications introduced at various points for experimental purposes, produced utterances using the system's lexicon and grammar.

Admittedly, Wooffitt et al.'s (1997) study of human–WOZ interactions opens itself up to scepticism about the validity of simulation-based studies by suggesting that research such as theirs can assist designers in building better systems by revealing the kinds of behaviour humans engage in when interacting with what is believed to be a computer. As they recognize (pp. 11–12, 23), this argument is in danger of being circular: the designers of the simulation are already building in assumptions about the system's behaviour which may constrain the tester to interact in ways required by the simulated system, rather than its being a neutral test-bed for the development of hypotheses.

But the real value of the Bionic WOZ simulations lies in a quite different area. Although it is not brought strictly to the fore by Wooffitt et al., this work offers an interesting insight into the kinds of interfaces there may be between human conversational practices and the interactional affordances of real-time conversational machines. Since the humans apparently believed they were interacting with a computer, and since the simulation was constructed according to the criteria of 'possibility' and 'specifiability', we can look at these interactions according to the terms I have outlined in this book. That is, rather than treating the data as a (possibly flawed) resource for building improved system designs, we can see it as an exemplar of the kind of talk humans may produce as they attempt to communicate in the light of the affordances offered by a computerized interlocutor.

To be sure, many other speech-based systems have been designed, and a good number have been implemented without having to resort to WOZ techniques. But in this field ideas currently outstrip the state of the art in speech recognition technology by a long way, and practical implementations are still relatively crude. Even though the SUNDIAL system is more ambitious than most, its conversational abilities, as we will see, remain quite rudimentary. Nevertheless, SUNDIAL too awaits major advances in technology before it can be fully implemented. In other words, although entirely believable as a machine (and not a human pretending to be a machine like the fictional examples at the start of this chapter), the Bionic WOZ experiments simulate capabilities that are too advanced to be built using current technologies. For this reason, I treat it as the most interesting example of a device that, though identifiably 'non-human', affords the possibility of conversational interaction.

The persistence of conversation

SUNDIAL's designers worked on numerous prototypes exhibiting different levels of competence and different interactional styles. Their designs were informed by many of the principles of CA; that is, they sought to incorporate within the algorithm for the dialogue manager module a representation of the 'rules' of turn-taking and other phenomena that conversation analysts have described (see Gilbert et al. 1990). As already remarked, part of the aim was to build a speech-based interface that engaged in interaction in ways that human users might recognize from their own conversational experience. In testing these design ideas, some of the WOZ and Bionic WOZ simulations were more 'human-like' in their behaviour than others (for a discussion of some technical issues, see Wooffitt et al. 1997: 169–82).

For present purposes, I want to focus on one of the more 'computer-like' variations. One of the problems that designers of speech-based computers face is that speech recognition systems are not really capable of dealing with talk that overlaps their own utterances. As we have seen at various points in preceding chapters, overlapping talk is extremely common in everyday talk-in-interaction; moreover, humans are capable of dealing not just with momentary overlaps but with relatively extended periods of overlapping talk. We seem to find little difficulty in producing our own utterance and hearing and understanding an interlocutor's utterance produced simultaneously (see, for example, Schegloff 1988/9; Hutchby 1992). In order to discourage human users from 'interrupting' the system, in which case parts of their utterance would be irretrievable because the system cannot be in 'listening' mode and 'speaking' mode at the same time, the designers experimented with introducing a short beep to indicate when the system was ready for a next user utterance (see Wooffitt and MacDermid 1995). Users would be instructed at the start of each call to 'speak after the tone' (much like the experience most people have of leaving messages on answer machines; except that here, the 'machine' would speak back to the human).

To be sure, this is a relatively crude device, and does not sit well with our perception of speech-based computers as state-of-the-art technology. Nevertheless it is intriguing as a strong case for exploring my basic question. If the computer goes to some lengths to make it clear that it is not capable of interacting in an entirely human-like manner – that is, that it has only some of the affordances of a conversationally competent entity – the question can be put: how might humans attempt to interact verbally with such a machine? What are the ways in which the normative structures of talk-in-interaction are brought to bear in the light of this particular range of affordances?

Extract 5 is a complete exchange between a human and the Bionic WOZ simulation of this computer system (which, like all SUNDIAL variants, was designed to deal only with airport enquiries about flight arrivals and departures).

(5) S8 Apsland 1:1:1–2

```
 1              ((ring))
 2  System:         Hel↑lo.
 3              (0.6)
 4  System:         This is British Airways flight inquiries service,
 5              (0.6)
 6  System:         I can only give you information on British Airways
 7                  flight arrivals and departures.
 8              (0.6)
 9  System:         Please speak after the tone.
10              (0.5)
11                  ----                              ((tone 0.4 seconds))
12              (0.6)
13  User:           Can you tell me when fli:ght B.A. (.) four eight
14                  one from (Dusseldorf) is expected to arrive.
15              (12.6)
16  System:         You ↑want to know the arrival ti:me?
17              (0.4)
18  User:           Ye[s:.
19                    [----                           ((tone))
20              (10.9)
21  System:         Plea:se speak a:fter the tone.
22              (0.5)
```

23		----	*((tone))*
24	(2.2)		
25 User:		↑C<u>ou</u>ld you tell me when flight <u>B</u>.A. f<u>ou</u>r eight	
26		↓<u>o</u>ne from ↑<u>Doo</u>sseldorf is exp<u>e</u>cted <u>to</u>: <u>arr</u>↓ive,	
27	(5.4)		
28 System:		Fl<u>i</u>ght B.<u>A</u>. four eight <u>one</u>?	
29	(0.5)		
30		-[---]	*((tone))*
31 User:		[Yes.] Yes.	
32	(4.8)		
33 System:		From D<u>oo</u>sse<u>ld</u>orf?	
34	(0.2)		
35 User:		Yes.	
36	(.)		
37		----	*((tone))*
38	(0.4)		
39 User:		Y<u>es</u>.	
40	(3.6)		
41 System:		To L<u>o</u>ndon?	
42	(0.5)		
43		----	*((tone))*
44	(0.3)		
45 User:		Y<u>e</u>↑:s,	
46	(6.9)		
47 System:		Fl<u>i</u>ght B.A. four eight <u>one</u> from <u>Doo</u>sseldorf arri:ves	
48		at London Heathrow at eighteen oh f<u>i</u>:<u>ve</u>.	
49	(0.5)		
50		----	*((tone))*
51	(2.5)		
52	((caller replaces receiver))		
53	(3.8)		
54 System:		Good ↑<u>bye</u>.	

This extract illustrates a number of interesting points. One of the most noticeable features, in comparison with earlier extracts cited in this chapter, is the relatively disjointed nature of the exchanges. There is a marked pause of some length between every one of the turns, and often these pauses are of what, in conversational terms, is an extreme length (12.6 seconds in line 15, 10.9 seconds in line 20, and 6.9 seconds in line 46). One reason for this is that the earlier extracts come from text-based interactions and thus do not reproduce any sense of the temporal organization of the exchanges: the length of time it took for participants to type in their words, for example (an issue I return to in chapter 9). Here, by contrast, the transcript is of a tape-recorded verbal interchange which means that the temporal aspect is able to be represented. Another reason has to do with the nature of the simulation itself: most of the very long pauses precede system turns, and they indicate such things as that the system is searching its database, or parsing the previous utterance of the user, or compiling its own next utterance. The marked slowness of these procedures reflects the problematic state of the art in speech recognition technology at the time of the experiment. Many of the shorter pauses are associated with the between-turn tone, and whether or not the user is appropriately orienting to its significance (an issue I discuss presently).

We could assume that the pause-ridden nature of the interchange may prove problematic for the user. As someone who is competent in human–human conversation, where as we saw in chapter 4, the turn-taking system is designed to minimize between-turn gaps and overlaps, the user may be primed to hear in such gaps signs of some form of communicative problem. For instance, conversation analysts (e.g. Davidson 1984; Pomerantz 1984) have shown that speakers may orient to pauses of only fractions of a second as indicating upcoming disagreement with what they have said, or declination of an invitation offered (both actions which they describe as 'dispreferred'). For the most part, in this call, the user seems capable of accepting the system's pauses as a function of its status as a computer, and not as indicative of a problem.

But that is not always the case. As Wooffitt et al. (1997) show, there are occasions when users produce talk during the system's silences (that is, following a recognizable syntactic completion of the user's utterance and a substantial silence of more than two seconds). This talk reproduces actions undertaken in human–human conversation to repair a situation where the speaker judges their interlocutor to be having a problem understanding some aspect of what they themselves took to be a complete utterance. In that situation, the pauses themselves can be relatively short, as the following extract from a telephone conversation shows.

(6) Holt: Xmas 85:4:2

((Lesley has announced that she wishes to tell a story about something that happened recently))

```
1      Lesley:        Well that sa:le.
2   →             (0.2)
3      Lesley:        At- at (.) the vicarage.
4   →             (0.6)
5      Joyce:         Oh ye[:s,
6      Lesley:            [.t
```

```
7              (0.6)
8    Lesley:    u (.) ihYour friend 'n mi:ne was the:re
9  →           (0.2)
10   Joyce:     (h[h hh)
11   Lesley:       [mMister::, R:,
12   Joyce:     Oh y(h)es, (hm hm)
```

Lesley makes successive attempts to get Joyce to recognize (a) the
context of the story she is about to tell (a vicarage sale), and (b) its
key protagonist (someone referred to as 'Mister R'). It is notable that
both her first attempts are very vague: 'that sa:le' (line 1) and 'Your
friend 'n mi:ne' (line 8); also, that both these attempts fail. The first,
'that sa:le', could potentially refer to any sale in any place, although
Lesley clearly believes that Joyce is capable of pinpointing the precise
sale in question. The subsequent pause in which Joyce displays no
such recognition indicates that this assumption is probably incorrect,
and Lesley produces an utterance which provides more explicit contextual information. After a further pause, Joyce finally shows that
she realizes what Lesley is referring to (line 5).

Immediately after this, Lesley embarks on the same trajectory,
beginning with a first mention of the key protagonist in the story
which is extremely vague (line 8). While 'Your friend 'n mi:ne' is a
conventionally ironic way of referring to someone who is not a friend
at all, it leaves the recipient a lot of work to do in order to establish
which non-friend exactly is being mentioned. Again, the subsequent
pause indicates that Joyce has not pinpointed the reference. Lesley
then produces her next attempt: 'Mister::, R:,' (line 20). At this point,
Joyce recognizes the referent (line 21), and the story subsequently
proceeds.

Similar features are visible in the following extract from a
human–WOZ interaction (in this case the simulation did not involve
the between-turn tone found in extract 5).

(7) WOZ 1:6:F [Transcript from Wooffitt et al. 1997: 144–5]

```
1    User:      I'm enquiring about em the flights coming from Crete
2               .h there's one due in: (.) to Gatwick (0.2)
3               approximately ten o'clock this morning .h but I've
4               heard (.) there's some problems (.) do you know if
5               there's any flight delays
6              (4.0)
7    System:    Please wait
8              (27.0)
9    System:    Please (0.3) repeat (.) the (.) point (.) of departure
```

10		(1.2)
11	User:	.hh Well >th-< the- it's flying from Crete
12		(4.3)
13 →	User:	To Gatwick
14		(1.2)
15 →	User:	Arriving at Gatwick
16		(4.3)
17	System:	I'm (.) sorry (0.7) British (.) Airways (0.5) do
18		not have (.) any (.) flights (0.5) from (.) Crete
19		(0.3) arriving (.) this (.) morning

Notice here that, in line 9, the system has requested the user to repeat one part of their inquiry, the point of departure. The user does this apparently adequately, saying 'it's flying from Crete'. There is next a silence: usual for the system while it searches its database or parses an utterance. Just over four seconds in, however, the user elects to offer more information, saying 'To Gatwick'. Then, another second later, 'Arriving at Gatwick'. Why might the user have produced these utterances?

Wooffitt et al. (1997: 142–6) propose that, like the example I provided in extract (6), these are indications that the user takes it her initial answer to the question, in line 11, is inadequate and that the system is having difficulty understanding. Like Lesley in the conversational extract, the user seeks to repair this inadequacy by offering further information that will help disambiguate the supposedly problematic turn.

What we find here is an example of what I want to call the 'persistence of conversation' in these interactions between humans and (simulated) computers. The computer system has (some of) the affordances of conversational competence, even though these are circumscribed by such non-human behaviours as pausing routinely for many seconds, or (to return to extract 5) requiring the human to speak only following a beep. The interesting thing is that while humans are evidently capable of dealing with conversational interaction within these constraints, the machine's affordances are such that at certain points the normative structures of talk-in-interaction override the system's attempts to 'technologize' the interaction. In extract (7), the normative practice comes into play after the system has indicated that it might have a problem with the user's inquiry and the user has tried to solve that problem, but, significantly, the system has given no indication that the user's turn satisfactorily helps with the problem. The user therefore acts according to the ordinary conversational expectation that, no uptake having been provided, more information is needed.

In the earlier extract involving the between-turn beeps, we find another kind of example of the persistence of conversation. Notice the following details from that transcript.

(8) Detail of Extract 5

```
16      System:              You ↑want to know the arrival ti:me?
17                  (0.4)
18 →  User:                  Ye[s:.
19                              [----                            ((tone))
20                  (10.9)
21      System:              Plea:se speak a:fter the tone.
```

(9) Detail of Extract 5

```
28      System:              Flight B.A. four eight one?
29                  (0.5)
30                           -[--- ]                             ((tone))
31 →  User:                    [Yes.] Yes.
32                  (4.8)
33      System:              From Doosseldorf?
34                  (0.2)
35 →  User:                  Yes.
36                  (.)
37                           ----                                ((tone))
38                  (0.4)
39      User:                Yes.
```

At each of the arrows, the user, who has been instructed by the system to speak after the tone, fails to do that. That is, she fails to comply with what Wooffitt and MacDermid describe as the 'social control mechanism' designed to ensure that 'the system's output will facilitate those forms of human verbal behaviour which, given the current speech recognition limitations, the technology can cope with ... [that is] to ensure the user's speech is *system-friendly*' (Wooffitt and MacDermid 1995: 126–7, emphasis in original).

Wooffitt and MacDermid show that this failure to observe the system's tone tends to occur in certain sequential environments. Principally, it occurs when the user is responding to a *confirmation request* from the system; either when the user is confirming or, alternatively, seeking to *correct* the system's displayed understanding of what they have said. The details found in extracts (8) and (9) represent examples of the first sort. In line 16, the system asks for a confirmation that it has correctly understood that the user is calling about a plane's arrival time. After a brief pause, the user confirms this. It may be that during the pause she is in fact monitoring for the tone, but judges that it will not occur (perhaps deciding that, like a telephone answering machine, the beep only occurs once). The tone, however, starts up in overlap with her confirmation. Nonetheless, having heard the tone, the user does not repeat her turn in the clear space after it has ceased, and there ensues a long silence. The system, having heard nothing (since it is only in 'hearing mode' following the tone) orients to this as occasioning the re-production of its original instruction (line 21).

Similarly, in lines 31 and 35, the user responds to confirmation requests from the system by speaking without waiting for the tone. In line 31, she immediately repeats the response following the tone. In the very next exchange, however, the error is reproduced (line 35), and it is only after a pause following the tone's cessation that the user repeats, with emphasis, her response (line 39). The emphasis itself may be of interest here. There is a sense in which an emphatic repetition such as this can indicate a degree of irritation on the speaker's part. It may be that the user is annoyed with her own repeated 'missing' of the tone, itself an indication of the involuntary nature of the error. But there may be good organizational reasons for such mistakes to occur where they do.

Wooffitt and MacDermid themselves offer what they describe as a 'speculative' account (1995: 134) based on the idea that confirmation sequences are clearly supplementary to the central business of the call – the attempt to get an answer to the caller's inquiry – and this may mean that users' sensitivity to the relevance of the tone is diminished, because the tone was initially introduced in relation to the call's main business, the initial inquiry. This would not seem to explain cases such as extract (9), where the user executes self-repair on her missing of the tone in line 31, but immediately goes on to repeat the error in the next exchange (line 35).

There may be a more structural account for this practice. Confirmation sequences are examples of adjacency pairs (Schegloff and Sacks 1973). As we saw in chapter 4, one of the normative rules associated with adjacency pair sequences is that the production of a first part (for instance, a question) makes conditionally relevant the production in the next turn of its matched second part (that is, an answer). The notion of conditional relevance means that non-production of a second part in the next turn is accountable: it may have moral consequences in the sense that the producer of the first part may seek reasons for the second part's non-production. A request for confirmation that the previous utterance has been correctly understood (such as the system's 'Flight B.A. four eight one?') 'prefers' agreement (Sacks 1987) in the sense that the system is not assuming that it *has not* understood but is double-checking that it *has* understood. As Sacks shows, the difference between answers that agree with the preference in the question and those that disagree is that '"agreeing" answers come early in their turns and are thereby contiguous with their questions, whereas "disagreeing" answers are deferred in their turns and are *not* contiguous with their questions' (1987: 65, emphasis in original). Given these features, it is more or less natural for the user in our extract to produce her agreeing response quickly in order to avoid what, in conversation, may be an inference that she is not going to go along with the confirmation as offered. What is intriguing, of course, is that we find this practice coming into play, apparently involuntarily, in the course of an interaction with a machine that is only partially conversationally competent.

In the second kind of case, Wooffitt and MacDermid (1995) found that users would override the tone when they needed to correct something the system had said. As the following examples show, this is not related to any inability on the user's part to orient to the tone, but again is tied quite specifically to sequential contexts.

(10) Wooffitt and MacDermid 1995: 135

1	User:		I would like to know (0.3) WHAt time (.) it
2			arrives (0.4) a::nd which (.) terminal
3		(5.0)	
4	System:		Please tell me where the flight leaves from?
5		(0.5)	
6			---- *((tone))*
7		(0.7)	
8	User:		Ibi̱:za,
9		(2.2)	
10	System:		From Cairo?
11		(0.2)	
12 →	User:		I̱:[:(.)b]i̱:za
13			[----] *((tone))*
14		(0.5)	
15	User:		>Ibiza<
16		(3.3)	
17	System:		I am having trouble with the name of the
18			departure city (0.3) Can you please spell it for me?

Notice here that in lines 4–8, the user displays the ability to interact within the system's constraints by waiting (line 5) for the tone (line

6) and then pausing again (line 7) before answering the system's question in line 8. When the system 'mishears' the word Ibiza as Cairo, however, the user reverts to the normative conversational expectation for doing other-correction (note that 'correction' is a different kind of activity from 'disagreement' in the sense outlined above, and involves expectations that in many ways clash with those operating for agreeing and disagreeing with a turn's preferences). As Schegloff, Jefferson and Sacks (1977) show, in order to avoid confusion about what precisely is being corrected, there is a need in conversation for other-correction to be placed as closely as possible to the prior turn's trouble source, and that means that the correction should be done in the very next turn following the erroneous utterance, and should be placed right at the start of that next turn. At the point where the system says 'From Cairo?' this set of normative expectations comes into play for the user, and he shifts from treating the computer appropriately as an interactionally limited non-human device to interacting with it as if it possessed the normal human set of conversational competencies.

The same features can be seen in extract (11).

(11) Wooffitt and MacDermid 1995: 135–6

```
1     User:              Ehm: the question I wanted to ask is: *urh .h
2                        when the flight from Athens is scheduled to arrive
3              (0.3)
4     User:              The flight number is B.A (.) four (.) six (.)
5                        fi:ve.
6              (7.5)
7     System:            You want to know the arrival time?
8              (0.5)
9                        ----                                   ((tone))
10    User:              Yes:
11             (8.8)
12    System:            Flight B.A. four five six from Amsterdam to
13                       London?
14 →  User:              >Fr'm< from Athe[ns
15                                       [----=             (tone))
16    User:              =From Athens
17             (0.7)
18    User:              To London
19             (4.2)
20    System:            From Athens?
```

Once more, in the first exchange the user appropriately orients to the tone. But once the system makes a mistake, substituting Amsterdam

for Athens, the user embarks on the correction immediately following the completion of the system's turn.

It is notable that in both these cases the users repeat their corrections immediately after the tone which they had originally over-
lapped (lines 15 and 16 respectively). By this action they seek to
show that they have not 'forgotten' about the instruction to speak
after the tone. Rather, these overlapping corrections are treated as
mere lapses. What is significant is not just that such 'lapses' do indeed
occur; but the light they shed on the interface between the normative structures of talk-in-interaction and the communicative affordances of a technology. Both types of lapse occur in the context of
a conversational routine – the confirmation sequence – which is
enormously recursive in inquiry service calls such as these simulations are intended to model. Whalen and Zimmerman (1987) show
that calls to inquiry and emergency services have a distinctive
structure in which the main business of the call comprises a
'request–response' adjacency pair with the caller making the request
at the start of the call and the service agent providing the required
response at the end. Between the parts of this adjacency pair there
may be inserted any number of question–answer sequences in which
further information is obtained by the agent. One of the major
sequence types involved in this information-gathering exercise is the
confirmation sequence, in which either the caller or, more usually, the
call-taker, seeks to confirm that they have correctly received a
segment of information.

The system designers incorporated series of confirmation
sequences into the dialogue manager module not just in order to
make the system approximate more closely the human–human
exchanges, but simultaneously to deal with a technical difficulty.
Speech recognition systems are plagued by the problem of mis-
recognition of human verbal input. Because of this, confirmation
sequences are a way of countering technological limitations within
an easily manageable interactional format. Yet as Wooffitt and
MacDermid (1995) point out, it is precisely here that communicative
problems may arise because humans bring into play conversational
expectations which, momentarily, supplant the more technologically
circumscribed forms of turn-taking into which the system is attempting to socialize them. Following on from the discussion in chapter 7,
we can say that once again, here, the system's communicative affordances reveal a disparity between design-features and features-in-use.
The system is designed to exhibit a form of conversational competence, but only within clearly signalled technical parameters. In use,

however, those very conversational affordances lead human users at certain junctures to 'forget' the technical parameters; or, put slightly differently, to seek to attribute greater degrees of conversational competence than the system in fact affords.

This may be a reflection of a general human propensity to assume that, if a device or organism gives the appearance of intentionality, agency and/or conversational competence, then it must in fact be capable of ordinary interaction. Remarking on just such a propensity, Gilbert et al. (1990: 244) suggest that this means that 'if we, collectively, choose to regard computers as social beings, then they will be so'. As they point out:

> The possibility of the ascription of 'sociality' to apparently unpromising material is nicely illustrated in Garfinkel's experiment (1967) in which he persuaded students seeking advice to visit a new form of counselling service. The students were told that they could ask only questions expecting a 'Yes' or 'No' answer and that their questions should be addressed to a hidden 'counsellor' sitting behind a curtain. Unknown to the students, the 'counsellor' responded to their questions with answers chosen at random, yet almost without exception the students were able to make sense of the answers, did not doubt the competence of the counsellor and professed themselves well satisfied with the session. (Gilbert et al. 1990: 244)

However, Gilbert et al.'s constructivist conclusion from this – that 'whether an entity is a "social being" . . . is not [therefore] a characteristic inherent in the entity, but an ascription by the observer or participant' (ibid.) – is not quite accurate. We have seen that, indeed, sociality and interactional competence can be ascribed to conversational computers by humans, and that the affordances of interactional competence may lead humans to bring into play normative expectations that the system turns out to be unable to manage. But the issue of ascription of competence is only one side of the coin. The communicative affordances of such devices may enable the ascription of competence, but they also disenable many of the degrees of competence that are bound up with the management of basic interactional routines such as confirmation sequences. In this sense, it is inadequate to focus exclusively either on the entity's inherent characteristics or on the observer's ascriptions. Affordances are complex phenomena at the interface between these two poles. An entity's affordances are aspects of its materiality as an object in the world, but they are also functional properties which are revealed in and through encounters with the entity and attempts to interact with it. In human–machine encounters, whether a machine is treated as a social entity therefore depends not just on whether it affords sociality; but also on the extent to which its affordances match up with the expectations generated by the normative structures of interaction.

9

Virtual Conversation

I began my series of case studies in chapter 5 by looking at the telephone. We saw that there are numerous ways in which telephone technology can be said to have an impact on the nature of conversational interaction. Since its introduction in the nineteenth century, the telephone's communicative affordances have encouraged the development of novel forms of talk-in-interaction and patterns of social identities (though the novelties themselves are seen in the details rather than being grossly apparent). I conclude now by looking at some features of a relatively new form of technology for communication, known as Internet Relay Chat (IRC).

On one level, IRC is a technology that affords communication in a similar way to the telephone. The participants are not physically co-present; instead interaction is carried out via computer terminals hooked up to a central server. Unlike other forms of computer-mediated communication such as e-mail, IRC enables participants to be online simultaneously and to interact with one another in a way that approximates real-time turn-taking. But there are also a number of differences. For instance, the 'conversation' is carried on through the means of typed text rather than speech; and typically, IRC channels involve a multiplicity of participants attempting to interact at any one time. The number involved in an IRC session can be in the hundreds, rather than the two-party colloquy characteristic of the telephone.

There are other parallels between the two technologies for communication. Much as sociologists have argued that, at the start of the twentieth century, the telephone had a widespread cultural impact, altering the spatial and geographical frameworks of interpersonal communication (Pool 1981), so at the century's end it was being argued that the internet (of which IRC is a part) is altering not just the quality of interpersonal relations but the spatial and temporal frameworks of our sense of individual identity and selfhood (Poster 1995).

My aim here is not to become involved in such theoretical debates. Rather, I will use some of the more interesting sociological claims as a background against which to consider in detail some features of the structural organization of IRC, which I will describe as a form of technologized or 'virtual' conversation. In line with the general orientation of the book, I want to ask: (a) what are the distinctive communicative affordances of IRC; (b) how do these interface with the normative structures of conversation; and (c) what forms of participation, identity and intersubjectivity are observably available to interactants in the IRC environment?

I begin with a discussion of some of the basic parameters of virtual conversations, drawing in part on studies which combine sociological interpretation with observation of the forms of communication that can be found on IRC. More recent studies (for example, Garcia and Jacobs 1999) have brought to bear a conversation analytic perspective by comparing the turn-taking systems of IRC with that described for conversation by Sacks et al. (1974). I will also draw on my own research to argue that questions of identity and of turn-taking can usefully be combined within an analytical framework that focuses on IRC's range of communicative affordances, and how those may enable novel forms of participation in a multi-party virtual conversation.

Parameters of virtual interaction

A number of claims have been made in support of the view that the rapid growth of information technologies at the turn of the twentieth century is leading to a revolution in the nature of communication. First, computer-mediated communication is said to constitute a new form of community which brings with it significant implications for interpersonal relations, social identities and frameworks of participation (Jones 1995). Second, this form of text-based communication involves a distinctive combination of individuality and anonymity which enables participants to 'play' with social identities, along with a relatively unconstrained capacity to breach social norms associated with face-to-face interaction (Reid 1991). Third, in that it is a relatively new development, IRC is thought to provide a promising resource for examining both the formation and the substantive features of new electronically-mediated social networks and 'internet cultures' (Shields 1996).

Baym (1995, 1996) has explored these issues in the context of an e-mail bulletin board or 'newsgroup' centred around discussions of the topic of television soap operas (the group adopted the name 'rec.arts.tv.soaps', or r.a.t.s). As an indication of the sheer size of r.a.t.s as an online presence, Baym (1995) notes that in 1994 it had some 52,000 members who collectively posted an average of 5,000 messages per month. Baym claims that such online bulletin boards constitute 'communities' even though their members are geographically distributed, their interaction is temporally dislocated (typically, one posts a message to the group when one is logged in but might not receive responses to that message until the next log-in, which may be the following day), and there is no actual need for them to be in physical co-presence (though occasionally some members do organize get-togethers in what they themselves call the 'real world').

The status of the newsgroup as a community has to do with a number of factors. First, there are specific, evolved *norms of behaviour* which inform appropriate participation in the community. On r.a.t.s, these include naming the specific soap that is the subject of your message in the message header so that those whose interests are in other soaps may elect to delete the message without reading it; avoiding excessive quotations of others' contributions in one's reply (e-mail programs give the user the option to 'include the original message' in a reply or not); or avoiding the danger of giving away plot developments to those whose TV schedules may run weeks or months behind one's own. Breaching such norms of behaviour can, as in ordinary everyday interaction, lead to sanctions of various sorts.

Second, the group has evolved specific *forms of expression*. As in other types of text-based electronic exchange, 'emoticons' are widely used. Emoticons are textual configurations that are included in a message to lend certain pragmatic or interpersonal effects to what is being conveyed. They generally represent facial expressions, and are best appreciated by looking at them with one's head tilted to the left. So, for instance, there are emoticons for anger:

>:-|

smiling:

:-)

winking:

;-)

being upset:

(:-(

and many more. These are used to accomplish such effects as avoiding giving offence if one's words may be read as insulting, softening a rebuke in the course of an argument, and so on.

Third, newcomers to the group are specifically inducted into these ways of behaving and of expressing oneself. For example, there exist online glossaries of emoticons which so-called 'newbies' are encouraged to consult in the course of registering as a member of the newsgroup.

For Baym (1995, 1996), the most important factor in all of this is the centrality of language – specifically, written language – in the formation of these communities. As we saw in chapters 5 and 6, the absolute reliance of telephone conversationalists on (spoken) language in the absence of gaze or physical gesture leads to the development of new cultures of talking, new ways of accomplishing routine actions such as mutual identification and recognition. Online, the presence of language is equally key, except that here all participants have access to are the typed words appearing on their monitor screen. In Baym's account, it is through the building up of systematic structures in language use within the technical and regulatory constraints of the medium – that is, the physical organization of the internet and the server administrators themselves – that new forms of community can be said to be coming into existence on the internet.

A major difference between newsgroups and IRC is that turn exchange in the former is asynchronous and so does not have the same appearance of approximating a text-based version of conversation as we can find on IRC. The metaphor of the 'bulletin board' captures this distinction well. On r.a.t.s, people post messages which can be read at any subsequent time by other members, who in turn may or may not decide to post a rejoinder to the board. One does not physically 'visit' the board: rather, the messages are conveyed electronically to one's monitor screen. There is thus a significant sense in which participation in newsgroups is not just spatially distributed, but temporally disjointed.

By contrast, IRC is a form of online communication that allows real-time, apparently synchronous interactions between multiple users in any geographical location from where the program can be run (I discuss presently the extent to which the interaction is in fact synchronous). The system works by a number of participants logging in, via one of the many IRC networks, to a server on which a 'channel' has been set up by an 'operator'. There are thousands of these channels open at any one time.

The only way of sending a message to the channel is by means of a 'talk-line' provided by some proprietary IRC software (usually downloadable from an internet shareware site). The software also places a main window on the monitor screen, in which one watches all the contributions of other participants, which scroll up and out of the window at varying rates according to the volume of messages being sent.

In one of the first empirical studies of IRC, Reid (1991) observed that IRC enables a kind of escape from traditional paradigms of social interaction, which are based on the centrality of presence (even on the telephone, our interactant is 'present' at the other end of the line). This is because IRC allows interaction that may be characterized as 'formally anonymous'. As in all online communication, participants interact through the medium of computer terminals hooked up to a server, and the convention is that participants identify themselves by a 'nickname'. Clearly, this nickname can be almost anything – so, for instance, a male user can easily masquerade as a female, and vice versa. Thus, while participants are always identifiable, either by their nickname or (more technically) by another participant sending a 'finger' request to the server to discover their 'real' log-in name (which itself may be a nickname . . .), there remains the systematic possibility that one can enter this domain in a guise of one's choosing. Participants are generally not visually accessible to others, though as we see below, they often exchange digitized snapshots of themselves, and there are now 'webcams' which can send live images of one participant, albeit extremely jerkily, to the terminal of another. But unless participants choose one of these ways to take up a visual presence, there is no way that their online identities can be pinned to an actual person in the world.

For Reid, one upshot of this relative anonymity is that users can feel freer than in co-present interaction to breach the social boundaries which humans ordinarily place around interaction with strangers. For instance, 'conversations on IRC can be sexually explicit, in blatant disregard for social norms regarding the propositioning of strangers' (Reid 1991: 11).

(1)   Reid 1991: 11 ((Slightly modified))

```
1 Han:   does this compu-sex stuff really happen?
2 Lola:  Han *smooch*
3 Han:   mmmmmmmmm . . . hehehe you alone ;)?
4 Lola:  Han certainly am! I'm dialling in from home
5 Han:   me tooo . . . are you horny today at all ;)?
6 Lola:  Han today? It's the middle of the night where I am . . .
7        as for the adjective, well, do what you can ;-)
8 Han:   mmmmmmmmmmmmmmmm . . . when did you last get off?
```

Reid offers no information about the context of this single example – for instance, at what point in the interchange between the two participants Han's compu-sex invitation comes; whether or not this was the first encounter between the two; or whether the type of IRC channel from which the exchange was drawn encourages sexual predilection. But it is certainly intriguing that two individuals who (a) are geographically distant (note the reference to different time-zones in line 6), and (b) cannot be sure of the 'real' gender of their inter-locutor, seem to agree so readily to engage in a (pretend) sexual encounter. It is probably too strong to call it a 'blatant disregard' for social norms since there is evidence of a good deal of negotiation between the participants. Once Lola has indicated, in line 2, that she may be interested in 'compu-sex' (conventionally, participants may indicate that they are producing actions as opposed to utterances by enclosing their words within asterisks, as here), Han proceeds to embark on a series of preliminary moves which can be characterized as 'setting the scene' or establishing the 'mood'.

However, along with the apparent breaking down of social bound-aries on IRC, new conventions have grown up which represent new forms of social boundary, and these boundaries are 'policed' through various means. Like the newsgroup, IRC involves normative con-ventions governing the forms of expression for participants. In the following extract from my own data, we see one participant being inducted into the rules governing the use of capital letters.

(2) IRC:MG:22.5.98

1	Balou Gal:	how is everyone
2 →	Timgodden:	MICHAEL JOLLIFFE
3	EGLV:	I want to go to school and major in advertising
4 →	Timgodden:	HES COOL
5	EGLV:	lol Fan
6 →	EGLV:	tim please lower your caps
7	Panther:	what time is it up there then?
8 →	Timgodden:	MICHAEL JOLLIFFE
. . . ((4 lines omitted)) . . .		
13 →	DragonRder:	Timgodden, UPPERCASE is normally used for
14		adding EMPHASIS! Otherwise it's considered
15		SHOUTING (and is harder to read)!

Timgodden's contributions are submitted in capital letters, an un-acceptable practice on IRC. After being invited to 'lower [his] caps' by a more seasoned participant, EGLV (line 6), Timgodden persists in his contribution at line 8. Finally, in lines 13–15, DragonRder rebukes Timgodden, at the same time providing an account of why this practice is frowned upon.

This extract also illustrates a number of other features of inter-action on IRC. For instance, the widespread use of abbreviations and acronyms, such as EGLV's 'lol' (standing for 'laughs out loud') in line 5; or, more significantly for my purposes, the fact that multiple con-versations tend to be sustained at any one time. In particular, EGLV can be seen in this short extract to be involved in three interactions almost simultaneously: answering an earlier question in line 3, laughing aloud at something Fan has said in line 5, and rebuking Timgodden's raised caps folly in line 6. I return to the issue of multiple conversations in a later section.

Reid (1991) also points out that interaction on IRC is mediated not only by the technology of internet servers and computer termi-nals, but also by a unique hierarchy of participant statuses. There are important differences between the categories of 'user', 'channel operator' (or 'chanop'), and 'system operator' (or 'oper'). Users are the ordinary participants on IRC. Chanops are those who initiate one of the many channels which those who log in are able to join (although it is also possible for trusted regulars to be awarded the status of chanop in order to help in moderating the channel). Chanops have a certain amount of power. For instance, they can limit access to the channel only to certain users, or they can 'kick off' a channel participant – that is, shut down their access. Opers are those who operate the systems which run the IRC program, and they have privi-leges not available to anyone else – for example, to send a message to all users, or to kick someone off the IRC network altogether.

Again, chanops and opers have evolved normative codes of conduct which are observed whenever they exercise their power to eliminate a user from the channel. One of the principal norms is that 'kicking' should not be done without a reason, and the reason should be communicated along with the announcement that a user has been kicked. For example, in extract (3), a user logs on with the nickname 'Jack_Shit' (in this extract, only actual talk lines are numbered: opers' and other system messages are on unnumbered lines).

(3) IRC:ENG:17.6.99:3 ((Slightly simplified))

1 →	JayBee:	jack – change that nick please
2	Sammi:	ha ha jb, you are such a short arse lol
3	JayBee:	i told you sammi!
4	Jack_Shit:	5 + 5 = 11
5	GateCrashed:	40 piddlin quid a week if they accept my claim
6	SCOUSER:	I am stale
7	zazoo18:	hello

8	Jack_Shit:	try = www.11.com
9	zazoo18:	ô¿Ù
10	Jack_Shit:	hi zazoo
11	aninha:	since when, jack-shit?
12	Nikki4:	hi there GC
→		*aninha has been kicked off the channel by GateCrashed (u came,*
→		*u saw, u swore so I kicked ya)*
13	Jack_Shit:	since today
14 →	JayBee:	jack – 60 seconds to change that nick, otherwise
15		i'll kick you out
16	GateCrashed:	allo nikki :)
17	Nikki4:	how r u GC?
18	Jack_Shit:	UUUUHHHHH im so scared
19	Nikki4:	kick him
20	Rianda:	you should be..lol
→		*Jack_Shit has been kicked off the channel by JayBee (sort yer life*
→		*out)*

Once more we find the participants involved in multiple conversations. At the start of the extract, JayBee (a chanop) is interacting with Sammi about a digitized snapshot that JayBee has sent out, while at the same time requesting Jack_Shit to change the inappropriate nickname that he or she has used. Often, IRC operators will have automated systems running on their terminals which will alert them to unaccepted forms of behaviour. In this case, there is a 'no swear words' rule on the channel, and part of Jack_Shit's name breaches that rule. System operators may also run automatic kicking-off scripts on their machines which will eliminate a user if, for instance, they have not contributed to the discussion for more than 30 minutes (thereby freeing up server space); or, in the first example of a kick found in extract (3), if a user sends a line containing a banned word. In this case, of course, the auto-kick eliminates a totally innocent user, since all that aninha had been trying to do (in line 11) is to offer a response to Jack_Shit. Her turn relates back to Jack_Shit's cryptic assertion, in line 4, that '5 + 5 = 11'. However, aninha's response, 'since when, jack-shit?', inadvertently contains the illicit word and she is kicked off by GateCrashed.

Jack_Shit, having remained on the channel and ignored JayBee's instruction to change the name (lines 14–15), subsequently taunts JayBee in line 18, and is finally kicked off with a message to 'sort yer life out'. Interestingly, we find here another indication of the sense of community fostered by some IRC channels. Both Nikki4 (in line 19) and Rianda (in line 20) react to Jack_Shit's taunt, Nikki4 in particular by encouraging JayBee to 'kick him'. Not only does this clearly show that only certain participants have the ability to eliminate other users; it also illustrates that Nikki4 has been monitoring the exchange while engaged in his or her own exchange with GateCrashed (lines 12, 16 and 17) and judges that JayBee is perhaps being too lenient with the interloper who is breaching the rules of participation in this interactive space.

In Reid's (1991) account, these would represent ways in which IRC users, faced with what Reid sees as the 'impossibility' of replicating the social boundaries of conventional communication, respond by developing new forms of ethics, new ways of relating to each other. Aspects of IRC encourage users to play with the conventional limits of expression, breaking the boundaries of social etiquette. At the same time the participants appear to be attempting to form themselves into 'communities' with differently structured behavioural norms, forms of expression, and the rest.

What I want to stress in this discussion is the fact that, in all sorts of ways, social interaction on IRC remains normatively bounded. In some ways those norms may appear different from the conventions underpinning interaction in everyday life. But on closer inspection they may not be so distinct. What remains to be done is to attempt a comparison between what we know of the normative structures of ordinary talk-in-interaction and what we can observe in the context of IRC and its communicative affordances. In the remainder of this chapter, I go into the IRC data in further detail and suggest some relevant comparative points. We will see that it may not be the best strategy to assume from the outset that 'virtual' conversations, whether as a result of the technology's configuration of users, or users' configuration of the technology, are inherently different. In order to understand the distinctive characteristics of virtual conversation it is more fruitful to investigate how users manage their interactions at the interface between the norms of conversation and the communicative affordances of the technology.

Sequential order in multi-party IRC

IRC is often characterized as a form of computer-mediated communication that involves synchronous online interaction, as opposed to the asynchronous interaction of such forms as bulletin boards, newsgroups and email. It is true that IRC is synchronous in the sense that all the participants on a channel are online at the same time. When a user joins a channel, he or she enters a space in which there is an ongoing conversation. The user has no access to anything that was said before he or she joined, and on leaving has no knowledge of anything further that is said as the conversation carries on.

But the interaction is not synchronous in the sense of there being the possibility of overlapping contributions, as in co-present verbal interaction. There is, however, the possibility of something quite different – 'lag', or a temporal gap between a turn's production (transmission to the server) and its reception (distribution to logged-on terminals). For this reason, we can follow Garcia and Jacobs (1999) in referring to IRC as 'quasi-synchronous'. It appears, particularly when we look at page-bound transcripts of IRC logs as in the present chapter, that the interaction is managed on a turn-by-turn basis such that participants have access to the same sequential organization of turns as the analyst does (much as, in chapter 4, I argued was the case in transcripts of telephone conversation). But as Garcia and Jacobs (1999) point out, participant B may be in the course of typing a response to a particular turn of participant A at the same time as A is sending a next turn to the server, which perhaps modifies their previous turn and so renders problematic many aspects of the relationship between B's contribution and A's.

Garcia and Jacobs (1999) videotaped students at work at their terminals in a small, classroom-based discussion group in which IRC was used as a form of computer-assisted education. They could thereby gain access not just to the words appearing on the screen but also to the typing out of contributions. Since participants' turns do not appear in the IRC environment until they have finished typing and pressed 〈Enter〉, Garcia and Jacobs were able to observe some of the ways in which contributors may engage in self-repair even before they have actually 'uttered' (that is, sent) their turn, in the light of other contributions addressed to the same topic which appeared in the course of their typing. Comparing some of the findings of Sacks et al. (1974) as to the means by which turns in oral conversation are sequentially related, they propose that it is often problematic for participants in this environment successfully to relate 'current' and 'prior' or 'current' and 'next' turns, partly because participants tend to 'import the organisational procedures of oral conversation to the [IRC] environment, with some problematic results' (Garcia and Jacobs 1999: 360).

Garcia and Jacobs make only passing reference to the role of the technology itself in this, when they say in their conclusion that the IRC turn-taking system 'results in different possibilities for sequential organisation [from face-to-face talk], in part because of the software's system-generated constraints' (1999: 360). But it seems clear to me that the technology, the specific combination of computer hardware and software (the IRC program and its interface), lies at the very heart of the issue. More specifically, the range of affordances of this combination of hardware and software for those who seek to interact by means of it are key to an account of the (possibly) distinctive features of 'virtual' conversations on IRC.

Participants may indeed encounter difficulties in establishing such things as sequential orderliness or mutual reference in their exchanges. Garcia and Jacobs (1999) seek to 'look behind' the production of turns in the public arena that is accessible to everyone else involved in an IRC session, to suggest that such problems may be generic features of attempts at participation in IRC. From a slightly different angle, it is possible to mirror the argument of chapters 3 and 4, where I proposed that far from having to rely on the thought processes that went on prior to the actual enunciation of an utterance, participants in talk-in-interaction maintain communication (problematic or otherwise) on the basis of utterances as they are actually produced. The same thing can be said about IRC: while participants may indeed 'change their mind' about (i.e. self-repair) the form their next turn will take in the course of its production, what every other participant on the channel has access to in their attempts to make sense of what is going on is precisely, and only, the turns themselves as they appear in the public discursive arena: that is, the scrolling window on their monitor screen. The key thing then becomes to look at how they repair – or more often, as we will see, ignore – potentially problematic events in the course of their mutually available (and publicly accessible) exchange of turns.

The affordances of the technology are centrally involved in this. Like other artefacts discussed in this book, IRC affords a version of conversational interaction, but only within technologically circumscribed constraints. For present purposes, I want to emphasize four specific constraints which serve to distinguish IRC interaction from the normative order of ordinary conversation:

1 Participants can only 'take a turn' in the ongoing conversation by typing something in their talk-line box and pressing ⟨Enter⟩.
2 That 'turn' only reaches all others on the channel once it has been accepted and distributed by the server (temporal lag).
3 There is a difference between a turn's course of production (typing in) and its public 'enunciation' (sending), such that other turns may appear in the interim which disrupt the turn's sequential relationship with its intended prior.

4　While all this is happening, the conversation is going on in a scrolling window on the monitor screen; which means that, on occasions of high traffic through the server, the prior contribution to which a turn is intendedly tied may have scrolled off the screen by the time the second contribution appears.

In the light of these features we can ask, what is the locus of order which lends a turn its sense in the public course of IRC interaction (as opposed to its 'private' course of production)? In ordinary conversation, the locus of orderliness for a current turn is, largely speaking, its relationship to the prior turn – or, at a push, the prior-turn-but-one. This is most evident in two-party conversation. It is two-party conversation that Garcia and Jacobs (1999) use as their baseline for comparison with IRC. But IRC, as we have already seen, is a complex form of multi-party conversation, and when there are more than two people talking, it might be thought that things will get a little more complicated. Looking at multi-party conversation, we find that, as in IRC, multiple single conversations tend to be going on simultaneously (see, for example, Egbert 1997). The way in which these multiple conversations are managed exhibits key differences, but also some basic similarities, in the two contexts.

Consider extract (4), in which a group of people are gathered for an alfresco dinner outside their house. I want to focus on the interaction between Ross and Susi (arrowed), which takes place amidst another interaction between Kathy, Dwayne and Matt.

(4) Goodwin: PD: 18

```
 1 →   Susi:          Where's the sa[:lad
 2     Dwayne:                       [Some of u[s weren't so lucky.
 3     Kathy:                                  [DIALLING for DOLLARS.
 4 →   Susi:          Wudje do with the salad.
 5               (0.4)
 6     Kathy:         It['s over (            )
 7 →   Ross:            [I dint do anything [with   [the salad.
 8     Dwayne:                              [m-hmh[m-hm
 9 →   Susi:                                       [Kathy pass the]=
10     Matt:                                        [How long's it ]=
11     Susi:          =[s a l a d.]
12     Matt:          =[g'nna tal:ke,
13     Martha:                       [Start [with the gra:vy w]illy[uh,
14 →   Ross:                                [Quit   cra::bbin'.]  |
15     Kathy:                                                      [WHA:T?
```

```
16                    (1.6)
17    Matt:           How long did he sa:y?
18                    (0.4)
19    Ross:           AN HOU:R.
20    Frank:          NO[WER:
21    Dwayne:             [WE- WI'LL CALL Y'IN CO:ME PICK Y'UP.
```

In line 1, Susi's question, 'Where's the sala:d', can be heard as directed to the company in general. Lines 2 and 3 show Dwayne and Kathy carrying on an exchange with Matt, who is not on the porch with the others but has been calling out to ask 'when dinner might be ready'. In line 4, Susi redirects her question specifically towards Ross, who responds in line 7 ('I dint do anything with the salad'). But before he does so, Kathy has also responded by starting to point out the location of the salad. In purely serial terms, then, Ross's turn in line 7 follows Kathy's in line 6 (or, at least, its onset). In sequential terms, however, it relates to the prior turn but one (Susi's in line 4).

A similar point can be made about Kathy's turn in line 15, 'WHA:T?'. Serially, this turn follows Ross saying 'Quit cra::bbin''. But sequentially it does not relate to that turn at all; nor, in this case, to the prior turn but one, Martha's 'Start with the gra:vy willyuh' (line 13) (even though the same utterance could conceivably act as a response to either of those turns). Rather, it relates to the turn before that, in which Matt again asks about how long 'dinner' might take. Evidence for this is provided in line 17, when Matt responds by re-iterating his question.

One of the reasons why it is possible to link to the prior-turn-but-*two* in this way in multi-party conversation comes from the fact that much of the talk is overlapping. We can perhaps see this with Ross's turn 'Quit cra::bbin'' (line 14). While it may seem that this is a response to the previous completed turn, Matt's complaint, 'How long's it g'nna take', there is evidence (even in the absence of the corresponding video record) that it is directed towards Susi. Two or three times in the preceding talk (data not shown here) Susi has instructed Ross to 'quit crabbin''. It seems likely that he is echoing that as a follow-up to his response to her implicit complaint that he has 'done something' with the salad. A number of overlapping voices have spoken between his 'I dint do anything with the salad' and its follow-up 'Quit cra::bbin'', but the actual time elapsed is little more than a second. Indeed, it is worth observing that the turn begins almost immediately following the transition-relevance place in Susi's own prior turn, 'Kathy pass the salad.'

I am proposing, then, that the sequence goes like this:

Susi (to Ross):   <u>W</u>udje do with the s<u>a</u>lad.
Ross (to Susi):   I dint do <u>any</u>thing with the s<u>a</u>lad.
Susi (to Kathy):   Kathy p<u>ass</u> the s a l a d.
Ross (to Susi):   Qu<u>i</u>t <u>cra</u>::bbin'.

and that while there are other utterances which occur serially in between these four, the exchange can be straightforwardly managed because of three factors: (a) the possibility of overlapping talk; (b) the resulting fact that the turns in the sequence can retain the close temporal relationship they would have if Ross and Susi alone were co-present; and (c) the fact that, in this situation, the participants have access to the additional resource of gaze to disambiguate an utterance's intended addressee.

The affordances of IRC lead to a contrasting situation on each of these dimensions. In IRC, turns can only make their appearance in the interactive space in the serial order in which they are distributed by the server. And from the users' perspective, they may not retain the same temporal order in which they are sent to the server. Hence, different kinds of work are needed in order to establish or cement their *sequential* order. Extract (5), from an IRC session, illustrates something of this, along with some of the interactional issues that can potentially arise as a result of the sequential ambiguity that IRC affords. As in extract 3, for ease of reference only actual talk lines have been numbered.

(5) IRC: ENG: 17.6.99: 1–2

```
1  |JayBee|:     ere sam, wanna see a pic of me with some hair?
   prince-uk has left the channel
2  SCOUSER:   (:
   Lenny_ has joined the channel
   osama_ has left the channel
3  ^Sammi^:   sure jb :)
4  SCOUSER:   anyone got any pics for me
5  {aninha}:   someone wants to speak?
6  SCOUSER:   ?
7  Emaly:     Is here somebody else from germany?
8  zazoo18:   yes
9  zazoo18:   scouser
10 |JayBee|:   ((sends URL))
   Signoff: C-Quence (Quit: Quantum physics my bu*t! ;))
   julie^^ has joined the channel
   sudi has joined the channel
```

11 |JayBee|:   you got a pic then zazoo?
   Lenny_ has left the channel
   Nikki4 has joined the channel
12 |JayBee|:   allo Nikki
13 Nikki4:   has anyone seen MTV?
   Jack_Shit has joined the channel
14 {aninha}:   me!me!me!
15 |JayBee|:   i could've laid money on you asking that
   Signoff: squall_911_stevie (Quit: Leaving)
16 Jack_Shit: Hello
   wieried has joined the channel
17 zazoo18:   nope sorrry
18 stakis: any english living in england??????????????
   GateCrashed has joined the channel
   Mode change "+o GateCrashed" by ChanServ
19 zazoo18:   no pic
20 stakis: *:)))
   straker has joined the channel
21 |JayBee|:   hes gone to lunch
22 zazoo18:   still working on it

One of the most obvious ways of handling the potential ambiguity of
address associated with this form of interaction (which is not just
rigidly serial, but also lacking resources such as eye-gaze or gesture
which would help in directing a turn towards its intended recipient)
is by using next-speaker selection techniques such as naming. Thus
in line 1 JayBee directs a question that acts as an invitation towards
Sammi (on IRC, 'exchanging' digitalized pictures of various kinds is
a routine activity). In line 3 (i.e., the next-but-one talk line), Sammi
accepts the invitation and reciprocally disambiguates the turn by
naming JayBee as its recipient.

In the meantime, another participant, SCOUSER, has contributed
a turn (line 2) which takes the form of an emoticon: the equivalent
to a non-verbal contribution in face-to-face conversation. The emoticon in line 2 expresses dismay (most emoticons are designed to be
approximations of facial expressions to be read sideways with the
head tilted to the left – hence this looks like two eyes with raised eye-
brows). While this contribution serially follows JayBee's invitation for
Sammi, it is not immediately clear where its sequential reference lies:
it could, for instance, be directed at another user in response to something said earlier.

However, apart from there being no obvious turn in the preceding
interaction (not shown here) to which it might relate, there are good
reasons for taking this to be an interjacent response to JayBee's invitation. Principally, SCOUSER's next turn in line 4, 'Anyone got any

pictures for me?', indicates that he or she may feel slightly put out by not being included in JayBee's picture invitation. Note that the call for a picture is not directed at JayBee but to the company in general, thereby displaying some form of orientation to the fact that JayBee has initiated a private deal with Sammi. It is possible on IRC to initiate private conversations by 'paging' a particular participant and inviting them into a separate 'room' where the exchange is not visible to other users on the channel. This, in fact, is another of the key affordances of IRC: the ability to hold one conversation 'in camera' while still maintaining a presence – both as listener and as speaker – in the main group interaction. One of the main activities of many IRCers is to search for people to have private conversations with in this way.

Yet while nominalization is one good strategy for dealing with ambiguity in address and sequential ordering, IRCers do not do this all that often. As we can see in this extract, many turns are produced without any explicit 'targeting' devices. This makes it much more problematic (not just for observer–analysts, but for participants themselves) to determine the locus of order – and often also the meaning – of a given turn. One example in extract (5) is provided by zazoo18's turn in line 8. In serial terms, zazoo18's 'yes' follows three questions from different participants: SCOUSER's 'anyone got any pics for me', aninha's 'someone wants to speak?' (line 5) and Emaly's 'Is here somebody else from germany?' (line 7). To which is it a response? On one level, zazoo18 offers an answer in her next turn (line 9), in which she names SCOUSER. This is readable/hearable as a disambiguation; rather than, for example, as a vocative seeking to initiate a new exchange with SCOUSER. This is not simply my reading/hearing of the turn: note that JayBee orients to zazoo18 as having responded affirmatively to SCOUSER's request, in line 11 ('you got a pic then zazoo?').

However, things turn out not to be as clear cut as they might be, since it appears that zazoo18 does not, in fact, have any pictures: note her response to JayBee, in lines 17 ('nope sorry') and 19 ('no pic'). This in itself is highly ambivalent. It may be that zazoo18 orients to JayBee's question as asking whether she has succeeded in downloading the picture that JayBee previously made available, and responds by indicating that she has not yet done so. Note, however, that JayBee refers to 'a pic' rather than 'my pic' or 'the pic'. Whereas the latter two options would tie the turn back to a previously intro-duced referent, 'a pic' seems to introduce a new referent, that is, not the earlier mentioned pictures. It may, then, just be that zazoo18 was attempting to engage in interaction with SCOUSER, and that her 'nope sorrry' is an apology for having given the impression that she was responding to SCOUSER's request rather than simply trying to get involved in a conversation. The upshot is that it remains ambiguous what zazoo18's turns in lines 8 and 9 were 'actually' doing. What is intriguing is that it is not only unclear to us as observers what is going on here, but the 'meaning' of zazoo18's contributions is not 'pinned down' by the participants in the interaction either.

It might be the relative anonymity of IRC that affords the possibility for ambiguities to remain unproblematically open. Some writers have argued that due to this anonymity, IRC enables participants to ignore, or avoid observing, normative conventions characteristic of ordinary conversation. The assumption here seems to be that participants in IRC *want* to evade communicative norms and conventions, and use the affordance for anonymity as a means of doing that. This, of course, may be the case; and writers such as Turkle (1995) and Reid (1991) have argued that many regular IRC and MUD users do enjoy exploiting the relative freedom from constraint that can be involved when interaction is mediated by distributed computer terminals. I would favour a more structural, less individualistic account. Such an alternative is possible if we begin from the standpoint that this is one of the affordances of the technological medium itself, around which participants are evolving ways of interacting.

Another element of this affordance for anonymity and open ambiguity can be seen in extract (6). Here, zazoo18 again appears, trying to initiate interaction with one particular participant. This extract is even less straightforward to offer a grounded description of than the previous exchange; however, I want to suggest that it illustrates the affordance for what could be called 'serendipitous' ambiguity in IRC.

(6) IRC: ENG: 17.6.99: 8–9

> |Sexy-Guy| *has joined the channel*
> o300501202 *has joined the channel*
> miss_Dee *has left the channel*
> yashi *has joined the channel*
> Mode change "+b *.*" by ^Viking^
> yashi *has been kicked off the channel by* ^Viking^ *(banned: JamesBates)*
> |Sexy-Guy| *is now known as Cool-dude*
> 1   zazoo18:   hello
> Signoff: webcty (Quit)
> Signoff: MaRyy (Quit)

> *Signoff: clever24man (Quit: Leaving)*
> *Cool-dude is now known as Cool-DudE*

2   zazoo18:   hi cool dude
3   zazoo18:   sup
4   zazoo18:   wan chat
5   zazoo18:   witha n 18 f

> *MEERSON has left the channel*

6   wieried: ok

> *|PinkFloyd| has left the channel*

7   zazoo18:   hi
8   zazoo18:   msg ok
9   zazoo18:   plz

> *Cool-DudE is now known as Guest15660*
> *Lady_Lady has joined the channel*
> *simbat has joined the channel*
> *SURGEON has joined the channel*

10   FaVuS: yeech colour . . .

> *Signoff: jamesdean1 (Ping timeout)*
> *Signoff: simbat (Quit: Leaving)*
> *Goldi has joined the channel*
> *I-AM-PRINCE has joined the channel*

11   wieried: what u do

> *Guest15660 is now known as {Sexy_Guy}*
> *ixxorra has left the channel*
> *Signoff: Hamid' (Ping timeout)*
> *simbat has joined the channel*
> *gurdalgo has joined the channel*
> *p3ace has been kicked off the channel by ^Viking^ (idle 30 min)*
> *Guest51864 has joined the channel*
> *p3ace has joined the channel*
> *^FisherKing^ has been kicked off the channel by ^Viking^*
> *(idle 30 min)*
> *Mode change "+b *.*" by ^Viking^*
> *p3ace has been kicked off the channel by ^Viking^ (You*
> *autorejoined after getting kicked. Not that smart indeed.)*
> *Rianda has left the channel*
> *Guest10949 is now known as sarhos*
> *JamesUK has joined the channel*

12   FaVuS: in and out..   and in and out and lurk..
13   muuhuuhu

What appears to happen in this extract is that zazoo18 attempts to
initiate a conversation with Cool-dude (lines 2–5). Cool-dude at no
stage responds to this – what he or she does is spend their time altering their nickname (from Sexy-Guy to Cool-dude to Guest15660 and
back to Sexy-Guy). However, in line 6, another participant, wieried,

appears to do so. Zazoo18 next invites her target, which at this stage could be either Cool-dude or wieried, to 'msg' her (line 8) – that is, to begin a private conversation. At this point, without the possibility of using the Garcia and Jacobs (1999) video-recording technique since participants are logging in from disparate geographical locations, we cannot say whether zazoo18 in fact embarks on a private conversation. Like the other participants on the channel, we do not have access to that aspect of her activities from our standpoint; although it is worth noting that shortly after this extract ends, zazoo18 can again be found attempting to initiate conversation with yet another participant.

Nevertheless, leaving out of account FaVuS's turn in line 10 which relates to a contribution that appeared slightly earlier (in which the contributor had written his or her message in garish colours – another potentially interesting affordance of IRC), I want to draw attention to wieried's turn, 'what u do', in line 11. Once again, there is substantial ambiguity in that it is not clear whether or not this turn is directed towards zazoo18; that is, as a next sequential move following wieried's previous apparent agreement to engage in chat with zazoo18. The ambiguity is compounded because it is not zazoo18 who responds but another participant, FaVuS, whose turn in line 12, 'in and out.. in and out and lurk', looks strange as a free-standing contribution, but can be made sense of as a response to the request, 'what u do?'. It might, that is, be unpacked as 'I move in and out of channels, and occasionally lurk' ('lurking' is a practice whereby a user logs on to a channel but does not contribute, instead merely observing what others say. It is in order to combat this that non-contributing participants in this particular channel are automatically kicked off after being 'idle for 30 minutes'). Following this, FaVuS's 'muuhuuhu' can be read as a textual rendering of a laugh.

It seems, then, that rather than being inherently problematic, the ambiguities that emerge from the technologically-based separation between serial and sequential order in IRC turn-taking can in fact be serendipitous. In this case, whereas zazoo18 began by trying to get a conversation going with Cool-dude, she almost found herself in conversation with wieried, who, in turn, finally ended up in an exchange with FaVuS. Interaction can thus emerge serendipitously from IRC's affordance for open ambiguity both in sequential order and in interpersonal address.

There is currently an inordinate amount of sociological interest (one might even say hype) focused upon the internet and its possible impacts in terms of social change. There is believed to be an inherent novelty and an intrinsic difference in the ways that the internet enables communication and the formation of social groupings, or even communities. Optimists believe that the internet is leading to wholly new forms of democracy, of politics, and of subjectivity in which people are freed from the one-sided versions of reality handed out by powerful voices through the traditional mass media of newspapers and broadcasting (for example, Poster 1995). Pessimists argue that the internet, and personal computing in general, are merely extensions of the deleterious effects that mass media such as television have had on the quality of everyday social life, especially for children (for example, Postman 1987).

Whatever the perspective, it appears that the internet and computer-mediated communication represent the prime example of what, in chapter 1, I described as the move into an era of technologized interaction. For this reason, it is fitting to end a book about the relationships between conversation and technology with a consideration, however exploratory and provisional, of the forms of interaction that can actually be observed in this arena for (text-based) 'talk' in interaction. Throughout the book, I have argued that if we look in close empirical detail at what people actually do when they attempt to interact through, around or with technologies for communication, we may find that things are somewhat different from the way that theorists might assume they are. In looking at 'virtual conversations' I have shown that there are both similarities and differences between the organization of participation in this setting and in ordinary face-to-face multi-party conversation. It is not enough to announce that IRC is representative of a technologically-driven 'revolution' in the very nature of communication. The nature of communication on IRC reveals its impact, and its interest, at a much more mundane level. As I have tried to show, the affordances of IRC as a technological medium for interaction shape the nature of sociality – as manifested in the sequential organizations of conversation – that users are involved in. I illustrated how the different dynamics at work in managing the separation between the serial and the sequential aspects of turns can mean that a contribution's ambiguity, far from being problematic, can turn out to be serendipitous for the course of interaction. But such phenomena can only be seen once we tune the focus of the analytic lens down to the level of individual actions and their interrelationship in ongoing real-time sequences of 'technologized' interaction.

10

Conclusion: A Reversion to the Real?

The overall theme of this book has been, on one level, relatively simple. It has been to argue for what might be called a 'reversion to the real' in the sociology of technology and culture: an acceptance that our interpretations and uses of technological artefacts, while important, contingent and variable, are constrained in analysable ways by the ranges of affordances that particular artefacts, by virtue of their materiality, possess. The social constructivist consensus outlined in chapter 2 has usefully brought to the fore the recognition that social processes are involved in all aspects of technology, and not simply in its effects upon society. But we can become too fixated on the social shaping of technology at the expense of an equally pressing, though differently framed, concern with the technological shaping of sociality.

In the course of making that argument, many more complex themes have been brought into play. In thinking through the nature of the relationship between conversation and technology, I have had to develop working definitions of what both 'conversation' and 'technology' themselves are. I stress the term *working* definitions, since it has not been my aim to forward supposedly definitive statements on either of these widely contested concepts. The book should not be read primarily as an intervention into theoretical or philosophical debates, but as a theoretically-grounded empirical investigation of the ways in which our ordinary conversational practices may be shaped by, and/or shape the properties of 'technologies for communication'.

I proposed an empirically usable working definition of such technologies – that they could be analysed in terms of their communicative affordances – and of ordinary conversation itself – that it could be analysed as a structured set of practices underpinned by describable normative conventions. The latter drew from the field of conversation analysis (CA), and in chapters 3 and 4 I defended CA's resolutely praxiological approach against those who would import computational metaphors into the very study of conversation itself. A major part of the point here was to establish an empirically workable distinction between the 'conversational' and the 'technological'. Indeed, throughout the book these two tropes have been held in mutual tension. It has been my aim to demonstrate that in order to think about the relationship between technologies and social practices it is neither useful to hold one or the other as an independent variable, as determinists tend to do; nor it is of any use to offer in-principle challenges to the stability of both as real phenomena, as relativists and some constructivists are wont to do. While, theoretically speaking, the affordances of technologies and the normative structures of talk-in-interaction are flexible, variable and open (over time) to change, in the empirical moment of engagement between a human and a technological artefact, or of a human with another human via a technological artefact, both may be treated as equally stable for all practical purposes. At this point of engagement, norms may come into conflict with affordances, or vice versa. It is in these worldly moments that we can observe at a new level the 'impacts' of technological forms on the nature of social life; and it is towards these moments that I have tried to direct attention in this book.

In chapter 2 I took issue with those perspectives in the sociology of technology which argue for a radical constructivism in attempts to analyse the social dimensions of technological artefacts. While I agreed with these approaches in their opposition to the unidirectional determinist emphasis on the impact of technology on society, I challenged the view that this necessarily means that it is wrong, pointless or obfuscating to talk in any sense about such impacts. The aim was not to deny the relevance of constructivism in all contexts and for all purposes (for instance, as a technique for investigating the history of a technological form), but to propose a shift in analytical emphasis in order to clear the ground for the specific empirical project that followed. I used Grint and Woolgar's (1997) strong version of constructivism – 'anti-essentialism' – as a foil against which to develop an alternative perspective on the relationship between technologies and social practices.

In response to the debate framed so well by Grint and Woolgar, I developed a vision of technologies for communication which sees them neither in terms of their 'interpretive textual' properties nor of their 'essential technical' properties, but in terms of their affordances. In my interpretation, affordances are functional aspects which frame, while not determining, the possibilities for agentic action in relation to an object. In this way, technologies for communication can be understood as artefacts which may be both shaped by, and shape the practices humans use in conversation with, around and through them. This 'third way' between the (constructivist) emphasis on the shaping power of human agency and the (determinist) emphasis on the constraining power of technical capacities has enabled me to argue that the affordances of technological media for interaction shape the nature of sociality – as manifested in the sequential organizations of conversation – that users are involved in.

In this concluding chapter I want to tie up some of the loose ends that may have been left dangling in the course of the main discussion. At the beginning of the book, I proposed that a question could be put as to what kind of relationship there could be between conversation and technology, and wondered whether it might be meaningful to say that developed capitalist societies are now moving into an era of 'technologized interaction'. It will be clear by this stage that I seek to distance my position from the more hyped-up journalistic versions of 'technological revolution', 'depersonalized communication' and 'information overload' that in themselves simply echo, under a new guise, technophobic and technophiliac concerns that have been with us since at least the 1950s. I suggested in the introduction that my perspective would cut a path between such determinist or semi-determinist views and the more sceptical or, better, agnostic stance taken by many constructivist critics of 'technological determinism'.

In order to clarify the direction that path takes, I conclude by considering some anticipated objections to different aspects of my argument. First, relativist or constructivist objections that might focus on my invocation of the reality or materiality of artefacts as a significant factor in humans' attempts to communicate through, around or with them. Here I draw on an exemplary paper in the relativist tradition by Edwards, Ashmore and Potter (1995). Second, possible objections to my stress on the normative structures of talk-in-interaction as a type of reality involved in human communication. The ethnomethodologists Lynch and Bogen (1994) have objected to the version of CA utilized in these pages, arguing that the ethnomethodological roots of CA have been abandoned by analysts who aim to give the discipline the appearance of an 'objective science'. My aim is not just to show that these kinds of objection are wrong, but to use them in order to clarify the stance that I am defending.

Death and furniture

Because the argument developed in this book involves notions of 'materiality' and therefore has a 'realist' slant, there will be those who will maintain that it is of necessity an example of what Edwards, Ashmore and Potter (1995) call the 'death and furniture' critique of relativism and constructivism. Edwards et al. describe (in a rather entertaining manner) how those who oppose the relativist or constructivist emphasis on reality as a 'construction', 'interpretation' or 'persuasive account' like to refer to furniture ('Surely you don't deny that this table is real') or death ('Surely you don't deny that people actually die') as a 'bottom line' beyond which interpretive accounts cannot go. As avowed relativists themselves, Edwards et al. do not provide any decisive argument against this appeal to the bottom line; rather, they offer a series of accounts of the rhetorical uses of this kind of argument and propose that any appeal to the intransigent reality of worldly objects is itself, of necessity, a construction of those objects as 'real'.

In responding to this anticipated criticism, some of the complexities of my case can be drawn out. To begin with, it is important to stress that I have not sought to engage in a debate about the relative merits of realist and relativist epistemologies. In my view, this is ultimately a philosophical issue. Although, in chapter 3, I imported some philosophical arguments into my discussion of the differences between computational and interactional models of communication, the ultimate aim was not to attempt a resolution of those philosophical issues, but to lay the groundwork for one of the central pillars of my case: namely that the normative structures of talk-in-interaction, described within the interactionist perspective of CA, represent the main conditions of possibility within which attempts to communicate among humans are managed.

As outlined in the final section of chapter 4, I consider the normative structures of talk-in-interaction to be a reality for participants in talk-in-interaction. Edwards et al. (1995) might object that it is not possible for me, as an analyst, to point to an 'adjacency pair', for instance, and say 'Surely you don't deny the reality of that?', since the only thing that could actually be 'pointed to' would be a set of words on a page of transcript. But does that mean that we must deny that, for the participants themselves, an 'adjacency pair first part' (so-called by analysts: see discussion below) is a real event in the world? It has, after all, been uttered; it has been heard; it makes relevant (because of the normative structure of this aspect of talk-in-interaction) a second part; and the non-production of such a second part is an accountable phenomenon for which this particular person may well be taken to task ('Did you hear me? I asked you a question').

The 'reality' of such normative structures is to be seen in terms of their status as conditions of possibility for mutually intelligible action.

It is possible for humans to ignore them, or to avoid observing them. But such behaviour, if taken too far, is open to the threat of moral sanction. As Sacks showed in a number of analyses (1975, 1984), humans are free to act freely, but if they value that freedom and wish to protect it, they will only exercise it within the normative constraints of recognizably 'ordinary' behaviour. As Garfinkel (1967) showed, in an experiment where he asked students to respond to everyday 'How are you?' inquiries as literal questions rather than ritual actions (recall the discussion in chapter 5), it is not necessary to go very far in this in order to have gone *too* far.

(1) [Garfinkel 1967: 44]

```
1 S:   How are you?
2 E:   How am I in regard to what? My health, my finances, my
3      school work, my peace of mind, my . . .
4 S:   ((Red in the face and suddenly out of control)) Look!
5      I was just trying to be polite. Frankly, I don't give
6      a damn how you are.
```

The fact that the sanctions involved here are described as *moral* sanctions may mean that I am falling into the relativist's trap. After all, social norms, morals and the rest appear to be historically contingent, culturally variable and intrinsically open to challenge and change. In short, they are constructed and relative. How can I claim these as evidence of a non-constructed reality?

The answer lies in different notions of what sense of reality is relevant, and what kind of analytic purchase we seek to get on that reality. Edwards et al. (1995) seem content to treat the whole issue as an elaborate academic game. At one point they focus on an earlier published version of Grint and Woolgar's (1997) debate with Kling (1992), which I described in chapter 2. Recall that the debate centres around Kling's claim that 'it is much harder to kill a platoon of soldiers with a dozen roses than with well-placed, high speed bullets' (1992: 362); and Grint and Woolgar's concerted effort to show that 'every successive attempt to reach a final, uninterpretable "effect" (hole in the head, falling body, wound, pain, death) from a determinate "cause" (pointed gun, loaded bullet, pulled trigger) can, with enough stubbornness, counter-intuition and effort, be construed as (yet another) social construction' (Edwards et al. 1995: 37).

Asking themselves what the point of all this is, Edwards et al. come to the conclusion that:

> The point is academic. In everyday parlance, 'academic' implies point-
> less, empty, inconsequential. But *we are* academics, for whom it is
> proper, essential even, to care about the epistemic and ontological
> status of claims to knowledge. And it is far from inconsequential. If
> even ostensibly bottom-line instances of brute reality are demonstra-
> bly social accomplishments, then academics are dealing with some
> powerful machinery: the possibility of critique, denial, deconstruction,
> argument, for any kind of truth, fact, assumption, regime or
> philosophy – for anything at all. Relativism is the quintessentially aca-
> demic position, where all truths are to-be-established. (Edwards et al.
> 1995: 37, emphasis in original)

The reference to 'powerful machinery' here is itself, of course, a
highly effective rhetorical move. In everyday parlance, the words
'powerful' and 'machinery' each denote things which are large,
important, to-be-taken-notice-of and therefore significant. But the
question is, for whom are the to-be-established truths to be established, other than academics? This is ultimately another variant of
the tendency in the sociology of technology which I argued against
throughout chapter 2: a perspective for which the only phenomena
of interest are the interpretations and representations of artefacts
produced (largely) by academics. My response to Edwards et al.'s
philosophical relativism is the same as my response to the radical constructivist position in technology studies. I have sought to place the
focus on what ordinary people themselves do with, and in the presence of, technologies, rather than on how the 'truth' of the technology is established. For all the in-principle possibility that humans may
doubt the essential reality of a telephone, it appears that in everyday life such scepticism is rarely, if ever, seriously exercised. Rather,
people rely on the very materiality of the telephone, its stability as
an object in the world, and its predictability as a functioning medium
of communication, in order to carry out the tasks for which they seek
to use it.

   In order to examine in detail human action and interaction in the
presence of technologies for communication, it is necessary to take
the analytic step of observing the world, as far as is methodologically
enabled, as the participants themselves orient to it. This is precisely
what relativists are wary of doing, preferring instead to debate the
status of epistemological claims *about* the world. But it is exactly what
conversation analysts attempt to achieve. From within the perspective of CA, we see that the world of interaction is bounded by
oriented-to normative rules and structures which themselves constitute a transcendent reality for participants in terms of which individual actions are produced and understood. This reality may not be

of the same order as the obdurate physical reality of nature, as adduced for instance in Collins's (1990) assertion that 'rocks provide causal constraints on our physical movements . . . we do not have to *decide* not to walk through [a rock]. . . . A rock instructs everyone equally . . . without needing to be recognised' (Collins 1990: 50, cited in Edwards et al. 1995: 28, emphasis in original). In a sense, therefore, Edwards et al. (1995) are right to assert that appeals to nature or solid objects ('death and furniture') can be inappropriate when the subject matter is the world of human sociality. Indeed, as they end up remarking, most of their targets in the 'death and furniture' category are not so much realist as *objectivist* arguments (1995: 37).

In order to avoid objectivism I have brought into play a conception of the affordances of artefacts. Following Gibson (1979), I proposed that affordances are functional and relational aspects of an object's material presence in the world. Affordances are *functional* in the sense that they are enabling, as well as constraining, factors in a given organism's attempt to engage in some activity: for instance, walking, or hiding, or photocopying a document, and so on. Certain objects, environments, or artefacts have affordances which enable the particular activity while others do not. But at the same time the affordances can shape the conditions of possibility associated with an action: it may be possible to do it one way, but not another. The *relational* aspect, on the other hand, draws our attention to the way that the affordances of an object may be different for one species than for another. Water surfaces do not have the affordance of walk-on-ability for a lion or a crocodile, but they do for an insect water-boatman.

Yet while it may be relatively unproblematic to see the affordances of a technology as a reality (both enabling and constraining) in terms of which actions are shaped, what does it mean to say that the normative order of talk-in-interaction itself constitutes a reality (even if not the same kind of reality as the rock which we trip over)? Earlier I referred to adjacency pairs – or, more strictly, the normative conventions governing appropriate interaction within the adjacency pair format – as a reality for participants in talk-in-interaction. The argument here is that these normative conventions represent structural constraints on action which participants cannot move outside except with the threat of sanction; except with the danger of being asked and even constrained to do something which they may not wish to, for instance answer the question, or account for why they have not answered it. But surely 'adjacency pair' is itself an analyst's construct, a category imposed from outside on the intrinsic organization of the participants' collaborative interaction?

Normative structures and grounded analytic accounts

This issue has been construed as a serious problem for the kind of analysis CA wishes to engage in (for example Lynch 1993: 203–64; Lynch and Bogen 1994). Yet rather than seeing it as a problem that conversation analysts engage in developing generalizable constructs as descriptions of observable human behaviour, I see that as an essential element of any attempt to produce an appropriately grounded analytic account of the practices of everyday life.

As Lynch and Bogen (1994) observe, CA consciously draws on the ethnomethodological principle that the practices which members of society show themselves to be oriented to in everyday life, and the methods they use in ensuring the understandability or accountability of those practices for one another, are organized phenomena which should not be treated ironically or sceptically by social scientists but taken seriously as sociological phenomena in their own right (see Garfinkel 1967; Heritage 1984a). Yet they argue that the overall analytical logic of CA leads its practitioners to violate that very principle, by 'reducing' members' embodied real-time practices to the status of mere exemplars of 'patterns' of the generic activity of talk-in-interaction. CA, in other words, becomes a formalist mode of thinking in which the analyst, contrary to his or her own epistemological commitments, comes to play the major role in constructing the kind of reality to which the participants are said to be orienting.

This critique again invokes the demon of sociological realism, in opposition to which ethnomethodology itself grew up. In sociology, the dominant forms of realism, which derive ultimately from either Durkheim or Marx, posit underlying causal structures which invisibly drive the surface phenomena of social life (the canonical twentieth-century example is found in the work of Parsons (1937, 1951)). In this perspective, the aim of sociology is to uncover these 'unobservable' forces, which the sociologist is apparently able to retrieve by virtue of his or her position as an external observer and generalizer.

As I argued in chapter 4, CA, like ethnomethodology, does not accept this picture of social life or the role of the sociologist. But for CA, unlike more recent versions of ethnomethodology, this does not mean that any reference to underlying regularities or structurally organized practices is thereby ruled out of court. In early ethnomethodological writings there was also the acceptance of something along such lines. For instance, Garfinkel (1967) famously proposed the 'documentary method of interpretation' as a generic procedure for achieving the 'repair of indexicality', by which he meant pinning down the context-dependent features of an utterance or action so that its sense is coherent in *this* context, in the moment-ary present, the here-and-now. Since, for Garfinkel, all actions are necessarily indexical (dependent for their meaning on the context in which they occur), it would seem that such a method is important (for members) in avoiding the dangerous abyss of total arbitrariness.

In more recent years, ethnomethodologists have favoured an emphasis on what they call the 'lived orderliness' of social practices (for example Garfinkel 1986). These later works draw on a distinc-tion between 'classic studies' in ethnomethodology (the studies carried out by Garfinkel and others in the 1950s and 1960s and pub-lished in Garfinkel 1967), and a perspective focusing on 'radical phe-nomena'. Earlier studies dealt with generic organizational practices (such as the documentary method of interpretation) which can be found across different concrete situations; while the later work is pre-occupied with *occasioned* organizations: the local, endogenous prac-tices that provide any singular concrete event with what Garfinkel (1991) calls its 'haecceity' – its 'just this-ness'.

Lynch (1993), following this second strand, argues that we cannot properly describe the production of social action in any specific situation if we seek to generalize the array of resources, because this necessarily means that we import a 'technical' vocabulary in the course of making sense of singular occurrences in the 'vernacular' world. For instance, in the specific context in which one participant utters 'Why don't you come and see me sometimes' it is of course a matter for the participants whether that constitutes a question, an invitation, a complaint, or whatever. For Lynch, crucially, these cate-gories of action ('question', 'invitation', 'complaint') are vernacular categories and we as analysts rely on our own vernacular language skills, as well as the vernacular skills of our readers, in managing to establish that 'Why don't you come and see me sometimes' is, on a given occasion, an invitation rather than a question. However, once we import the technical notion of 'adjacency pair first part' to describe this utterance, we are moving beyond the demonstrable rele-vancies at work for the participants in that particular situation, and are in danger of slipping back into an ironicizing sociological stand-point. Lynch (1993: 247–54) argues that the use of the term 'adja-cency pair first part' represents an unnecessary – indeed illegitimate – transmutation of perfectly adequate vernacular terms (question, invitation, and so on) into a technical category which serves mainly to buttress conversation analysts' sense that what they are engaging in is 'scientific' analysis.

Beginning from the position of later 'radical' ethnomethodology, then, Lynch argues that CA has abandoned its ethnomethodological roots and become a 'professional analytic community' in which the verifiability of analytic observations and findings is based not in the 'lived orderliness' of the participants' own world but only in the professional community of CA practitioners itself: the material technology of tape-recording and playback devices, the 'literary technology' of the transcription system, and the technical vocabulary of concepts and turn-taking formats (Lynch 1993: 241–7). This complaint is based on a reading of some remarks by Sacks, CA's founder, about the way he saw the work that he was engaged in (see Sacks 1972, 1984).

Sacks, according to Lynch (see also Lynch and Bogen 1994) had a conception of CA as a 'primitive natural science': a pursuit the relevance of whose observations 'anyone' could see, without the necessity of specialist training in techniques or descriptive vocabulary. For example: 'one of the ways that we may get to see that we have something in an analysis is that it's of that order of primitiveness that anybody can go out and look, and see that the thing seems to be as we said' (Sacks 1992, vol. 1: 487). Such a statement seems, on the face of it, to be defending an enterprise of 'pure' observation, unmediated by any kind of analyst's construct. Sacks compares this possibility to a suggested situation 'in biology in the 19th century', where

> there were all these amateurs around, and these were people who could look at results and find another; look at an object and see that it was as people said it was. They could see it with their eyes, they didn't need a lot of equipment. And they knew what an account would look like. So they could learn as the field was learning. And it must have been like that earlier in other fields, like at some point in astronomy, for the Egyptians, etc. As compared to now, where that's not so. (Sacks 1992, vol. 1: 487)

Note that in the second part of this quote, Sacks implies that there is a historical development to fields of scientific inquiry, such that 'as the field is learning' the possibility of such 'amateur' observations becomes less, presumably because the field grows in conceptual sophistication and the various observational technologies needed to discover new phenomena grow more complex. At the time this lecture was given (in 1966), Sacks saw the nascent discipline of CA as being in the 'amateur' stage; but there is no indication, either in the above citation or in the surrounding comments which are much too extensive to quote here, that Sacks felt that CA should remain in this mode, nor that he viewed it as a problem that the field should move into a stage where its knowledge becomes more systematized. Sacks was, after all, the main author of the overtly systematizing paper 'A simplest systematics for the organisation of turn-taking for conversation' (Sacks et al. 1974), discussed in chapter 4. Indeed, there is a clear indication of Sacks's more 'professional' analytic inclinations slightly earlier in the very same 1966 lecture:

> What I want to do is to . . . use what 'we' know, what any Member knows, to pose us some problems. What activity is being done, for example. And then see whether we can *build an apparatus* which will give us those results. Where that is *not to be decided as to its adequacy by what a Member knows*, but may well look quite non-intuitively (i.e., in terms of our Members' intuition) strong (or weak, or irrelevant, for that matter). (Sacks 1992, vol. 1: 487, emphasis added)

Lynch's (1993) main point (full discussion of which would take us far outside the concerns of the present book) is that the model of scientific inquiry implicated in Sacks's remarks is wrong. Not only wrong: it leads inevitably to the development of a 'professional analytic community' in which, as remarked, the analyst's constructs come to substitute for the embodied activities they purport to offer an account of. Yet as the latter comments from Sacks clearly indicate, the aim in CA has never been to produce accounts of action that are isomorphic with the accounts participants themselves might have, or might give if asked. In my view, this would leave the whole enterprise with little point. There *is* a point. It is to describe the ways that participants in talk-in-interaction organize the mutual intelligibility of their talk, in a formal, abstract, yet empirical, observationally based (in other words, scientific) way. CA thus maintains its ethnomethodological roots in the earlier sense of the 'classic studies'. Lynch's sleight of hand is to claim that CA should be commensurate with the later ethnomethodological programme in which it is the singularity, the haecceity, of a situation which is of interest – and then to chastise its practitioners for not living up to that programme.

Conversation analysts argue that their data (recordings of events that did indeed occur in the world) show human verbal interaction to be recursively patterned: the same kinds of events can be seen to occur in widely differing contexts involving different participants engaging in different specific activities. Although individual cases always differ to varying degrees, they can still legitimately be described as individual cases of a class. But the aim is not simply to list and categorize utterances or turn-types along the lines of saying

'Well, there's another adjacency pair first part'. The technical concept of 'adjacency pair' (as only one example) evolved as a means of systematizing accumulated knowledge of how participants in talk-in-interaction routinely solve certain sequential problems: for instance, the problem of getting another person to speak next, in the next turn, on a topic of the first speaker's choosing (one solution to which is to ask them a question). To be sure, on any of the indefinitely large number of occasions in which one participant asks a question of another, that is done in unique, context-sensitive ways and for contextually-specific purposes. But the organizational problem itself is context-free: in any conversation, for any set of participants, there exist the generic issues of 'Whose turn is it to speak now?' and 'How do I take my turn to say what I want to?' Sacks's early lectures (1992, vol. 1; originally given between 1964 and 1968), which for Lynch and Bogen (1994) exemplify a version of CA which has subsequently been abandoned in favour of a more 'formalist' version, in fact are organized around demonstrating the omnirelevance of these sequential–organizational issues.

Indeed a telling indication of the necessity of formal descriptions at some level in the enterprise comes in a passage from another work by Lynch and Bogen (1996) themselves. In their analysis of the controversial Iran-Contra hearings in the USA in 1987, Lynch and Bogen state that:

> we have not set out to interpret the videotaped 'surface' of the testimony by reference to one or another abstract cultural framework or code. Instead, we describe how *a whole array of possible legal, cultural and discursive resources were available, and were in fact used, by the parties to the hearings*. These resources included various binary oppositions, linguistic categories, procedural rules and protocols, [as well as] references to cherished constitutional rights and ethical values, invocations of national interest, and popular media themes. . . . [We] are not denying that we must interpret the videotapes and written texts that make up our materials; we are, instead, denying that it is necessary to organise such an interpretation around a core theory or cognitive model. (Lynch and Bogen 1996: 266, emphasis added)

Conversation analysts would certainly agree that one should not organize accounts around a single core theory or cognitive model (recall my criticism of the computational model for communication). But surely the 'array of . . . resources' that were 'available', and the way that they are described in this passage, necessarily involves a formal characterization of both the array and its possible constituents. Without, at some level, utilizing a formal analysis of resources that goes beyond the specific instance of a specific 'device' in a specific context, Lynch and Bogen would be unable to come to such a (useful and interesting) conclusion.

It is in this sense, then, that I invoke the concept of normative structures of talk-in-interaction, and in this sense that I construe them as a 'reality'. I freely admit my reliance on analytic constructs in order to establish a case for considering those normative structures as a feature of talk that is observably oriented to by participants. It is not enough simply to be able to point to a phenomenon at a level of prim- itiveness such that 'anyone' could see it and agree; though on one level I believe CA can still do that: there are still those kinds of novel phenomena to observe. But if we set ourselves to live by that con- straint it is difficult to see what we could do other than generate more and more elaborate schemes of classification. In order for a social science to have any relevance its observations need to have upshots that add to knowledge of wider questions such as the nature of social organization, of social interaction, of human communication itself. We need, I believe, to be able to say 'These *kinds of* things can be seen to be done by humans in managing these *kinds of* activities, which are bound up with these *kinds of* elements of social life'.

In this light, my aim has been to describe the kinds of actions that humans undertake in managing the activities of interaction through, around or with certain forms of technology. An empirically-grounded notion of the normative structures of talk-in-interaction has allowed me to look for aspects of that interaction where it appears that the technology, or more strictly its affordances, comes to play a role in the exchange of turns at talk, in the structures of those turns, in the actions accomplished by those turns, and so forth.

Ultimately, then, I argue that the perspective adopted in this book lies somewhere between the poles of realism and relativism. Both the normative structures of talk-in-interaction, and the communicative affordances of artefacts, are relative in the sense that they are func- tional aspects which only become relevant, and hence visible, in the light of particular actions. But they are also real, in the sense that they nevertheless exist as perennial potentials. To Gibson's remark: 'the walk-on-ability of a surface exists whether or not the animal walks on it' (1982: 409), we can add: the surface's affordance of walk-on- ability becomes manifest *when* the animal walks on it.

I will therefore characterize the general standpoint I have adopted as a 'relational' perspective. This entails neither a commitment to the 'stubborn anti-realism' (Edwards et al. 1995: 43) of the relativist nor to the rock-like, death-and-furniture insistences of the (objectivist) realist. It is a perspective that is comfortable with the idea that the world, and most of the objects in it, exhibit a stable reality that, in given circumstances, can be an intransigent obstacle in the way of some intended action or, in others, can act as a flexible resource in the pursuit of an action. Applied to the specific domain of technology and conversation, this means that technologies can never amount simply to what theorists reconstruct them as, nor solely to what their users seek to make of them. And here is the rub. Technologies do not impose themselves on society, mechanistically altering the pattern of human relations and social structures. Neither does human agency encounter technologies as blank slates, as infinitely malleable forms. Technologies for communication possess materiality not only in the physical sense but in the sense of their very conditions of possibility. Technologies do not make humans; but humans make what they do of technologies in the interface between the organized practices of human conversation, and the technology's array of communicative affordances.

Appendix: Transcription Conventions

Most of the transcripts reproduced in this book use the Conversation Analytic conventions, originally developed by Gail Jefferson. Occasionally, other modified systems are used; the relevant modifications are explained in the main text. Below is a glossary of the more important transcription symbols. For a fuller glossary, together with an explanation of how transcripts are produced in CA, see Hutchby and Wooffitt (1998: chapter 3).

(0.5)	Numbers in brackets indicate a gap timed in tenths of a second.
(.)	A dot enclosed in brackets indicates a 'micropause' of less than one tenth of a second.
=	Equals signs are used to indicate 'latching' or absolute contiguity between utterances, or to show the continuation of a speaker's utterance across intervening lines of transcript.
[ ]	Square brackets between adjacent lines of concurrent speech indicate the points of onset and cessation of overlapping talk.
(( ))	Double brackets are used to describe a non-verbal activity, for example ((banging sound)). They are also used to enclose the transcriber's comments on contextual or other relevant features.
( )	Empty brackets indicate the presence of an unclear utterance or other sound on the tape.
.hhh	'h's preceded by a dot are used to represent audible inward breathing. The more 'h's, the longer the breath.
hhhh	'h's with no preceding dot are used in the same way to represent outward breathing.

huh heh hih	Laughter is transcribed using 'laugh tokens' which, as far as the transcriber is able, represent the individual sounds that speakers make while laughing.
:	Colons indicate the stretching of a sound at the preceding lexical item. The more colons the greater the extent of the stretching.
-	A dash indicates a sudden cut-off of the prior sound.
. , ?	Punctuation marks are not used grammatically, but to indicate prosodic aspects of the talk. A full stop indicates a falling tone; commas indicate fall-rise or rise-fall (i.e. a 'continuing' tone); question marks indicate a marked rising tone.
↑↓	Upward and downward arrows are used to mark an overall rise or fall in pitch across a phrase.
a:	Underlining of a letter before a colon indicates a small drop in pitch during a word.
a:	Underlining of a colon after a letter indicates a small rise in pitch at that point in the word.
Under	Other underlining indicates speaker emphasis.
CAPITALS	Capitals mark a section of speech markedly louder than that surrounding it.
→	Arrows in the left margin point to specific parts of the transcript discussed in the text.
°°	Degree signs are used to indicate that the talk between them is noticeably quieter than surrounding talk.
< >	Outward chevrons are used to indicate that the talk between them is noticeably slower than surrounding talk.
> <	Inward chevrons are used to indicate that the talk between them is noticeably quicker than surrounding talk.

Bibliography

Atkinson, J. M. 1978: *Discovering Suicide: Studies in the Social Organisation of Sudden Death*. London: Macmillan.

Atkinson, J. M. 1984: *Our Masters' Voices: The Language and Body Language of Politics*. London: Methuen.

Atkinson, J. M. and Drew, P. 1979: *Order in Court: The Organisation of Verbal Interaction in Judicial Settings*. London: Macmillan.

Atkinson, J. M. and Heritage, J. (eds) 1984: *Structures of Social Action: Studies in Conversation Analysis*. Cambridge: Cambridge University Press.

Baum, F. [1900] 1974: *The Wonderful Wizard of Oz*. London: Collins.

Baym, N. 1995: From practice to culture on UseNet. In S. L. Star (ed.), *The Cultures of Computing*, Oxford: Blackwell, 29–52.

Baym, N. 1996: Agreements and disagreements in a computer-mediated discussion. *Research on Language and Social Interaction*, 29, 315–45.

Berger, C. 1997: *Planning Strategic Interaction*. Hillsdale, NJ: Lawrence Erlbaum Associates.

Bijker, W. E. and Law, J. 1992: General introduction. In W. E. Bijker and J. Law (eds), *Shaping Technology/Building Society: Studies in Sociotechnical Change*. Cambridge, MA: MIT Press, 1–14.

Braverman, H. 1974: *Labour and Monopoly Capital: The Degradation of Work in the Twentieth Century*. New York: Monthly Review Press.

Brooks, J. 1975: *Telephone: The First Hundred Years*. New York: Harper and Row.

Button, G. 1990: Going up a blind alley: Conflating conversation analysis and computational modelling. In P. Luff, N. Gilbert and D. Frohlich (eds), *Computers and Conversation*, London: Academic Press, 67–90.

Button, G. 1993: The curious case of the vanishing technology. In G. Button (ed.), *Technology in Working Order: Studies in Work, Interaction and Technology*, London: Routledge, 10–28.

Button, G. 1998: Review of *Humans, Computers and Wizards* by R. Wooffitt, N. Fraser, N. Gilbert and S. McGlashan. *Sociology*, 32, 896–8.

Button, G. and Harper, R. 1993: Taking the organisation into accounts. In G. Button (ed.), *Technology in Working Order: Studies in Work, Interaction and Technology*, London: Routledge, 98–107.

Callon, M. 1980: Struggles and negotiations to define what is problematic and what is not: The sociologic of translation. In K. Knorr, R. Krohn and R. D. Whitley (eds), *The Social Process of Scientific Investigation* (vol. 4), Dordrecht: Reidel, 197–219.

Callon, M. 1986a: Some elements of a sociology of translation: Domestication of the scallops and the fishermen of St Brieuc bay. In J. Law (ed.), *Power, Action and Belief: A New Sociology of Knowledge?*, London: Routledge and Kegan Paul, 196–233.

Callon, M. 1986b: The sociology of an actor-network: The case of the electric vehicle. In M. Callon, J. Law and A. Rip (eds), *Mapping the Dynamics of Science and Technology: Sociology of Science in the Real World*, London: Macmillan, 19–34.

Carroll, R. 1987: *Cultural Misunderstandings*. Chicago: University of Chicago Press.

Chomsky, N. 1959: Review of *Verbal Behaviour* by B. F. Skinner. *Language*, 35, 26–58.

Chomsky, N. 1965: *Aspects of the Theory of Syntax*. The Hague: Mouton.

Churchland, P. 1986: *Neurophilosophy: Toward A Unified Science of the Mind/Brain*. Cambridge, MA: MIT Press.

Clark, H. H. and Clark, E. V. 1977: *Psychology and Language: An Introduction to Psycholinguistics*. New York: Harcourt Brace Jovanovich.

Clayman, S. 1988: Displaying neutrality in television news interviews. *Social Problems*, 35, 474–92.

Collins, H. 1990: *Artificial Experts: Social Knowledge and Intelligent Machines*. Cambridge, MA: MIT Press.

Coulter, J. 1979: *The Social Construction of Mind*. London: Macmillan.

Coulter, J. 1983: *Rethinking Cognitive Theory*. London: Macmillan.

Coulter, J. 1989: *Mind in Action*. Cambridge: Polity Press.

Davidson, J. 1984: Subsequent versions of invitations, offers, requests, and proposals dealing with potential or actual rejection. In J. M. Atkinson and J. Heritage (eds), *Structures of Social Action: Studies in Conversation Analysis*, Cambridge: Cambridge University Press, 102–28.

Dennett, D. 1991: *Consciousness Explained*. New York: Little, Brown and Company.

Descartes, R. [1664] 1953: Traite de l'homme. In *René Descartes, oeuvres et Lettres*. Paris: Editions Gallimard, 807–73.

Drew, P. 1984: Speakers' reportings in invitation sequences. In J. M. Atkinson and J. Heritage (eds), *Structures of Social Action: Studies in Conversation Analysis*, Cambridge: Cambridge University Press, 129–51.

Drew, P. 1989: Recalling someone from the past. In D. Roger and P. Bull (eds), *Conversation*, Clevedon: Multilingual Matters, 96–115.

Drew, P. 1997: 'Open' class repair initiators in response to sequential sources of trouble in conversation. *Journal of Pragmatics*, 28, 69–101.

Drew, P. and Heritage, J. (eds) 1992: *Talk At Work: Interaction in Institutional Settings*. Cambridge: Cambridge University Press.

Duncan, S. and Fiske, D. W. 1977: *Face-to-Face Interaction: Research, Methods and Theory*. Hillsdale, NJ: Lawrence Erlbaum Associates.

Durkheim, E. [1897] 1951: *Suicide* (trans. J. A. Spaulding and G. Simpson). London: Routledge and Kegan Paul.

Edwards, D., Ashmore, M. and Potter, J. 1995: Death and furniture: The rhetoric, politics and theology of bottom line arguments against relativism. *History of the Human Sciences*, 8, 25–49.

Egbert, M. 1997: Schisming: The collaborative transformation from a single conversation to multiple conversations. *Research on Language and Social Interaction*, 30, 1–51.

Fitch, K. 1998: Text and context: A problematic distinction for ethnography. *Research on Language and Social Interaction*, 31, 91–107.

Fodor, J. 1975: *The Language of Thought*. Scranton, PA: Crowell.

Frissen, V. 1995: Gender is calling: Some reflections on past, present and future uses of the telephone. In K. Grint and R. Gill (eds), *The Gender–Technology Relation*, London: Taylor and Francis, 79–94.

Garcia, A. C. and Jacobs, J. B. 1999: The eyes of the beholder: Understanding the turn-taking system in quasi-synchronous computer-mediated communication. *Research on Language and Social Interaction*, 32, 337–67.

Garfinkel, H. 1967: *Studies in Ethnomethodology*. New York: Prentice Hall.

Garfinkel, H. (ed.) 1986: *Ethnomethodological Studies of Work*. London: Routledge.

Garfinkel, H. 1991: Evidence for locally produced, naturally accountable phenomena of order, logic, reason, meaning, method, etc. in and as of the essential haecceity of immortal ordinary society (I): An announcement of studies. In G. Button (ed.), *Ethnomethodology and the Human Sciences*, Cambridge: Cambridge University Press, 10–19.

Gibson, J. J. 1979: *The Ecological Approach to Perception*. London: Houghton Mifflin.

Gibson, J. J. 1982: *Reasons for Realism: Selected Essays*. Hillsdale, NJ: Lawrence Erlbaum Associates.

Giddens, A. 1981: Agency, institution and time–space analysis. In K. Knorr-Cetina and A. V. Cicourel (eds), *Advances in Social Theory and Methodology*, London: Routledge, 161–74.

Giddens, A. 1984: *The Constitution of Society: Outline of the Theory of Structuration*. Cambridge: Polity Press.

Gilbert, N., Wooffitt, R. and Fraser, N. 1990: Organising computer talk. In P. Luff, N. Gilbert and D. Frohlich (eds), *Computers and Conversation*, London: Academic Press, 235–58.

Godard, D. 1977: Same setting, different norms: Phone call beginnings in France and the United States. *Language in Society*, 6, 209–19.

Goffman, E. 1961: *Encounters*. New York: Bobbs-Merrill.

Goffman, E. 1971: *Relations in Public*. New York: Basic Books.

Goffman, E. 1981: *Forms of Talk*. Oxford: Blackwell.

Goodwin, C. 1981: *Conversational Organisation: Interaction Between Speakers and Hearers*. New York: Academic Press.

Goodwin, C. 1986: Between and within: Alternative sequential treatments of continuers and assessments. *Human Studies*, 9, 205–17.

Goodwin, C. and Heritage, J. 1990: Conversation analysis. *Annual Review of Anthropology*, 19, 283–307.

Goodwin, M. H. 1990: *He-Said-She-Said: Talk as Social Organisation Among Black Children*. Bloomington, IN: Indiana University Press.

Greatbatch, D. 1988: A turn-taking system for British news interviews. *Language in Society*, 17, 401–30.

Greatbatch, D., Luff, P., Heath, C. and Campion, P. 1993: Interpersonal communication and human–computer interaction: An examination of the use of computers in medical consultations. *Interacting with Computers*, 5, 193–216.

Grint, K. and Woolgar, S. 1997: *The Machine at Work*. Cambridge: Polity Press.

Harris, R. 1982: *The Language Myth*. London: Duckworth.

Harris, R. 1987: *Language, Saussure and Wittgenstein*. London: Routledge.

Haugeland, J. (ed.) 1981: *Mind Design: Philosophy, Psychology, Artificial Intelligence*. Montgomery, VT: Bradford Books.

Heath, C. 1986: *Body Movement and Speech in Medical Interaction*. Cambridge: Cambridge University Press.

Heath, C. and Luff, P. 1993: Disembodied conduct: Interactional asymmetries in video-mediated communication. In G. Button (ed.), *Technology in Working Order: Studies of Work, Interaction and Technology*, London: Routledge, 35–54.

Heritage, J. 1984a: *Garfinkel and Ethnomethodology*. Cambridge: Polity Press.

Heritage, J. 1984b: A change-of-state token and aspects of its sequential placement. In J. M. Atkinson and J. Heritage (eds), *Structures of Social Action: Studies in Conversation Analysis*, Cambridge: Cambridge University Press, 299–345.

Hirst, G. 1991: Does conversation analysis have a role in computational linguistics? *Computational Linguistics*, 17, 211–27.

Hopper, R. 1992: *Telephone Conversation*. Bloomington, IN: Indiana University Press.

Horton, D. and Wohl, R. R. 1956: Mass communication and para-social interaction: Observations on intimacy at a distance. *Psychiatry*, 19, 215–29.

Houtkoop-Steenstra, H. 1991: Opening sequences in Dutch telephone conversations. In D. Boden and D. Zimmerman (eds), *Talk and Social Structure*, Cambridge: Polity Press, 232–50.

Hughes, T. 1983: *Networks of Power: Electrification in Western Society, 1800–1930*. Baltimore, MD: Johns Hopkins University Press.

Hughes, T. 1988: The seamless web: Technology, science, et cetera, et cetera. In B. Elliott (ed.), *Technology and Social Process*, Edinburgh: Edinburgh University Press, 9–19.

Hunter, J. F. M. 1973: *Essays After Wittgenstein*. Toronto: University of Toronto Press.

Hutchby, I. 1992: Confrontation talk: Aspects of 'interruption' in argument sequences on talk radio. *Text*, 12, 343–71.

Hutchby, I. 1996: *Confrontation Talk: Arguments, Asymmetries and Power on Talk Radio*. Mahwah, NJ: Lawrence Erlbaum Associates.
Hutchby, I. and Wooffitt, R. 1998: *Conversation Analysis*. Cambridge: Polity Press.
Jefferson, G. 1978: Sequential aspects of storytelling in conversation. In J. Schenkein (ed.), *Studies in the Organisation of Conversational Interaction*, New York: Academic Press, 219–48.
Jefferson, G. 1980: On 'trouble-premonitory' response to inquiry. *Sociological Inquiry*, 50, 153–80.
Jefferson, G. 1984: Stepwise transition out of topic to inappropriately next-positioned matters. In J. M. Atkinson and J. Heritage (eds), *Structures of Social Action: Studies in Conversation Analysis*, Cambridge: Cambridge University Press, 194–222.
Jefferson, G. 1986: Notes on latency in overlap onset. *Human Studies*, 9, 153–83.
Jefferson, G., Sacks, H. and Schegloff, E. A. 1987: Notes on laughter in pursuit of intimacy. In G. Button and J. R. E. Lee (eds), *Talk and Social Organisation*, Clevedon: Multilingual Matters, 152–205.
Jones, S. (ed.) 1995: *CyberSociety: Computer-Mediated Communication and Community*. London: Sage.
Kendon, A. 1990: *Conducting Interaction*. Cambridge: Cambridge University Press.
Kendon, A. and Ferber, A. 1973: A description of some human greetings. In R. P. Michael and J. H. Crook (eds), *Comparative Ecology and the Behaviour of Primates*, London: Academic Press, 591–668.
Kling, R. 1992: Audiences, narratives and human values in social studies of technology. *Science, Technology and Human Values*, 17, 349–65.
Koffka, K. 1935: *Principles of Gestalt Psychology*. London: Routledge.
Latour, B. 1987: *Science in Action: How to Follow Scientists and Engineers through Society*. Milton Keynes: Open University Press.
Latour, B. 1988: *The Prince* for machines as well as for machinations. In B. Elliott (ed.), *Technology and Social Change*, Edinburgh: Edinburgh University Press, 20–43.
Latour, B. 1992: Where are the missing masses? The sociology of a few mundane artefacts. In W. E. Bijker and J. Law (eds), *Shaping Technology/Building Society: Studies in Sociotechnical Change*, Cambridge, MA: MIT Press, 225–58.
Latour, B. 1997: On actor networks: A few clarifications. Centre for Social Theory and Technology, Keele University.
Latour, B. 1998: Thought experiments in social science: From the social contract to virtual society. First Annual *Virtual Society?* Public Lecture, Brunel University, April 1st.
Law, J. 1987: On the social explanation of technical change: The case of the Portuguese maritime expansion. *Technology and Culture*, 28, 227–52.
Levinson, S. 1983: *Pragmatics*. Cambridge: Cambridge University Press.
Luff, P., Gilbert, N. and Frohlich, D. (eds) 1990: *Computers and Conversation*. London: Academic Press.

Lynch, M. 1993: *Scientific Practice and Ordinary Action.* Cambridge: Cambridge University Press.

Lynch, M. and Bogen, D. 1994: Harvey Sacks' primitive science. *Theory, Culture and Society*, 11, 65–104.

Lynch, M. and Bogen, D. 1996: *The Spectacle of History: Speech, Text and Memory at the Iran-Contra Hearings.* London: Duke University Press.

McBarnet, D. 1981: *Conviction: Law, the State and the Construction of Justice.* London: Macmillan.

Mauldin, M. 1994: Chatterbots, TinyMUDs and the Turing Test: Entering the Loebner Prize Competition. *Proceedings of the Twelfth National Conference on Artificial Intelligence.* AAAI/Cambridge, MA: MIT Press, 16–21.

Maynard, D. 1984: *Inside Plea Bargaining: The Language of Negotiation.* New York: Plenum.

Maynard, D., Schaefer, N. and Cradock, R. 1995: Gatekeeping as a feature of declinations to participate in the survey interview. Unpublished MS.

Mehan, H. 1979: *Learning Lessons: Social Organisation in the Classroom.* Cambridge, MA: Harvard University Press.

Mill, J. S. 1968: A system of logic. In M. Cowling (ed.), *J. S. Mill, Selected Writings*, New York: New American Library. (First published 1843.)

Miller, G. 1981: *Psychology.* Harmondsworth: Penguin.

Moerman, M. 1988: *Talking Culture: Ethnography and Conversation Analysis.* Philadelphia, PA: University of Pennsylvania Press.

Orlikowski, W. J. 1992: The duality of technology: Rethinking the concept of technology in organisations. *Organisation Science*, 3, 398–427.

Parsons, T. 1937: *The Structure of Social Action.* New York: McGraw-Hill.

Parsons, T. 1951: *The Social System.* New York: The Free Press.

Perakyla, A. 1995: *AIDS Counselling.* Cambridge: Cambridge University Press.

Pomerantz, A. 1980: Telling my side: 'Limited access' as a 'fishing' device. *Sociological Inquiry*, 50, 186–98.

Pomerantz, A. 1984: Agreeing and disagreeing with assessments: Some features of preferred/dispreferred turn-shapes. In J. M. Atkinson and J. Heritage (eds), *Structures of Social Action: Studies in Conversation Analysis*, Cambridge: Cambridge University Press, 57–101.

Pool, I. de Sola 1981: *The Social Impact of the Telephone.* Cambridge, MA: MIT Press.

Poster, M. 1995: Postmodern virtualities. In M. Poster, *The Second Media Age*, Cambridge: Polity Press, 23–42.

Postman, N. 1987: *The Disappearance of Childhood.* London: W. H. Allen.

Potter, J. 1996: *Representing Reality: Discourse, Rhetoric and Social Construction.* London: Sage.

Prescott, G. 1884: *Bell's Electric Speaking Telephone: Its Invention, Construction, Application, Modification and History.* New York: D. Appleton and Co.

Psathas, G. (ed.) 1979: *Everyday Language: Studies in Ethnomethodology and Conversation Analysis.* Hillsdale, NJ: Lawrence Erlbaum Associates.

Randall, D. and Hughes, J. 1995: Sociology, CSCW and working with customers. In P. Thomas (ed.), *The Social and Interactional Dimensions of Human–Computer Interfaces*, Cambridge: Cambridge University Press, 142–60.

Reid, E. 1991: Electropolis: Communication and community on Internet Relay Chat. Unpublished MS.

Rutter, D. R. 1989: The role of cuelessness in social interaction: An examination of teaching by telephone. In D. Roger and P. Bull (eds), *Conversation*, Clevedon: Multilingual Matters, 294–312.

Ryle, G. 1949: *The Concept of Mind*. Oxford: Oxford University Press.

Sacks, H. 1972: On the analysability of stories by children. In J. J. Gumperz and D. Hymes (eds), *Directions in Sociolinguistics: The Ethnography of Communication*, New York: Holt, Rinehart and Winston, 329–45.

Sacks, H. 1975: Everyone has to lie. In M. Sanches and B. Blount (eds), *Sociocultural Dimensions of Language Use*, New York: Academic Press, 57–80.

Sacks, H. 1984: Notes on methodology. In J. M. Atkinson and J. Heritage (eds), *Structures of Social Action: Studies in Conversation Analysis*, Cambridge: Cambridge University Press, 21–7.

Sacks, H. 1987: On the preferences for agreement and contiguity in sequences in conversation. In G. Button and J. R. E. Lee (eds), *Talk and Social Organisation*, Clevedon: Multilingual Matters, 54–69.

Sacks, H. 1992: *Lectures on Conversation* (2 vols. ed. by G. Jefferson). Oxford: Blackwell.

Sacks, H., Schegloff, E. A. and Jefferson, G. 1974: A simplest systematics for the organization of turn-taking for conversation. *Language*, 50, 696–735.

Samson, C. 1999: Biomedicine and the body. In C. Samson (ed.), *Health Studies: A Critical and Cross-Cultural Reader*, Oxford: Blackwell, 3–21.

Saussure, F. de [1915] 1984: *Course in General Linguistics*. London: Fontana.

Schegloff, E. A. 1968: Sequencing in conversational openings. *American Anthropologist*, 70, 1075–95.

Schegloff, E. A. 1979: Identification and recognition in telephone conversation openings. In G. Psathas (ed.), *Everyday Language*, Hillsdale, NJ: Lawrence Erlbaum, 23–78.

Schegloff, E. A. 1980: Preliminaries to preliminaries: 'Can I ask you a question?' *Sociological Inquiry*, 50, 104–52.

Schegloff, E. A. 1982: Discourse as an interactional achievement: Some uses of 'uh huh' and other things that come between sentences. In D. Tannen (ed.), *Analysing Discourse: Text and Talk*, Washington DC: Georgetown University Press, 71–93.

Schegloff, E. A. 1986: The routine as achievement. *Human Studies*, 9, 111–52.

Schegloff, E. A. 1987: Recycled turn-beginnings. In G. Button and J. R. E. Lee (eds), *Talk and Social Organisation*, Clevedon: Multilingual Matters, 70–85.

Schegloff, E. A. 1988: Presequences and indirection: Applying speech act theory to ordinary conversation. *Journal of Pragmatics*, 12, 55–62.

Schegloff, E. A. 1988/9: From interview to confrontation: Observations on the Bush/Rather encounter. *Research on Language and Social Interaction*, 22, 215–40.

Schegloff, E. A. 1991: Reflections on talk and social structure. In D. Boden and D. Zimmerman (eds), *Talk and Social Structure*, Cambridge: Polity Press, 44–70.

Schegloff, E. A. 1992a: To Searle on conversation. In H. Parret and J. Verschueren (eds), *(On) Searle on Conversation*, Amsterdam: John Benjamins, 113–28.

Schegloff, E. A. 1992b: Repair after next turn: The last structurally provided defence of intersubjectivity in conversation. *American Journal of Sociology*, 97, 1295–345.

Schegloff, E. A., Jefferson, G. and Sacks, H. 1977: The preference for self-correction in the organisation of repair in conversation. *Language*, 53, 361–82.

Schegloff, E. A. and Sacks, H. 1973: Opening up closings. *Semiotica*, 7, 289–327.

Schutz, A. 1962: *Collected Papers I: The Problem of Social Reality*. The Hague: Martinus Nijhoff.

Schutz, A. 1972: *The Phenomenology of the Social World*. London: Routledge and Kegan Paul.

Searle, J. 1990: Is the brain's mind a computer program? *Scientific American*, 262, 26–31.

Shannon, C. E. and Weaver, W. 1949: *The Mathematical Theory of Communication*. Urbana, IL: University of Illinois Press.

Shields, R. (ed.) 1996: *Cultures of Internet*. London: Sage.

Silverman, D. 1996: *Discourses of Counselling*. London: Sage.

Suchman, L. 1987: *Plans and Situated Actions*. Cambridge: Cambridge University Press.

Suchman, L. 1990: What is human–machine communication. In S. P. Robertson, W. Zachary and J. B. Black (eds), *Cognition, Computing and Cooperation*, Norwood, NJ: Ablex, 25–55.

Terasaki, A. 1976: Pre-announcement sequences in conversation. Social Sciences Working Paper 99, University of California at Irvine.

Thomas, P. (ed.) 1995: *The Social and Interactional Dimensions of Human–Computer Interfaces*. Cambridge: Cambridge University Press.

Toffler, A. 1981: *The Third Wave*. London: Collins.

Turing, A. 1950: Computing machinery and intelligence. *Mind*, 59, 433–60.

Turkle, S. 1986: *The Second Self: Computers and the Human Spirit*. New York: Simon and Schuster.

Turkle, S. 1995: *Life on the Screen: Identity in the Age of the Internet*. London: Weidenfeld and Nicholson.

Weber, M. 1968: *Economy and Society*. New York: Harcourt Brace. (First published 1922.)

Webster, F. 1995: *Theories of the Information Society*. London: Routledge.

Weizenbaum, J. 1966: A computer program for the study of natural language communication between man and machine. *Communications of the Association of Computing Machinery*, 9, 36–45.

Weizenbaum, J. 1970: *Computer Power and Human Reason*. San Francisco, CA: W. H. Freeman.

Whalen, J. 1995: Expert systems versus systems for experts: Computer-aided dispatch as a support system in real-world environments. In P. Thomas (ed.), *The Social and Interactional Dimensions of Human–Computer Interfaces*, Cambridge: Cambridge University Press, 161–83.

Whalen, J. and Zimmerman, D. 1987: Describing trouble: Practical epistemology in citizen calls to the police. *Language in Society*, 19, 465–92.

Winch, P. 1958: *The Idea of a Social Science and its Relation to Philosophy*. London: Routledge and Kegan Paul.

Winner, L. 1984: Do artefacts have politics? In D. MacKenzie and J. Wajcman (eds), *The Social Shaping of Technology*, Milton Keynes: Open University Press. (First published 1977.)

Wittgenstein, L. 1958: *Philosophical Investigations*. Oxford: Blackwell.

Wittgenstein, L. 1981: *Zettel*. Oxford: Blackwell.

Wooffitt, R., Fraser, N., Gilbert, N. and McGlashan, S. 1997: *Humans, Computers and Wizards: Analysing Human (Simulated) Computer Interaction*. London: Routledge.

Wooffitt, R. and MacDermid, C. 1995: Wizards and social control. In P. Thomas (ed.), *The Social and Interactional Dimensions of Human–Computer Interfaces*, Cambridge: Cambridge University Press, 126–41.

Woolgar, S. 1985: Why not a sociology of machines? The case of sociology and artificial intelligence. *Sociology*, 19, 557–72.

Woolgar, S. 1991: The turn to technology in social studies of science. *Science, Technology and Human Values*, 16, 20–50.

Woolgar, S. and Cooper, G. 1999: Do artefacts have ambivalences? Moses' bridges, Winner's bridges, and other urban myths in science and technology studies. *Social Studies of Science*, 29, 433–49.

Zimmerman, D. H. 1992: The interactional organisation of calls for emergency assistance. In P. Drew and J. Heritage (eds), *Talk at Work*, Cambridge: Cambridge University Press, 418–69.

Index

actor-network theory 18–19, 21–2, 29
affordances 26–30, 32–3, 193–5, 199
artificial intelligence 146–74, 153–7
Ashmore, M. 32, 195, 196–9
Atkinson, J. M. 4, 65, 77

Baym, N. 174–6
Bell, A. G. 37, 41
Berger, C. 46–50
Bijker, W. E. 14, 19
Bogen, D. 195, 200, 204–5
Braverman, H. 14
Button, G. 13, 25, 32, 143–5, 155–6

Callon, M. 19, 21–2
Chinese room 154–5
Chomsky, N. 42–3, 54
Churchland, P. 55
Clayman, S. 65
Collins, H. 199
computational model of communication 35–53, 155; conceptual problems of 42–6; empirical problems of 50–3; strong version of 40–6; weak version of 46–50
constructivism 75–9; and conversation analysis 76–8; and realism 77–9
conversation analysis 55–79, 156, 193–4; and adjacency pairs 65–70, 200–3; and cognition 58–9, 75; and plan-based communication 70–5; and preference structures 67; and repair 132–4; and rules 61–4; and turn-taking 60–5; applications of 64–5; conditional relevance 66–7; realist epistemology of 76–9; transition-relevance places in 60–4; turn-construction units in 60–1; *see also* ethnomethodology
Cooper, G. 25
Coulter, J. 39, 40, 45, 132, 142

Davidson, J. 68, 163
Dennett, D. 155
Descartes, R. 35
Drew, P. 56, 65, 67, 70, 75, 76
dualism 36
Durkheim, E. 77

Edwards, D. 32, 195, 196–9, 205
ELIZA 147–9, 153, 154
Elizabots 147–53
ethnomethodology 200–5; and conversation analysis 200, 201–5; classical studies in 200–1; radical programme in 201–3
expert systems 132–9, 143–5; and interactional problems 134–9; communicative affordances of 141–2

Fitch. K. 106–7
Fodor, J. 40–1